# SWINBURNE

*A Biographical Approach*

FROM A DRAWING FROM LIFE, IN 1874,
BY CARLO PELLEGRINI

# SWINBURNE

*A Biographical Approach*

BY

## HUMPHREY HARE

KENNIKAT PRESS
Port Washington, N. Y./London

SWINBURNE

First published in 1949
Reissued in 1970 by Kennikat Press
Library of Congress Catalog Card No: 74-112314
ISBN 0-8046-1020-7

Manufactured by Taylor Publishing Company    Dallas, Texas

TO

R. H. H.

*"Quand on fait une étude sur un homme considérable, il faut oser tout voir, tout regarder, et au moins tout indiquer."*

SAINTE-BEUVE

# PREFACE

"I AM told," remarked Queen Victoria upon Tennyson's death, "that Mr. Swinburne is the best poet in my dominions." But Mr. Gladstone demurred and the laureateship went eventually to Alfred Austin. Nevertheless, it was the measure of a surrender, the reward of conformity. Watts-Dunton, as chaperon, might be justly proud. Already, like a garden Apollo, Swinburne's nakedness was hedged about with the variegated laurels of nineteenth - century propriety. The shrubbery was to grow more dense. By 1909 twenty-five unimpeachable volumes had issued from Putney, while upon the poet's death Edmund Gosse added the camouflage of a whimsical, if official, biography. A portrait was presented of an excitable elfin creature with flaming hair and green eyes, fluttering hands and "epileptiform" fits, the possessor of a talent which, since it was allied to a perfect gentility, was excusable if regrettably disconcerting. A label was invented to discount the outcry with which *Poems and Ballads* had been received in 1866—an outcry which still lingered in elderly memories. What had it all been about? *Songs before Sunrise* gave the cue. Swinburne became "The Poet of Revolt".

In a sense this was perfectly true, but in a sense quite other than was intended and infinitely more subtle. It was not until *La Jeunesse de Swinburne* appeared in 1928 that Swinburne was exhumed from the dank concealing clay to which the literary sextons had consigned him. Without Lafourcade's imaginative scholarship Swinburne would still remain what Gosse and Mr. Harold Nicolson were content to have him be: an inexplicable phenomenon. "There will be those, doubtless," wrote the latter, "who . . . will trace depressing and essentially erroneous analogies to Dr. Masoch and the Marquis de Sade. . . ."

The artist, like the saint and the criminal, tends to be maladjusted. His sensitivity alone forbids him to accept unquestioned society's rules and taboos, its standards and ethics; for him its synthesis is either too exclusive or too inclusive. According to his temperament and capacity he seeks, consciously or not, to create a synthesis of his own. Essentially it is a rival one. He becomes a revolutionary, and society reacts with the brutality engendered by fear. When it becomes apparent, as in the case of Swinburne, that this rival synthesis is founded upon so apparently dangerous an aberration as algolagnia, the reaction is intensified. Society hits out wildly in a crisis of self-preservation. It may ban the books, burn the pictures and imprison the artist. But this is a confession of weakness. Swinburne was, perhaps, more fortunate. Nineteenth-century England was very conscious of its strength. It contented itself with the lesser forms of persecution; it could afford to wait. Patience was rewarded. The impotent husk of a poet at least was safely garnered. Mr. Gladstone need have had no fears; the royal instinct was, as ever, sure.

Perhaps no century was more conscious of its moral inhibitions than the nineteenth. Perhaps, too, this is the measure of its æsthetic achievement: great art is in its essence revolutionary and to revolt there must be something to rebel against. The grand moralities, the consciousness of an ordered world progressing evenly towards the power and the glory of an undefined Utopia, formed a citadel of complacency which the eccentric was irresistibly impelled to breach. In what, exactly, did Swinburne's eccentricity consist? The algolagnia, which was to become so notorious and acquire so European a reputation that no novelist in the last decade of the century could create a character who practised *le vice anglais* without attributing to him some of Swinburne's physical characteristics—an honour which, due largely to Maupassant, he shares with George Selwyn —was far more than a regrettable sexual aberration. The pornography of *The Flogging Block* and *The Whippingham Papers*, the ridiculous indecencies of the correspondence, were but symptomatic of an emotion which was infinitely more profound, of an anguished sensitivity which was of the very essence of his being, and with which he responded to an outer world, whose impressions he received with an overwhelming intensity, with a shock, which left pleasure and pain inextricably confounded.

This incapacity to formulate the normal dichotomy between pleasure and pain permeated his whole life. In the same way that masochism becomes so easily sadistic—in the sense that there is a desire to give the loved one pleasure by inflicting pain—so in Swinburne a submissiveness, evident in the hero-worship lavished upon Landor, Hugo and Mazzini, and the complete self-abandonment to the will of Watts-Dunton, is allied to a rebelliousness which caused him to leave prematurely both Eton and Oxford, to adopt in politics a violent republicanism, and to become embroiled in a continuous series of needless disputes. This is the clue to much in his life which would otherwise be incomprehensible. And if this is accepted as the basis of Swinburne's psychology, the history of his literary development will be found to assume a logic, an inevitability, which is not without significance.

Indeed, given the presence of poetic genius, Swinburne's psychology was eminently suited to the production of a romantic poet. "Since every 'classical' literature", wrote Mario Praz in *The Romantic Agony*, "represents a synthesis, a balance of forces, it makes at the same time a compromise, that is, it implies exclusions and sacrifices which sooner or later come to be resented. No sooner does a resentment of this kind achieve a certain degree of intensity than the classical idea breaks up, and new forms of imagination and feeling make themselves felt and demand expression: a 'romantic' period begins." This conception is, perhaps, less accurately applicable to movements than to individual writers or even to some period of their development. Nor are the terms "classical" and "romantic" to be accurately defined; in this sense they are perhaps best interpreted as "established" and "aspiring". In a world where Tennyson was the "established" poet there was one obvious *lacuna* in the accepted synthesis: erotic sensibility. And this was a basis of inspiration which Swinburne was peculiarly fitted to exploit.

He did not, however, exploit it exclusively at once. The innate rebelliousness, the resentment against society, that the tension of his awareness of peculiarity aroused in him, was expressed at first by an anti-theism and a republicanism which only gradually became dominated by the exploitation of his innate aberration. But having discovered the formula, its development was continuous. From the identification of himself with flagellated adolescents—schoolboys, choirboys, pages—as in *Laugh and Lie Down*, in the *Chronicles of Tebaldeo Tebaldei*, in *Rosamond* where the young chorister, Arthur, bears on his body the "stripes since last red week", and in *Lesbia Brandon*, he passed to the more elaborate fantasies of *Chastelard*, where the lover dies ecstatically by order of his royal mistress who is his prototype of the *femme fatale*. And this in turn, after a sympathetic study of Sade, developed into the intellectualized algolagnia of *Atalanta*, where the synthesis is ultimately achieved, and which, indeed, may be considered his masterpiece. But after the publication of *Poems and Ballads*, which in a sense is the commentary upon this process of development, a change becomes manifest. The synthesis is abandoned and with it the theory of Art for Art's sake, which was its necessary moral justification. The reasons for this *volte face*, partly spontaneous, partly due to the influence of Mazzini, will be explored, but its results are evident. *Songs before Sunrise* was an attempt to find a new basis for his inspiration. And, indeed, out of his passionate political beliefs, his revolutionary fervour, and his exaltation of liberty, he was able temporarily to achieve the semblance of a synthesis which enabled him to create a work of art. But it could not endure. It lapsed with the political circumstances that gave it cogency and with the withdrawal in death of Mazzini's intellectual domination.

Indeed, the essential basis of his inspiration could not be denied with impunity. By devoting his art to utilitarian ends he was capitulating to society. It was a fatal surrender. The algolagnic synthesis abandoned, his genius entered upon a decline: *Bothwell* is not comparable to *Chastelard*, *Erechtheus* to *Atalanta*, or the *Poems and Ballads* of 1878 to the first series of 1866. There are admirable passages in all these volumes, but it becomes increasingly clear that for all their fluent metres, their elaborate cadences, their brilliance of technique, the fire is lacking and the fervour forced. While at last, in 1879, weakened by alcoholic poisoning, he surrendered in his life as he had capitulated in his art. Society, triumphant in the shape of Watts-Dunton, acquired the remains. *Songs before Sunrise*, for all its merit, was prophetic of the long and sterile twilight of The Pines.

This, then, is the theme, indeed the excuse, for this book. It will be recognized by any student of Swinburne that it owes much, as any study of Swinburne must, to the scholarship of the late Georges Lafourcade—killed in an accident during the war—who devoted so much of his life, so much of his admirable talent, to the literature of this country. It would be effrontery to pretend to supersede his profound and detailed studies, it is vanity enough to hope to supplement them. Nevertheless, in reading his work, in following the guiding tape he so delicately laid through the massive labyrinth of Swinburniana, it becomes subtly apparent that though the ground is beautifully covered, though the revealing quotation is inevitably made, there is a certain hesitation before the logical conclusion, a certain reluctance in judgment. Was this due to a nice loyalty towards T. J. Wise (a loyalty which bibliographers may, since the revelations of 1934, feel was misplaced) and through him to Edmund Gosse, towards whose biography of Swinburne one may judge him to have been over kind? Certainly, in the greater freedom of the British Museum, where Wise's Ashley Library has now found its permanent resting-place, there is no need to sustain a loyalty or suspend a judgment. Of the latter's justice the reader must conclude.

# ACKNOWLEDGMENTS

MY thanks are due to Messrs. William Heinemann Ltd. for permission to quote from Swinburne's Works and published Letters; to Messrs. Macmillan & Co. Ltd. for permission to reproduce Pellegrini's drawing from *The Life of Algernon Charles Swinburne* by Sir Edmund Gosse; to the authorities of the British Museum for their skilled and courteous assistance, and similarly to the authorities of the London Library. The illustrations facing pages 144 and 192 are reproduced by kind permission of the Council of the Bibliographical Society. My gratitude is also due to those friends who have aided me with documents, reminiscences, suggestions and advice; and to those who have helped me in the reading and correcting of proofs.

H. H.

# CONTENTS

# ILLUSTRATIONS

# CHAPTER I

## (1837–1849)

ALGERNON CHARLES SWINBURNE was born at No. 7 Chester Street, Grosvenor Place, at five A.M. on 5th April 1837. He was the eldest of the six children of Charles Henry Swinburne, a captain in the Royal Navy of two years' seniority, and at this time forty years of age, and of his wife, Lady Jane Hamilton, fourth daughter of George, third Earl of Ashburnham, now aged twenty-eight. His parents had been married two years. On the authority of his family there is no evidence for the drama which Swinburne was later to ascribe to his entrance into the world. "I have heard," he wrote to E. C. Stedman in 1878, "that Goethe, Victor Hugo and myself were all born in the same condition — all but dead, and certainly not expected to live an hour." In compensation, perhaps, for his strange and puny physique, he was always inclined to dramatize his origins and enhance the romantic possibilities of his ancestry.

The incidence of inherited characteristics appears to be so arbitrary that nothing as a rule is to be gained by the detailed study of the forebears of genius. Any tree may, apparently, bear this sport, this sudden, embarrassing and unheralded fruit. That the combination of these two wealthy and aristocratic families should have resulted in their affliction by so curious a phenomenon remains as unaccountable to-day as it was to themselves. For, indeed, the Swinburnes and Ashburnhams were pure types of the aristocratic class— sportsmen, soldiers and county magnates. They had every right to expect a son of a similar stamp. The Swinburnes were an old Northumbrian family with a baronetcy dating from 1660. Their chivalry and romantic turbulence were to be greatly exaggerated by the poet. It was not quite accurate to say that they had given "their blood like water and their lands like dust for the Stuarts". It is possible that two of the younger sons may have taken part in the Rebellion

1

of 1745 and it is known that they were at this period ardent
Catholics and maintained contacts with the Court of Saint-
Germain.  The poet's great-grandfather, Edward Swinburne,
was, so it appears, living in France when he inherited the
title and estates from his brother in 1763, and had a few years
earlier, in 1756, been permitted to remain in Bordeaux in
spite of the war since he was "d'une famille catholique et
zélée pour les Stuarts".  The only point of real significance
in this family history, in so far as it affected the poet, was that
several members of the family were brought up in France,
including Edward's brother Henry, his sister Anne, who
became a nun at Montargis, and, most important of all,
Edward's son, Sir John Swinburne, the poet's grandfather,
the influence of whose French culture upon his grandson
was to be profound.  There is one other point that may be
mentioned in the history of the house of Swinburne.  The
poet's great-grandmother, Edward's wife, whom he married
in Bordeaux in 1761, was a Dillon.  This accounted for
"the Irish particles" in the poet's blood, while Christiana
Dillon's stepmother, a Miss Disconson, who was remotely connected with the Polignacs, was made *faute de mieux* to supply
both the "French particles" and that noble French ancestry
which Swinburne claimed with such alacrity though, since
there was no blood-relationship, it was demonstrably false.

The Ashburnhams, on the other hand, "a family of
stupendous antiquity", had been settled in Sussex before the
Norman Conquest.  It numbered amongst its members
one, John Ashburnham, who was "the closest follower of
Charles I till his death".  His son became a baron and the
earldom dates from 1730.  With the accretion of honours,
however, this family, unlike the Swinburnes, found it more
profitable to abandon the Stuarts.  Between Captain
Swinburne and Lady Jane there was a measure of blood-
relationship.  They were second cousins, their maternal
grandfathers being brothers.

Throughout his life Swinburne was far from being dissatisfied with his aristocratic origins, particularly since he
was able to decorate them with romantic fantasies.  The
family adherence to the Stuarts must, he felt, be accountable
in his heredity for his attachment to lost causes.  While

"all the French and Irish particles of his blood" were apt to "tingle" in moments of excitement, and was there not, too, a strange antithesis in the fact that he himself was a republican while descended from "a lady of the house of Polignac (a quaint political relationship for me, as you will admit)"? Not that there was, as he was at pains to make clear, anything really inconsistent between his background and his republican principles. Was he not merely following in a great tradition? "I was born," he wrote to Giuseppe Chiarini in 1872, "in the aristocratic class, an accident which I share with Byron and Shelley, the only two other English poets brought forth in these later generations who have had faith in republican peoples and Freedom." And these sentiments were supported with remarkable complacency by his mentor, Victor Hugo himself: "Vous avez raison: Vous, Byron, Shelley, trois aristocrats, trois républicains, et moi-même, c'est de l'aristocratie que je suis monté à la democratie, c'est de la pairie que je suis arrivé à la république; on va d'un phare à l'océan: ce sont là de beaux phénomènes." While as to the virility of his family, who could doubt it, when there was, so he assured Stedman, an ancestress, a Lady Swinburne, who "bore 30 children to one husband, people thronged about her carriage in the streets to see the living and thriving mother of thirty sons and daughters"? Evidently with such a heritage he might say with justice, "I think you will allow that when this race chose at last to produce a poet, it would have been at least remarkable if he had been content to write nothing but hymns and idylls for clergymen and young ladies to read out in chapels and drawing-rooms."

Though he was born in London, Swinburne's childhood was spent almost entirely in the country. His father rented East Dene, a large house at Bonchurch, in the Isle of Wight, whose rambling gardens descended in terraced lawns to the seashore. Here, or at Capheaton in Northumberland, or at Ashburnham Place in Sussex, he passed his early years in the serene, assured, charmed atmosphere that was the ambience of a privileged aristocracy. Nor was the companionship of other children lacking. During the first eleven years of his life Lady Jane produced five younger children. It is, perhaps, significant that none of the four sisters should have

married. Alice, the eldest, was, after Edith, Swinburne's
favourite. All their lives they wrote frequently and in-
timately to each other. Swinburne dedicated *Locrine* to
her in 1887. She died in 1903. Edith, the second sister,
was the one with whom he had the greatest affinity. She
had the same coloured hair as her eldest brother, an extraordinary and brilliant red-auburn. Her early death in 1863
affected him profoundly and served to enhance, perhaps, the
sombre fatalism of *Atalanta in Calydon*. With the third
sister, Charlotte, who lived till 1889, he seems to have been
out of sympathy. It is possible that she preferred her
younger brother, Edward. She has left no trace either in
Swinburne's works or correspondence. With the fourth
sister, Isabel, the only member of the family to survive him
—she died in 1915—his relations were perhaps more complex.
They corresponded frequently; less often on his side than
on hers; he dedicated a poem to her; but the narrowness of
her religion was a bar to any close intimacy. She deplored
her brother's anti-theism and even refused to admit that he
had quitted the embrace of the Church. At his death,
outmanœuvring Watts-Dunton, and contrary to Swinburne's
express wish, she succeeded in imparting a semblance of
the rites of religion to the ceremony of the funeral. The
youngest of all was Edward, born in 1848. This "brightest
of baby boys" was, however, to grow up into an
unsympathetic, if tragic, figure. He attacked his brother's
poems on the grounds that they were anti-aristocratic and
let it be known that he considered him in the ordinary affairs
of life as incompetent and irresponsible. It can hardly be
denied that this view was justified, but its expression was not
conducive to any mutual regard. As far as is known they
never corresponded. Edward travelled unceasingly about
Europe: in France, Germany, Italy, Turkey even. In 1879
he married a cousin, Olga Thurmann, the daughter of a
German professor. The marriage was not a success. One
day, in July 1891, he returned suddenly to London and
startled the family with a telegram. Alice went to him and
found him dying of heart disease. Upon his death Swinburne wrote to Watts-Dunton: "I cannot but keep thinking
. . . how long since, how many years ago, I should have died

as my poor brother has just died if instead of the worst of wives I had not found the best of friends."

But the misunderstandings and disasters were still in the future. The impression left by these early years at East Dene is one of a happy band of children romping in a sunlit garden, in the woods, or along the seashore:

> *The many coloured joys of dawn and noon*
> *That lit with love a child's life and a boy's. . . .*

There were, too, cousins near by. Sir Henry and Lady Mary Gordon, Lady Jane's sister, lived with their children a few miles away at Northcourt, Shorwell. Mrs. Disney Leith, the author of *The Boyhood of A. C. Swinburne*, was one of these cousins. Visits between East Dene and Northcourt were constant. Or, again, the cousins would meet at The Orchard, Niton, also not far away, where lived Sir James Gordon, Mrs. Leith's grandfather. Here, it is recorded, might constantly be seen "Algernon, riding on a very small pony, led by a servant", come to spend the day.

Such early education as he received was perhaps more influenced by his mother than was usual in the well-to-do households of the period. Lady Jane had been educated in Florence and spoke fluent French and Italian, the fashionable third language of the day. From her he learnt to speak these languages in his childhood and to her, too, he owed his first introduction to their literatures. In later years Swinburne told Edmund Gosse that he knew the *Orlando Furioso* long before he had *heard* of the *Faerie Queene*. But English literature was not neglected. Shakespeare in the edition of Mr. Bowdler came into his hands at an early age and created a profound and enduring impression. At a later date he was to write: "More nauseous and more foolish cant was never uttered than that which would deride the memory or depreciate the merits of Bowdler. No man ever did better service to Shakespeare than the man who made it possible to put him into the hands of intelligent and imaginative children. . . ." Swinburne was such a child. His passion for reading awakened very early and, according to Mrs. Leith, he was "always privileged to have a book at meals". No doubt it was due to his early taste for

literature that he was able, with the wide and precocious
extent of his knowledge, to astonish the Reverend Foster
Fenwick, Rector of Brook, to whom he was sent to be
grounded in the classics before going to Eton.  Indeed,
French and Italian readings were not altogether sufficient
as a preparation for that narrow classical *régime*, supported
though they were by an extensive knowledge of the Holy
Scriptures.  In his own words he was brought up "quasi-
Catholic", and it was remarked at this time how beautifully
he replied to the Catechism and read aloud from the Bible,
entering even "passionately" into the religious exercises of
a Sunday.  Was there, perhaps, in Lady Jane a certain
narrowness of culture and outlook?  Her High Church
Anglicanism, profoundly affected by the Oxford Movement,
seems to have resulted in an intellectual timidity which,
nevertheless, is not altogether untypical of the age.  Novels
were placed on the Index and the young Algernon was made
to promise that never, never would he so much as open the
works of Lord Byron.  And later she was to fear that Hugo
and Mazzini were materialists and might destroy her son's
faith — a faith which by then had long been discarded.
Moreover, in 1881, when Swinburne had retired to The
Pines with Watts-Dunton, she wrote to the latter hoping
that in some obscure manner—her piety was perhaps always
a little vague—this retreat might bring Algernon back to his
youthful faith.  But for Swinburne, to whom perhaps the
sentiment of reverence came in general more easily than that
of affection, his mother was, amongst the members of his
family, the outstanding exception.  That something childish,
schoolboyish, which was so marked and enduring a feature
of his character, served in this instance to preserve a certain
spontaneity in his regard for her.  To her he dedicated
many of his works, and when she died in 1896, at Barking
Hall, in her eighty-seventh year, he expressed his profound
distress in an elegy:

> *But she, beloved above*
> *All utterance known of love,*
> *Abides no more the change of night and dawn,*
> *Beholds no more with earth-born eye*
> *These woods that watched her waking here where all things die.*

Swinburne's relations with his father are far less easy to
resolve. He himself has built up two distinct portraits.
They are divergent, though perhaps not altogether irreconcil-
able. On the one hand is the widely travelled sailor, the friend
of Lady Hester Stanhope, "Lord Collingwood's favourite
middy" (though the date of his entry into the service,
1810, casts a certain doubt on this typically Swinburnian
statement), who, though innocent of battle experience,
was able to recount exciting stories of the sea. The child
remembered, too, in later years, the enchantment of "being
held up naked in my father's arms and brandished between
his hands, then shot like a stone from a sling through the air,
shouting and laughing with delight, head foremost into the
coming wave. . . ." In fact it is a not unattractive portrait
of a retired sailor (he seems to have been at home on half-pay
during the whole of Swinburne's childhood and youth, being
placed on the reserve and promoted Admiral in 1857), who
enjoyed inventing mechanical contrivances in his garden
workshop, made his son's literary career possible by giving
him a small allowance, even financed the publication of his
early books, and in later years would dash up to London in
moments of crisis, the devoted parent, on missions of rescue.
And yet it is impossible to escape the conclusion that during
most of Swinburne's youth there was a morbid antagonism
between father and son. In the autobiographical novels,
the unpublished *Lesbia Brandon* and *A Year's Letters* (*Love's
Cross-Currents*), there is the same basic and significant
situation. Both Bertie Leyton and Reginald Harewood are
indubitably Swinburne himself. The situations described are
not, of course, to be taken as authentic, while the emotions
aroused in his characters are inhumanly exaggerated by the
fundamental perversity of his sensibility. Nevertheless it is
impossible not to suppose that they reflect a live relationship
which, in however attenuated a form, he was conscious of
having experienced. Bertie, the victim of an irresistible love
for his sister, Lady Wariston, is filled with hate for his tutor,
Denham, who flogs him unmercifully while deriving satisfaction from the boy's resemblance to his sister with whom
he, too, is in love. Or Reginald, in *A Year's Letters*, torn
between resentment of his father, Captain Harewood, and

love for Eleanor Ashburst.  It is difficult to refrain from reconstructing the classic situation by substituting Lady Jane for Lady Wariston and Eleanor Ashburst, and the Admiral for Denham and Captain Harewood.  Besides, the letters written by Captain Harewood to his son, it is not unreasonable to suppose, must often have resembled in tenor, if not in cruel severity, those received by Swinburne from the Admiral: "At the end of last autumn, I had the pleasure of reflecting as I looked back over my son's school and college days on three memorable features in them of which his friends loved to boast: that he had got himself constantly flogged, twice plucked and once rusticated.  The distinction was noble and well-merited; any boy and any father might be proud of it for life."  This was a more or less faithful picture of Swinburne's own scholastic career.  And since the novel was composed in 1862, at a time when his relations with his father had, as a result, been in a condition of strain for some years, it is not surprising to find as cold and terrible a letter—allowing always for imaginative exaggeration—as the following: "From childhood upwards, I must once for all remind you, you have thwarted my wishes and betrayed my trust. . . . Prayer, discipline, confidence, restraint, hourly vigilance, untiring attention, one after another failed to work upon you. . . . At school you were constantly in disgrace. Pain and degradation could not keep you right; to disgrace the most frequent, to pain the most severe, you opposed a deadly strength of sloth and tacit vigour of rebellion. . . ."

What in fact were the father's shortcomings, if shortcomings they were?  Beyond a certain failure in sensitivity, a certain lack of understanding—both, it must be admitted, hardly surprising in the circumstances—they appear to have been limited to intermittent attempts, whenever his natural kindliness was temporarily overwhelmed by shocked surprise, to resolve an insoluble problem by taking refuge in the standards of the quarter-deck.  Perhaps Swinburne's letter to W. M. Rossetti, written in 1870, on the subject of Shelley's relations with *his* father, is as sound a summing-up as can be made: "I think you are rather hard upon him as to the filial relation.  I have no more doubt that it may be said for Sir Timothy that his son was what Carlyle calls an 'afflictive phenomenon' than that I was the same to my father before, during and since my Oxford time; but I do not think you make allowance for the provocation given (as well as received) by a father who may be kindly and generous, to a boy or man between 17 or 21 or 30, with whom he has no deep or wide ground of sympathy beyond the animal relation or family tradition. You will allow me to say that I am sure you can never have felt at that age the irreparable, total and inevitable isolation from all that had once been closest to the mind and thought, and was still closest to the flesh and memory, the solitude, into which one passes from separation to antagonism of spirit, without violent quarrel or open offence, but by pure logical necessity of consequences, the sense that where attraction gradually ends repulsion gradually begins, which many besides Shelley, and as affectionate and faithful by nature and temperament as he, *have* felt at that age." One is left with the impression of a well-meaning, kindly but puzzled father, alternating between generosity and anxious reproof, confronted in his offspring with a sensitive psychology which he was totally unable to comprehend.

For Sir John Swinburne, his grandfather, the poet preserved always a particular reverence and admiration. Every year, from Swinburne's earliest childhood, the family spent part of August and September at Capheaton in Northumberland. Of this wild landscape, this ancestral background, Sir John was in the child's eyes the peculiar patriarch. He was to survive, upright and in command of his faculties, till 1860, and his ninety-ninth year. One may well wonder to what extent this particular grandson was singled out for attention out of the twenty-four to whom Sir John regularly extended his hospitality, but his urbane presence, which preserved always some flavour of the *ancien régime*, and his romantic past, were singularly well fitted to inspire pride of race, and a predilection for lost causes. Had he not with his father suffered in his youth what Swinburne chose to look upon as exile for the sake of the Stuarts? In fact, of course, Sir John was very much more sensible than his romantic grandson pretended to suppose. He had even, for political considerations, abandoned the family's traditional Catholicism. "It was absurd," he wrote, "to sacrifice my consideration in my own country, my prospects in life, to condemn myself to eternal insignificance and oblivion for Tenets I did not believe, and Ceremonies I never practised." As an advanced Whig he became a Member of Parliament, the friend of Wilkes and Mirabeau, and in 1814 wrote to Leigh Hunt, imprisoned for insulting the Regent, "with respect to the payment of the fine you may command me to the amount of from £2 to £300". But he never lost his admiration for France and French culture and this, with his own impeccable and fluent knowledge of the language, the possession of a library "the most extensive and best chosen collection in the north of England", which was "particularly rich in Spanish and French books", may well have awakened Swinburne's love for that country. In fine, Sir John was the first of that long line of old men, from Landor to Trelawny, upon whom Swinburne was to lavish his perpetually schoolboyish hero-worship. He was even, perhaps, the model by which they were to be judged.

Of Swinburne himself in these early and important years there is little knowledge to be gained from the external and sentimental records available. When we have noted the small boy with his tiny body, his fluttering hands, the large head with its aureole of red hair, the green eyes; when the personalities of his family have been recorded, the background against which he moved of Bonchurch and its sea, Northumberland and its fells, the libraries and works of art of Capheaton and Ashburnham, nearly all has been said: but not quite. At what moment in his boyhood did he realize the peculiarities of his physique—the puny, the apparently delicate body? Mr. Harold Nicolson has noted the presence of a "virility complex". Was there a certain raillery from the Gordon cousins, a tendency to look upon "Cousin Hadji" as effeminate and odd? And was it this that led to dangerous escapades among the cliffs, to an impetuousness in swimming or on horseback ("I never cared for any . . . sport . . . except . . . riding and swimming"), which amounted to showing-off? In compensating for his physical deficiencies, one may suspect, he could not afford to be otherwise than elaborately fearless. And in his relations with those girl cousins at Northcourt did he submit to a tender bullying which was already the basis of his devotion? In *The Sisters*, written in 1891, he has left us a nostalgic representation of himself as he would have liked to be but a few years later. Reginald Clavering, identifiable with Swinburne, is addressed by the love-struck Mabel in a tone of curious reminiscence:

> Well, you always were the best to me;
> The brightest, bravest, kindest boy you were
> That ever let a girl misuse him—make
> His loving sense of honour, courage, faith,
> Devotion, rods to whip him—literally
> You know—and never by one word or look
> Protested.

But in the unpublished novel *Lesbia Brandon*, begun some fifteen years later, there is a more precise picture of the boy's developing temperament. There can be little doubt that when Swinburne wrote it he was honestly endeavouring to recapture the emotions of his dead self. The early pages are a brilliant reconstruction of awakening awareness. In them he has opened a psychological vista upon his own youth, nor are they the less trustworthy because the lineaments of the man are distinguishable in the child. Bertie Letyon is "Well broken in to solitude and sensitive of all outward things, he found life and pleasure enough in the gardens and woods, the downs and the beach. Small sights and sounds excited and satisfied him; his mind was as yet more impressible than capacious, his senses more retentive than his thoughts. Water and wind and darkness and light made friends with him; he went among beautiful things without wonder or fear. For months he lived and grew on like an animal or a fruit: and things seemed to deal with him as with one of these; earth set herself to caress and amuse him; air blew and rain fell and leaves changed to his great delight; he felt no want in life." But in his apprehension of nature it was above all to the sea that he responded with an extraordinary sensitivity. "At the next turn they were in sight of [the sea]. . . . To this, the only sight of divine and durable beauty on which any eyes can rest in the world, the boy's eyes first turned, and his heart opened and ached with pleasure.  His face trembled and changed, his eyelids tingled, his limbs yearned all over: the colour and savour of the sea seemed to pass in at his eyes and mouth; all his nerves desired the divine touch of it, all his soul saluted it through the senses."  The boy received the spirit of the sea "with fleshly pleasure", with "a furious luxury of the senses" which "kindled all his nerves and exalted his life".  And bathing, the blood surges through his arteries: Bertie is "beaten into colour, his ears are full of music and his eyes of dreams".  Over and over again throughout his life Swinburne wrote of the sea in terms of physical passion, of mingling with the enveloping female body of the sea as in the famous passage from *The Triumph of Time*:

> *I will go back to the great sweet mother,*
> *Mother and lover of men, the sea.*
> *I will go down to her, I and none other,*
> *Close with her, kiss her and mix her with me;*
> *Cling to her, strive with her, hold her fast: . . .*

"I remember," Swinburne wrote in a letter, "being afraid of other things, but never of the sea . . . it shows the *truth* of my endless passionate returns to the sea in all my verse." Indeed, it was an enduring passion; but a passion of an altogether particular kind.  "The surging of the surf made [Bertie] . . . red from the shoulders to the knees and sent him on shore whipped by the sea into a single blush of the whole skin"; but "the knowledge of how many lives went yearly to feed with blood the lovely lips of the sea-furies who had such songs and smiles for summer, and for winter the teeth and throats of ravening wolves or snakes untameable, the hard heavy hands that beat out their bruised life from sinking bodies of men, gave point to his pleasure and a sheathed edge of cruel sympathy to his love.  All cruelties and treacheries, all subtle appetites and violent secrets of the sea, were part of her divine nature, adorable and acceptable to her lovers."

Indeed, the first manifestations of his temperament were probably pantheistic—a feeling of exaltation in the presence of nature, a heightening of perception, which was stimulated to an exaggerated degree by the apprehension of the pain and

suffering she could inflict—suffering which at the same time
was feared and ardently desired.   From the first he was intoxicated by "the pleasure there is in pain".   But here, too,
on these blue foolscap sheets, he was able to recapture the
mystical enchantment, the delicious anguish, of evenings in
the nursery at Capheaton when his mother read the Border
ballads, which were probably his first experience of verse.
The children listen with "intent faces and fiery pleasure".
When she has finished reading they are all in tears.   "Things
in verse hurt one, don't they?   Hit and sting like a cut. . . .
Verse hurts horribly:  people have died of verse-making
and thought their mistresses killed them—or their reviewers.
. . . Never write verses when you get big;  people who do are
bad or mad or sick. . . . It's odd that words should change
so just by being put into rhyme.   They get teeth and bite;
they take fire and burn.   I wonder who first thought of
tying words up and twisting them back to make verses, and
hurt and delight all people in the world for ever.   For one
can't do without it now. . . . It was an odd device. . . .
One can't tell where the pain or the pleasure ends or begins.
'Who shall determine the limits of pleasure?'   That is a
grand wise word."

    If the autobiographical truth of *Lesbia Brandon* is accepted,
it becomes possible to identify in the child much that later
becomes evident in the man: the response to beauty and its
inseparable attribute of cruelty, the identification of pleasure
with pain, the creation, as yet but dimly perceived, of "a new
and credible mythology", a pantheism, which was "apart
and not averse from the daily religion taken and taught on
trust"; and thus, in his own words, "an example of infant
faith and infant thought", he was, at the age of twelve, sent
to Eton.

# CHAPTER II

## (1849–1853)

SWINBURNE has never made any impact upon the narrow culture of the Lilies. Gray is its laureate. The passion of Swinburne's poetry with its implications of "unhealthiness" has relegated him to join "mad" Shelley among the elm-shadowed foothills of the Eton Parnassus. How many boys at the end of their five years, receiving from the hands of the Headmaster the vellum-bound leaving-book of *Poems by Gray*, even know that Swinburne was a member of the school? It is the more remarkable that during his lifetime, in his old age, the Eton authorities at least attempted to honour him. For the school's Ninth Jubilee in 1891 he was asked to write an Ode for the occasion and to be present at the celebrations. "Here is my copy of verses," he wrote, "shown up in time as I understand—and I only hope I shall not be put in the bill for showing up too few." Dr. Warre, the Headmaster, asked him to stay the night, but Watts-Dunton "declined to sanction it". In the presence of A. J. Balfour, who was the guest of honour, a speaker at the dinner publicly deplored that "Mr. Swinburne has been *compelled* to refuse the invitation". Eighteen years later the Eton authorities sent a handsome wreath to the poet's funeral. Deprecation has since been the predominant attitude.

It was in April 1849 that the Admiral and Lady Jane took him to Mr. Joynes's house in Keate's Lane. Algernon Bertram Mitford, his cousin, who was only five weeks his senior, but had already been at the school for three years, was sent for, and Swinburne was placed in his care. This cousin, afterwards Lord Redesdale, gave Edmund Gosse a description of Swinburne's appearance: "He was strangely tiny. His limbs were small and delicate; and his sloping shoulders looked far too weak to carry his great head." Already he had the habit, when excited, of drawing his arms down from the shoulders and fluttering his hands—a habit

14

which was due, according to a specialist to whom Lady Jane, concerned, had taken him, to "an excess of electric vitality". Then he had a "tangled mass of red hair standing almost at right angles" to the head. It was "red, violent, aggressive red . . . unmistakeable, unpoetical carrots". But "his features were small and beautiful. . . . His skin was very white". And "under his arm he hugged his Bowdler's Shakespeare . . . bound in brown leather with, for a marker, a narrow slip of ribbon . . . with a button of that most heathenish marqueterie called Tunbridge ware dangling from the end of it". He had "an exquisitely soft voice with a rather sing-song intonation". But how was this little creature who walked about Windsor and Eton "with that peculiar dancing step", with "his hair, like the Zazzera of the old Florentines, tossed about by the wind", declaiming verses in English, French and Italian, to survive the *régime* of a mid-nineteenth-century public school? "Other boys," says Lord Redesdale, "would watch him with amazement. . . . None dreamt of interfering with him—as for bullying there was none of it. He carried with him one magic charm —he was absolutely courageous. He did not know what fear meant." But there were less sympathetic observers. Lord St. Aldwyn recalled "a horrid little boy, with a big red head and a pasty complexion, who looked as though a course of physical exercise would have done him good"; while Sir Osbert Sitwell records an old gentleman selecting from the memories of eighty years this perhaps apocryphal reminiscence: "I remember well when I went to Eton, the head boy called us together, and pointing to a little fellow with curly red hair, said 'kick him if you are near enough and if you are not near enough throw a stone at him',—I have often wondered what became of him—his name was Swinburne"! Indeed, as Sir George Young, one of his few Eton friends, remarked, "he was not at home among Eton boys" though, since "there was something a little formidable about him", perhaps he was not bullied overmuch.

The Eton into which Swinburne was plunged preserved still the elegancies and barbarities of the eighteenth century: a standard of impeccable classicism in which a false quantity was a solecism that could be expiated only by the birch.

It was a narrow system of education which "was entirely classical", wrote Oscar Browning, "resting on the foundation of the Greek and Latin languages. It had grown up by accident. It was out of touch with the age. But it was the best system of education which ever existed". Greek and Latin poetry were read extensively if uncritically, there were "saying-lessons" in which hundreds of ill-comprehended lines were learnt by heart and, most important of all, there were endless copies of Latin and Greek verses to be composed in which the height of achievement was the acrostic-like ability to include the maximum number of recognizable classical tags. Outside the classics there were no official subjects. There was, it is true, a master qualified to teach mathematics, but it does not appear that he in fact did so. Small boys were no doubt given sums in arithmetic to do, but algebra and geometry were totally ignored. It was not till 1851 that Dr. Hawtrey succeeded in introducing mathematics and even in 1864 only three hours a week were devoted to them. There was some instruction in history and geography below Sixth Form, but the geography consisted for the most part of lists of classical place-names. English literature was, of course, not taught at all, though it was conceded that benefits might accrue from the study of Shakespeare's plays provided it was conducted on the basis of translating them into Greek! The natural sciences were not considered proper to the education of a gentleman. The celebrated Mr. Tarver, however, had, with his son, "the privilege of instructing in the French language" and, it may be added, the Italian. He was not considered quite the social equal of the other masters; his lessons were not compulsory; his salary was inferior; he had no powers of enforcing discipline; and he was accustomed to refer to himself as "un simple objet de luxe". Discipline in the Eton tradition was still reasonably savage. Flogging was regarded "quite as a natural incident of the day" and, in the Lower School at least, was carried out in public. Fagging seems already to have been systematized, though games, by contrast, had not reached any high standard of organization and do not appear to have been compulsory.

What did Swinburne owe to Eton? Much must always

depend, in the peculiar Eton system of frequently changing masters and permanently remaining under the care of the same tutor, upon the personality of that tutor. Mr. Joynes was not perhaps quite the man to play much part in the development of nascent genius. He had no ideas or theories about education, as is evidenced in his panic-stricken refusal to succeed Dr. Hawtrey as Headmaster. He was a good disciplinarian but his teaching, according to A. C. Benson, was "sound old-fashioned Eton scholarship, which was a curious little exotic bloom of culture, conventional and narrow, and based upon a minute acquaintance with two or three authors". One of these authors was Horace, whom Mr. Joynes made his pupils learn by heart and thereby aroused in Swinburne an enduring antipathy: "My dislike of [Horace]," he wrote in 1888, "—dating from my school-days—is one of the very few points on which I find myself in sympathy with Byron." Despite his "kind and fatherly manner" and the kindness of Mrs. Joynes—who was German by birth—"at the age when I most needed kindness," it is impossible to escape the conclusion that Swinburne found both his tutor and Mrs. Joynes extremely dull. In later years Joynes remembered only that his former pupil had had red hair, and he would change the subject with obvious disapproval when Swinburne's poetry was mentioned. Not, perhaps, an altogether sympathetic or, indeed, inspiring character. Nevertheless, the fault may well have been in part Swinburne's. It is curious, for instance, that none of the masters to whom he was "up" during his time at Eton should have retained any very definite impressions of him. William Johnson Cory, that finished classical scholar and author of *Ionica*, whom Swinburne fortuitously sat under twice, in the Fourth and Fifth Forms, during his Eton career, retained apparently none at all. And yet it is impossible not to suppose that Swinburne owed to him much of his love of Greek literature, and very likely some of that restless experimenting with metre which was to distinguish his later work. Another distinguished scholar with whom he came in contact was W. G. Cooksley, whose editions of Pindar, Catullus, Tibullus and Propertius were always to remain among Swinburne's favourites. "Here comes the

rising sun at last!" he is reported to have remarked when
Swinburne, who had that peculiar faculty of never being
quite in time for anything, entered his schoolroom late for
early school.   Whatever may have been the shortcomings
of the Eton system of education, for Swinburne at least it
was not altogether unsuitable.   Though he may never have
learned any trigometry, though he reached old age without
being aware of the position of the bladder in the human body,
who dare say that those attainments would have been more
valuable to him than a profound love for, and knowledge of,
classical literature?   The charm of the *Poetæ Graeci*, the
official Eton anthology, appealed to him at once; Bion,
Moschus, Pindar, Theocritus and Sappho were read side by
side with Aeschylus and Sophocles.   Very early his critical
faculties were awakened: for Euripides he evinced an in-
stant aversion which was to last him all his life.   While in
Latin, though he disliked the *Æneid* and Horace, he
delighted in Ovid and Catullus.   A set of verses shown
up in that unorthodox metre, galliambics, resulted in
Mr. Joynes' disapproval and painful consequences.   His
scholastic career had nothing of the precocious.   He was
placed in the Upper Fourth on his arrival and moved up the
school at the normal rate.   Of his school compositions, a set
of eighteen Greek iambics and two sets of Latin verses, one
a translation of Falconer, have survived in an exercise-book.
Mr. Joynes has marked them: *Very well*; *Very well*; *Very
creditable*.   Twice he was "sent up for good"—a mark of
distinction conferred upon a particularly outstanding piece
of work—and once he was placed in "trials"—a terminal
examination—above the future headmaster, Dr. Warre.

In other directions, however, he displayed precocity
enough.   Availing himself of the luxury of Mr. Tarver, he
won, in 1852, the Prince Consort's Prize for Modern
Languages, a triumph which he, himself, attributed more
to the early teaching of his mother than to the efforts of
the schoolmaster.   Nevertheless, Mr. Tarver, who without
doubt had much literary sensibility, seems to have been the
first master to discover in Swinburne a similar bent.   He has
in any case the distinction of having first awakened in him
what was to become a passionate and lifelong enthusiasm

by introducing him to Victor Hugo's *Le Roi s'amuse*, *Notre-Dame de Paris* and *Lucrèce Borgia*. A year later *Les Châtiments* was to produce in Swinburne "a sort of rapturous and adoring despair ".

But the main impulse of his intellectual development was concentrated into the channels of English literature. To this Eton contributed nothing beyond the provision of good libraries. Much of his time was spent in the Boys' Library in Weston's Yard, where he might often be seen sitting in an embrasure with "some huge old-world tome, almost as big as himself". He even found his way into College Library, to which at that date few boys had access. And what was he reading? Astonishingly, this boy of thirteen was reading the rarer Elizabethan and Jacobean dramatists. The book which, so he told Edmund Gosse, "taught me more than any other in the world—that and the Bible," was Lamb's *Specimens of the English Dramatic Poets*. This was the foundation for the theme which was to prove itself a lasting excitement throughout his life. We know that while at Eton he read, besides Shakespeare and Ben Jonson, Nabbes, Webster, Middleton and Tourneur. But this was not all. By 1853, being comfortably supplied with pocket-money, he had acquired an almost complete set of the *Aldine Poets*, which included besides Spenser and Milton, Chaucer, Burns, Pope, Prior, Swift, Thomson and Young. Nor were the moderns forgotten: Wordsworth, Coleridge, Keats and Shelley, Moore and Southey were all explored. Only Byron appears still to have remained banned. Thomas Hood he disliked. Landor, on the other hand, whom he discovered with "inexplicable pleasure and a sort of blind relief", remained for ever a flashing enthusiasm. And these early enthusiasms cannot be overstressed. His love for Sappho, Theocritus, Pindar and Aeschylus, for the early English drama, for Hugo and Landor and Shelley, was to retain throughout his life its charged, pristine and adolescent quality. His literary tastes were formed at Eton. They remained, with very few additions, unchanged throughout his life. At Putney, half a century later, he would still evince an almost physical excitement at the stimulus of a name which had caused him rapture at thirteen.

Not much remains of the literary productions of his schooldays. Swinburne himself believed that he had destroyed "every scrap of manuscript" on leaving Eton. The "blood-curdling dramas" of which Mrs. Leith speaks as the compositions of his childhood no doubt continued through his years at school. Of these a fragment has, happily, survived: four acts of a tragedy, written in an exercise-book, entitled *The Unhappy Revenge*. Almost certainly it is the tragedy referred to in the letter to John Collins of December 1876: "Thank you sincerely (*ex imo corde*, as my master Victor Hugo once began a letter to me unworthy, with a most tremendous dash under the words) for so high a compliment and one that I shall always prize so highly as the dedication of Tourneur. Nothing could have given me more pleasure, whether on private grounds as your friend, or on public as a lover and student of Cyril Tourneur and all his kind from the ripe age of twelve, at which I first read *The Revenger's Tragedy* in my tutor's Dodsley at Eton (which he was actually kind enough to entrust to such a small boy) with infinite edification, and such profit that to the utter neglect of my school work, to say nothing of my duties as a fag, I forthwith wrote a tragedy of which I have utterly forgotten the very name (having had the sense at sixteen to burn it together with every other scrap of MS. I had in the world) but into which I do remember, with ingenuity worthy of a better cause, I had contrived to pack twice as many rapes and about three times as many murders as are contained in the model, which is not noticeably or exceptionally deficient in such incidents. It must have been a sweet work, and full of the tender and visionary innocence of childhood's unsullied fancy."

*The Unhappy Revenge*, having somehow escaped the flames, passed into the possession of Isabel Swinburne. She has annotated it: "Tragedy written by A. C. Swinburne soon after he went to Eton at about 13 years old." From perhaps an excess of prudery three pages have been removed. It is, indeed, a curious revelation of the romantic horrors among which the child's precocious imagination moved. The scene is set in the Rome of the Emperor Maximus and the revenge is that of Eudoxia, whose honour he had betrayed,

which she takes by handing over the city to the Huns. It is
an astonishing production for a child, revealing already a
highly developed literary sense in the fidelity to his
models. The influences of Tourneur, Massinger and
Webster can be confidently traced; as indeed can a
certain voluptuous pleasure in the pangs of martyrdom.
It is worth quoting the funeral chant of the Christians to
give the reader some idea of what Swinburne was capable
even as a child:

> *All must wither into dust,*
> *Snowy age and youth all must*
> *In the grave join bloodless hands,*
> *And in everlasting bands,*
> *Let worldly joys and sorrows vain*
> *Swell false fortune's glistening train . . .*
> *Angels tune a jubilee*
> *While we vainly mourn for thee;*
> *All must wither in the grave;*
> *No man can his body save.*
> *But the gloomy wave of Death*
> *Chills our hot and panting breath;*
> *Stoop from heavenly skies awhile;*
> *Bless us with one radiant smile.*
> *Those who stood on the world's rack*
> *Lie in Death's corrosive bands*
> *And their humble graves must lack*
> *Offices of pious hands.*
> *But the garland of thy grave*
> *Never a withering time shall have.*
> *Earth's cold weight can ne'er in ties*
> *Oppress the blossom of the skies.*

There is one other English composition that survives
from this period. Unlike *The Unhappy Revenge*, which was
written for his own pleasure, *The Triumph of Gloriana* was
written under instructions and for an official occasion. On
the Fourth of June 1851, the anniversary, still celebrated at
Eton, of her grandfather, Queen Victoria visited the school.
Cory himself commemorated the occasion in verse and the
boys were instructed to do likewise. Swinburne, now

aged fourteen, produced an almost impeccable *pastiche* of
Pope.

> *What Muse shall boldly raise a humble lay*
> *To celebrate the glories of this day?*
> *When glittering myriads flock, a countless crowd*
> *Confus'd with hearts upraised and voices loud.*
> *A thousand shouts the spacious triumph filled;*
> *No heart, no tongue was then by silence chilled;*
> *What means this pomp? and what this festal throng,*
> *That down the crowded way is borne along?*
> *'Tis Gloriana now her palace seeks,*
> *And in that single voice wide Albion speaks. . . .*

Shepherds give the pastoral suggestion; and Eton, Harrow
and the Duke of Wellington appear respectively in classical
disguise, as Athens, Thebes and Miltiades. The poem is
important only in that it shows he was already competent
to assume a style with astonishing skill. The manner of the
eighteenth century is managed with bewildering assurance.

These early essays in literature, the dawning realization,
perhaps, that he possessed a particular talent which only
needed development, were no doubt stimulated by his
contacts with famous writers. Already Charles Dickens
had stayed at Bonchurch and remarked upon "the golden-
haired lad of the Swinburnes", and Lady Jane had removed
his novels from the Index. And now, in September 1849,
during the holidays from Eton, accompanied by Miss
Elizabeth Sewell, a friend of the family, the Swinburnes
presented themselves at Rydal Mount with a letter of
introduction. Wordsworth was pleased to remark that
"there was nothing in his writings that would do the boy
harm, and there were some things which might do him good".
He then told them how General Wolfe, at the battle of
Quebec, had recited Gray's celebrated *Elegy*. The aged
Laureate was so kind and so venerable that when, on their
departure, he said, with the apparent conviction that they
would never meet again, that "he did not think Algernon
would forget him", Algernon burst into tears. Six months
later Wordsworth was dead. And then, in 1851, Lady Jane
took Swinburne one evening to St. James's Place to visit
Samuel Rogers, the poet and banker, who now aged eighty-

seven had refused, on the score of advanced years, to succeed
Wordsworth in the Laureateship. Lady Jane remarked
that she had brought Algernon "because he thinks more of
poets than of any other people in the world". Mr. Rogers
graciously laid his hand on Algernon's head and said, "I
prophesy that you will be a poet too." Algernon was much
gratified, though it may be doubted to what extent it
stimulated his appreciation of *The Pleasures of Memory*.

But these meetings with the old and famous were merely
incidents in his Eton career whose importance can be easily
exaggerated. The most that can be said is that they provided
an extra stimulus to a spontaneous necessity. And his life
at Eton—much less that of a normal schoolboy's than has
sometimes been supposed—was conditioned by the peculiarities of his rapidly developing temperament. His passion for
literature and, perhaps, the unsuitability of his physique gave
him neither the time nor the strength to play games. There
is a reference in a letter, written late in life, to scoring a
"rouge" at Eton football, but contemporary records agree
that he did not play games and never even "possessed a
cricket-bat". His early biographers cast an idyllic atmosphere about his time at Eton, an aura of *couleur de rose*.
They were misled for a variety of reasons. In the first place
Swinburne, himself, never renounced Eton as he was later to
renounce Oxford. Obviously, therefore, given his rebellious
temperament, their relations must, until the final break, have
been harmonious. And, if harmonious, must they not have
been both happy and desirable? In 1867 Swinburne wrote:
"I should like to see two things at Eton again." The first of
these was the river. As the sea at Bonchurch so the river
at Eton held much of his devotion. Though never a strong
swimmer—his physique forbade it—he was a courageous one.
Cuckoo Weir, Upper Hope and Athens were his goals on
summer afternoons and remained always cherished memories.
Comparing himself with Shelley, he wrote: "I am more than
ever amazed at Shelley's neglect of swimming . . . my one
really and wholly delightful recollection of the place and time
being that of the swimming lessons and play in the Thames.
I would have wagered that Shelley of all verse-writing men
and Eton boys would have been the one at least to match me

in the passion of that pursuit." But the second of those things he wished to see again was the flogging-block. And here, too, his early biographers have been misled: the continuous humorous references to this aspect of Eton discipline which may be found in the letters of the whole of his lifetime cannot be taken at their face-value—humorous treatment being but an evasion which presupposes attraction to the subject. *A Year's Letters*, *The Flogging-Block*, *The Whippingham Papers* and *Lesbia Brandon*, in most of which the victim can be identified with Swinburne himself—not to mention *Eton: another Ode* ("Swish, swish, swish! O I wish, I wish I'd not been late for lock-up last night!")—show a much more serious preoccupation. Indeed, it was to become an obsession. There is no doubt that at Eton indestructible associations were created in his mind and the tendencies already latent in his temperament were confirmed.

There is, of course, no direct evidence as to when he became fully conscious of the implications of his abnormality. But could he help being aware of it? This awareness caused him almost continuous uneasiness and, at times, considerable unhappiness. Those unusual reactions to sea-bathing, the curious fascination to be derived from the tender bullying of his girl cousins, the pleasurable agonies of the birch, began early to induce in him a sense of isolation. It became tragically and increasingly clear to him that he was differently constituted to other people. And this may well account for his not altogether coherent attitude towards Eton. On the one hand, we derive an impression that he never quite fitted in to the pattern of the school while he was there, that he was solitary and almost friendless. Sir George Young—"I should think I *did* remember," he wrote in after years, "the best friend of my schoolboyhood"—seems in truth to have been the only one. And Young was a day-boy with a comfortable house nearby in which Swinburne could take refuge. His cousin, Mitford, he does not appear to have seen much, while "the other fellows", occasionally referred to, remain anonymous. And then, why did he leave Eton prematurely? Was it as a result of some trouble with Mr. Joynes or was it simply that he did not wish to return, being no longer able to support the impassable barrier that his growing consciousness of eccentricity created between himself and his fellows? Gosse's explanation that he left "in consequence of some representations" does not take us much further. One thing, however, is quite clear, he was in no sense expelled: the initiative for his departure lay with himself and his family. On the other hand, he maintained throughout his life a certain nostalgia for the school. In retrospect at any rate that something enduringly adolescent in his character caused him to look upon Eton as a place of fulfilment, in his imagination at least the submissive trait in his temperament had responded avidly to an authoritarian society, had yielded with alacrity to the sanction of the "best of all punishments". It was upon this aspect of Eton that his mind liked to dwell. And thus gradually his algolagnia dictated in later years a view of Eton that was largely at variance with his actual experience. It is only thus that the paradox of his deliberately leaving a place which he loved can be explained. Having left for the summer holidays at Bonchurch, he did not return. The reasons for his leaving remained a mystery to his contemporaries.

# CHAPTER III

## (1853–1860)

CONSCIOUS of his isolation, of being differently constituted to other people, belonging, as he did, to a class that was becoming progressively more intolerant of the eccentric, Swinburne's instinct was to conceal his abnormality. What was to be done? The cloak he selected was the uniform of the Dragoons. Stimulated, perhaps, by his reading of the Elizabethan drama, he had formulated the illusion of a romantic and adventurous future, had identified his reading with the aspirations of real life. But the Dragoons, with his nervous and diminutive physique, were as a solution grotesque, and were promptly vetoed by his father. Denied, therefore, the anodyne of a fashionable profession and one—who could tell?—which might have conditioned him to that normality he so ardently desired, what was there for him to do? Inspired by the Balaclava Charge, symbolic of unattainable glories, his immediate reaction was to climb Culver Cliff "as a chance of testing my nerve in face of death which could not be surpassed". Throughout his life he hankered after military glory, regretted too, perhaps, the denial of this the first of his snatches at normality. The disappointment was permanent. Thirty years later, commenting to Gosse on his increasing deafness, he added, "so that, after all, I suppose I should not have done well to be a soldier"! But the problem of a profession had still to be considered. What, the Admiral and Lady Jane may well have asked—and were to ask again in similar crises—was to be done with Algernon? There were two possible professions: the Church and the Law. With these possibilities in view he was to be gently directed towards Oxford. And Oxford was to show him an alternative. Though the longing to conform was never altogether suppressed, was, indeed, to recur at intervals till ultimately it triumphed, he was to discover, with his first serious attempts

26

at creation, the true basis of his inspiration. The abnormality
was to be exploited.

But this was not yet. Having left Eton prematurely if
unspectacularly, there were still two years before he could
enter the University. There were rather vague scholastic pre-
parations with tutors, with the Reverend John Williamson,
vicar of Cambo and, later, with the Reverend James Wood-
ford, vicar of Kempsford and afterwards Bishop of Ely. But
in the main life at East Dene, Ashburnham Place and Capheaton was continued very much as in the holidays from
school: a healthy outdoor life of swimming, walking and
riding in the company of cousins; the writing of dramas for
amateur performance; and the wide reading within the limits
of the libraries of the family houses.

It was probably in Northumberland that he was happiest.
Did he not make it the background for *The Sisters*? The
wild austerity of its country-side, the presence of his Jacobin
of a grandfather, aroused in him the dual sensations of
reverence and enfranchisement. Besides, was not Wallington
close at hand? This house became for him a refuge and an
inspiration. Half-way between Capheaton and Cambo,
William Bell Scott has left us an account of seeing Swinburne
at Wallington on his way to or from the vicarage, mounted
on a pony with a long tail, his massed, flaming hair blowing
round his head and his school books strapped to his saddle.
At this date Wallington was the favourite residence of Sir
Walter Trevelyan, geologist and botanist. Their relationship is obscure, unless there is some hint of it in the character
of the naturalist Ernest Rudworth, who appears in *A Year's
Letters*. There cannot ever have been much sympathy
between them. Sir Walter, severe, acid and bigoted, contrived with a superb irony to possess one of the best cellars
in England and to be a fanatical teetotaller. Dining
his guests on the rarer of unpalatable fungi, gathered with
his own hands, he would conform so far to the customs of
the age as to produce one bottle of wine. Of this it was an
unforgiveable solecism to indulge in more than a single glass.
Between Sir Walter and Swinburne there can have been little
temperamental accord. But, in 1835, at Cambridge for the
Congress of the Association for the Advancement of Science,

Sir Walter had met Paulina Jermyn. Immediately, he had been deeply impressed. Did she not understand the most abstruse of lectures? Had she not read and criticized Doctor Whewell's *History of the Inductive Sciences*? Here, obviously, was the perfect wife; and he had married her. But Lady Trevelyan's masculine intelligence cloaked an equally profound and delicate sensibility. She wrote verses and studied painting. She admired Turner and, under the influence of Ruskin, followed with passionate interest the early efforts of the Pre-Raphaelites. Through her Swinburne was first to come into contact with this then esoteric school. Moreover she was "a woman of singular and unique charm; quiet and quaint in manner, nobly emotional, ingrainedly artistic, very wise and sensible, with an ever-flowing spring of the most delicious humour". At this date, 1854, she was thirty-eight years old and twenty years younger than her husband. In the opinion of William Bell Scott she was neither beautiful nor ugly but "as light as a feather and as quick as a kitten".

Lady Trevelyan encouraged Swinburne's visits to Wallington. She was intelligent enough to detect his talents. She encouraged him to write verses. He responded with a passionate devotion. For the first time he encountered the exquisite delights of understanding for his genius, of sympathy for his aspirations. Perhaps it was now, at the beginning of this friendship, that he first consciously decided upon the vocation of a poet. Many of his poems were to be heard for the first time in her drawing-room where, standing upon a chair, with rigid body and fluttering hands, his voice rising ever higher in almost hysterical excitement, the beholders would be impressed by the occult strangeness of this unselfconscious performance. Many years later Swinburne wrote of his "dear friend (and the first one my boyish verse ever had among adults) Lady Trevelyan". She had, during the short years of their friendship, a profoundly beneficial influence over him. She was his guardian angel, ready always with eagerly accepted criticism and advice both in the conduct of his art and of his life. It was a permanent misfortune for him that her early death took place in 1866.

It was, too, at Wallington that Swinburne first met her
young relative, George Otto Trevelyan, though the acquaintanceship had nothing but the sterility of mutually exclusive
interests. Here also he first met Ruskin, already at the
height of his fame, for Ruskin was a frequent visitor to
Wallington, though it seems impossible to determine whether
this first meeting took place before or after Swinburne
entered Oxford. It was, for the eminent critic, to be the
first step in a curious if one-sided relationship; the strange
and improbable combination of Swinburne's personality and
genius aroused in him emotions both of fascination and
repugnance which he was never quite able to resolve.

In July 1855 Swinburne for the first time went abroad.
In company with his uncle, General Thomas Ashburnham,
and Lord Sandwich he went to Germany for some weeks.
They went by Calais and Liége, where the country reminded
Swinburne of Northumberland, and then by Aix-la-Chapelle
to Cologne. He became, immediately, a passionate sight-
seer and insisted upon the company of his exhausted but
German-speaking uncle as interpreter. In witnessing the
Mass in Cologne Cathedral, so he wrote to his mother, he
felt like bursting into tears to think of the divisions and
jealousies which separated the great branches of the Christian
Church. Evidently the High Church doctrines of East Dene
were still very present to his consciousness. Then by way
of Coblenz, where there was the excitement of meeting a
veteran of Balaclava, and up the Rhine by boat to Wiesbaden,
that the General might take the cure.

After some more sightseeing, Swinburne and his uncle
—Lord Sandwich had left them—returned to England by
Ostend. Germany, except for the pleasure of sightseeing,
the castles of the Rhine perhaps, left very little impression
on him. The lessons he took in the language, no doubt all
too few, did nothing to ameliorate his ignorance. He could
never speak it or read it. He felt, apparently, no real
sympathy with the country or its inhabitants. At Oxford he
was to resist the influence of Carlyle and the Germanophiles.
Except for this one short visit Germany played no part in
his life.

But on the return journey, which took place towards the

end of August, he was to receive one of the most vivid and enduring impressions of his life. Not as a rule particularly sensitive to the world around him, not, indeed, much aware of it, he had, nevertheless, a selective faculty which could awaken in him at rare moments an ecstasy of concentrated observation. The impression, once acquired, remained ineffaceable. The ship on which they crossed was delayed for three hours by a thunderstorm which caught her in mid-Channel. The spectacle of the sea, with which he had always felt so profound an affinity, in this new and exciting guise with its "race and riot of lights, beautiful and rapid", as he was to write fourteen years later in a review of *L'Homme Qui Rit*, raised him "to the very summit of vision and delight". He remembered it always as a night of "such glory, such terror, such passion", and his verse is endlessly full of references to it. At last, in his old age, he was to describe it all over again in *A Channel Passage*:

*Three glad hours, and it seemed not an hour of supreme and supernal*
    *joy,*
*Filled full with delight that revives in remembrance a sea-bird's*
    *heart in a boy.*

On 23rd January 1856 Swinburne, now aged eighteen, went up to Balliol. Oxford at this date was still, looked at from the standpoint of to-day, almost medieval in her preoccupations. Indeed she was still suffering the aftermath of religious war. The great controversy of the Oxford Movement was still alive though its leaders had quitted the battlefield. The necessity for members of the University to subscribe to the Thirty-nine Articles had been abolished only two years before. Heresy-hunting was still the fashionable sport; and Jowett was to be accused of it by Pusey as late as 1863 and, more immediately, had failed to be elected to the mastership of Balliol which was clearly his due. In a day when the great majority of the Fellows of colleges were in Orders all discussion of reforms tended to be linked to theological controversy. Lectures, regulations, even the conversation of undergraduates were inclined to reflect the guerrilla tactics of religious discussion. Plunged suddenly into this alien atmosphere Swinburne, no doubt, was at first struck with a bewilderment which very soon turned to boredom. Perhaps this accounts for the reports that as a freshman he was "very reserved" and "rather sullen". Very likely the Anglican ritualism in which he had been brought up and which appears to have remained with him till now, if not fanatically practised at least outwardly unquestioned, received its first shock from this unexpected contact with Christian backbiting. The successive influences of "Old Mortality" and the Pre-Raphaelites were ultimately to destroy his faith.

In 1856 Balliol had not yet started upon that rôle of wet-nurse to the careers of famous men which was to obtain for her so distinguished a renown by the end of the century. Indeed at this time there might even have been discerned a certain intellectual torpor amongst her inmates. Scott, the Master, whose literary remains include a Greek Lexicon and the, at that date, indispensable volume of sermons, does not appear to have had any personality to impress upon his college, while Jowett, whose name is indissolubly connected with its future fame, was being violently attacked for his support of religious toleration. Nevertheless Jowett, who was now Regius Professor of Greek with a brilliant scholastic career behind him, had great influence amongst the younger dons and there was a feeling in the air that he was "a coming man". He was to exercise a beneficial effect upon Swinburne, who became devoted to him, but it was only after Swinburne had been up some time that he was to take any serious place in his life.

Though Swinburne's manner "had a particular charm of refinement and good breeding" it does not appear that his early days at Balliol were altogether satisfactory. No doubt his strangeness of appearance, his refusal to take part in any outdoor amusements, and the report that he was "engaged upon a tragedy" were not conducive to popularity in a society which in those days was probably much less tolerant than even Eton had been. We can well understand that his verse was "not much appreciated by the rank and file of the college". As a freshman he seems to have led a solitary life, "never appearing at wine-parties or at breakfasts". The isolation he had known at school evidently pursued him

in his early Oxford career. Nor did his application to the
official courses of study encourage any tutorial hopes.

It was mostly outside his college that his first contacts
appear to have been made. Already in May 1856 he was
dining at the Radcliffe Observatory with Mr. Johnson, the
astronomer, and from the reference to him as "a Balliol
friend of mine" in a letter of Birkbeck Hill's, who was also
present, it would appear that they were already acquainted.
Then, through Miss Sewell, he met her brother, who was
Warden of St. Peter's College, Radley. Swinburne was
invited to spend Sundays there and enjoyed talking to the
boys, recapturing perhaps that atmosphere of adolescence
which no doubt he already regretted. But soon he was to
be discovered corrupting Mr. Sewell's pupils by defending
Tennyson's *Maud*, and being guilty of "theories of free-
thinking". Reluctantly the gates of Radley had to be
closed against him. He might, so Mr. Sewell feared,
"inoculate boys with his sinister tenets".

And then there was the Taylorean—the Oxford citadel
of modern languages. Aurelio Saffi was responsible for
lecturing in Italian. He had been living in England in exile
since 1851, having had to leave Italy after the events of 1849.
Minister of the Interior, one of a triumvirate with Armellini
and Mazzini, he made his living by writing and speaking
for the cause and by instructing undergraduates in Italian.
Swinburne was profoundly impressed. Under the influence
of Saffi liberty, and particularly Italian liberty, began to
acquire a place in his mythology. Saffi, no doubt, constituted only an introduction to the worship of Mazzini, but
he never lost his place in Swinburne's affections. In 1886
he wrote:

> *Year after year has fallen on sleep till change*
> *Hath seen the fourth part of a century fade,*
> *Since you, a guest to whom the vales were strange*
> *Where Isis whispers to the murmuring shade,*
> *Above her face by winds and willows made,*
> *And I, elate at heart with reverence, met.*

He dedicated to him three poems and placed him in the
hierarchy of his admiration as: "In Dante's presence, by
Mazzini's side."

This republicanism was to be much stimulated by the association known as "Old Mortality" and, in particular, by its founder, John Nichol. Nichol was some years older than Swinburne, and indeed of most of the rest of the set of which he was the leader, and of which Swinburne now became a member. Having already spent four years at Glasgow University, where his father was Professor of Astronomy, he was, not only in age but in intellectual outlook and character, already much more formed than the others. He was a logician of parts: had travelled; admired Mill, Carlyle and Goethe, had met Kossuth and Mazzini, was free-thinking and republican. But there was also something a little sinister about him. His austere and ruthless intelligence was allied to a certain melancholy, a capacity for satire and a sardonic wit. Though he was only to become Professor of English Literature at Glasgow, though in his old age, when the disparity of intellectual attainment had been removed, Swinburne was to write from Putney, "I won't see Nichol again! He spent the time reading his own stuff to me", there is no doubt that at Oxford his influence was complete and dominating. At his instance that lingering Anglicanism that Swinburne had so far managed to maintain languished and was discarded for ever, and those vague libertarian emotions which had been burgeoning in that excitable mind, the fading Jacobinism of Sir John at Capheaton, the enthusiasm for Shelley, Landor and Hugo, the lectures of Signor Saffi, suddenly became integrated and fused in a blinding flash of light. From now on Mazzini became the centre of Swinburne's curious mythology; his portrait found its place on the wall of his rooms; while Napoleon III became a sort of Antichrist. Swinburne would scream with bird-like fury at the very mention of his name. And when Orsini made his attempt at assassination his portrait joined Mazzini's. Before them Swinburne would dance, pirouetting solemnly, and making formal acts of obeisance. And when, in 1858, Swinburne's family took him to Paris he gave them a solemn undertaking that while in France he would do nothing subversive to the *régime*. And though he handsomely kept his word not to endanger the Empire, a meeting, while driving in an open carriage in the Champs-Élysées, with the Emperor, proved altogether too much for his republican emotions. While the Admiral raised his hat and Lady Jane bowed, Algernon gazed steadfastly to his front, "not wishing", as he informed Gosse, "to be obliged to cut my hand off at the wrist the moment I returned to the hotel"!

Nichol founded the Old Mortality Society one evening in his rooms in Balliol. The original six members were: Nichol; Swinburne; Algernon Grenfell; the future Professor A. V. Dicey; George Birkbeck Hill, the future editor of the works of Dr. Johnson; and George Rankine Luke. This last, who was perhaps the most imposing figure of them all, for his great promise and "the beauty and originality of his character", was to meet a tragic fate. In 1862 he was accidentally drowned in the Isis. In 1881 his memory still haunted Swinburne:

> *His name who sorrow and reverent love recall*
> *The sign to friends on earth of that dear head*
> *Alive, which now long since untimely dead*
> *The wan grey waters covered for a pall.*

Other members were added later: Lord Bryce, Professor T. E. Holland, and the philosopher, T. H. Green. While after Swinburne had left Oxford, Walter Pater and J. A. Symonds joined.

In the minutes of the Society it is recorded that: "It was decided to call the society Old Mortality from the consideration that every member of the aforesaid Society was or has lately been in so weak and precarious a condition of bodily health as plainly and manifestly to instance the great frailties and so to speak mortality of this our human life and constitution and this name, therefore, was formally adopted." Further the intention of the society was defined as: "Object: stimulating and promoting the interchange of thought among the members on the more general questions of literature, philosophy, science as well as the diffusion of a correct knowledge and critical appreciation of our standard English authors." And the Society's proceedings were on a level with the future intellectual eminence of its members. On 23rd May 1857 there was a discussion on Hume's defence

of suicide; on 7th November Nichol read an essay on
Wycliffe; on 13th February 1858 there was a discussion on
the English satirists: Byron and Pope were praised; Swinburne proclaimed the superiority of Dryden. There were, too,
readings from modern works. Swinburne read Browning's
*The Statue and the Bust* and *The Heretic's Tragedy*; also
Morris's *The Defence of Guinevere*. Intellectually austere
though the proceedings of the Society may have been,
its meetings were enlivened with libations of claret and
brandy. The Society had its lighter moments. Hill writes
of a picnic on the river and "Old Mortality's" intention to
"make merry". But as they became better known in the
University they began to be looked at askance. Were they
not engaged in intellectual pursuits? Did they not refuse
to play games and despise physical exercise? Did they
not support the Italian patriots and attack Napoleon III?
And, more seriously still, it was whispered that "they read
Browning"! Singularity, obviously, could go no further.

In November 1857 the "Old Mortality", under the leadership as always of Nichol, took over a magazine which they
renamed *Undergraduate Papers*. The publishers were to
pay the contributors five shillings a page. We know that
all this time Swinburne was writing. Hill recorded in
March 1857: "Yesterday I was in Swinburne's room. I
wish you knew the little fellow. He is the most enthusiastic
fellow I ever met, and one of the cleverest. He wanted to
read me some poems he had written and have my opinion.
They are really very good and he read them with such an
earnestness, so truly feeling everything he had written that I
for the first time in my life enjoyed hearing the poetry of an
amateur." It is possible that these poems included the *Ode
to Mazzini* and *The Temple of Janus*, which later he entered
for the Newdigate but without success. Curiously enough,
though, his first appearance in print was in the form of prose
—a perhaps not unnaturally arid article on Congreve in
*The Imperial Dictionary* of 1857. The first number of *Undergraduate Papers* appeared on 1st December. Hill wrote
on that date: "The Magazine ought to have come out
last night, and we were a good deal disappointed that it was
late; for Swinburne had invited all the contributors to his

room, except Nichol, who had gone down to welcome in
the little stranger. Tho' we had not the satisfaction of
having the paper itself we still managed to drink its health in
very good claret as well as the health of each contributor,
and the absent editor also. So we made very merry indeed,
and tho' the baby was not there, still the christening was very
successful."

Swinburne contributed *The Early English Dramatists*,
*Queen Yseult* and *Modern Hellenism*, an article of which he
never admitted the authorship since it was in effect an attack
on Matthew Arnold who had recently been appointed
Professor of Poetry, to the first number; *The Monomaniacs'
Tragedy* to the second; and *Church Imperialism* to the third.
Of these *Queen Yseult* was particularly significant. It
was the beginning of a new phase, the acknowledgement
of a new influence and the opening of his Pre-Raphaelite
period.

That Swinburne should be drawn into the orbit of the
Pre-Raphaelites was inevitable. The appeal of a revolutionary artistic movement was irresistible. The atmosphere
of Oxford was oppressive. Even the "Old Mortality" was
apt to suffer from an incipient donnishness which could fill
him with ill-concealed tedium, as on the celebrated occasion
when T. H. Green read an essay on the development of
Christian Dogma—a subject, for Swinburne, of profound
irrelevance. A Romantic Movement—particularly one that
could satisfactorily combine Mazzini and Medievalism,
painting and poetry, wealth and Workmen's Colleges—was
exactly what he needed. The astonishing fact about the
P.R.B. was that its relative success as a movement was
combined with a complete lack of any community of artistic
practice. The nebulous ideals upon which the first Brotherhood had been founded had prevented its aims from ever
being quite clear, and this in turn had permitted its members
to interpret them in their own way. And to what extraordinary divergences this had led! Indeed, romantic
individualism had been the cause of the disintegration of the
first Brotherhood. It had drawn Hunt, who interpreted
its nebulous aims in terms of religion, to the shores of the
Dead Sea where, in ascetic if traditional surroundings, a

tethered, flea-bitten animal posed for *The Scapegoat*; it had
led Millais to seek the ultimate guerdon of success in the
hunting-field, the deer-forest and the drawing-rooms of
Mayfair; and it had led Woolner to the Antipodes.
Rossetti, though this was disputed by Hunt, was popularly
esteemed the leader of the Brotherhood. But by 1853, when
the P.R.B. had been in existence for five years, it appeared
that he alone remained. But though the Brotherhood was
dissolved, its vague romantic aspirations had taken root,
not only amongst the writers and artists of the capital, but
by a curious process of infiltration through all ranks of
society: amongst the business men of the Midlands, the
working masses of the industrial North. It became a focus
for every kind of idealism: for the new social worker whose
conscience was aroused by the appalling legacy of the
industrial revolution; for the millowner who sought to spend
his excess profits on culture; for the weaver, lifting his tired
eyes from the loom, who sought a sudden glimpse of an
unknown, unimaginable romance. Here and there throughout the land grey and overcast lives were suddenly lit by the
blinding flash of a mystical splendour. The ideal, whatever
it was, had become part of Victorian England. And in 1856,
through the accession of two young and ardent disciples,
Rossetti was able to reconstitute the P.R.B. With the
collaboration of Burne-Jones and Morris there was to be a
new and even more remarkable florescence. And a year
later Swinburne and Rossetti were to meet for the first time.

Already the foundations for this meeting had been laid:
contacts had been established, as it were, with the Pre-
Raphaelite perimeter. The Long Vacation of 1857 was spent
partly in Scotland with Nichol, where a visit to Skye in tearing
high spirits produced the most execrable puns—"we ran a
Muck—we made a Mull—it is a Rum go"—and partly at
Wallington with Lady Trevelyan, where he met Bell Scott,
who it appears from his rather obscure *Autobiographical
Notes* had already seen Swinburne some years before but
had apparently not been introduced to him. Bell Scott was
a drawing-master at the Government School of Design at
Newcastle, and had known Rossetti since 1848. It is
probable that it was also on this visit that Swinburne was

first personally presented to Ruskin, who is known to have
stayed at Wallington in that year on his way back from a
visit to the Highlands. A few months later at Oxford he
asked Swinburne to come to see him. But there was a more
direct line of approach even than this. Early in his Oxford
career Swinburne had met, probably through Birkbeck Hill,
Edwin Hatch of Pembroke. Hatch was now the dominating
personality of the "Birmingham Set", whose headquarters
were at Pembroke and which included Cormell Price, later
to become the headmaster to whom Kipling dedicated
*Stalky & Co.*; Faulkner, gifted both in the arts and mathematics; Dixon, poet and future canon, and some few others.
This set had recently suffered the loss of William Morris and
Burne-Jones, who, though at Exeter, had been the founders
of the group and had started *The Oxford and Cambridge
Magazine*, now edited by Faulkner, under the inspiration of
*The Germ*, which had been the organ of the first P.R.B.

Rossetti, in the intervals of painting, was at this time,
encouraged by Ruskin, busily engaged with the Working
Men's College. Still only twenty-eight, he seemed already to
have attained to the importance and position of successful
middle age. With a curiously personal blend of outward
high spirits and inner melancholy, with the magic of an
attitude and an unfaltering genius for enthusiasm, he was
capable of transforming the most diverse characters into
devoted disciples. With Morris and Burne-Jones the
transformation was effected without difficulty. The first
number of *The Oxford and Cambridge Magazine* contained
praise by Burne-Jones of *The Blessed Damozel* and *The
Story of Chiaro*. Rossetti was gratified. Burne-Jones went
to London and visited Rossetti at Chatham Place. Morris
met him a few months later. Rossetti contributed to their
magazine. They became Ned and Topsy and must, said
Rossetti, leave Oxford and paint. By the end of 1856 they
were installed in Red Lion Square painting hard. It was
Burne-Jones' "Wonderful Year". They were taken to see
the Madox Browns in Kentish Town, the Brownings in
Devonshire Place, the Prinseps and G. F. Watts, and one
glorious day at Chatham Place there entered "the greatest
genius that is on earth alive, William Holman Hunt"

Stimulated by this fortuitous contact with Oxford and by his admiration for the Fire Office in Chatham Place designed by Woodward, "a thorough thirteenth-century Gothic man", Rossetti and Morris went to Oxford and came back with the commission—though only living expenses and materials were to be paid—to decorate Woodward's debating hall for the Union Society. "Rossetti and Morris," wrote Burne-Jones, "came back full of schemes about the Union. Gabriel is hungry to fill all the blanks and the pictures are to be from the *Morte d'Arthur*, so wills our master." The team was soon recruited: Burne-Jones, Morris, Arthur Hughes, Pollen, Val Prinsep and Spencer Stanhope. They were young, and filled with an excess of those astonishing nineteenth-century high spirits. Oxford was besieged with a storm of facetious hilarity. She capitulated. Invitations poured into 76 High Street and, later, into 13 George Street. Rossetti's serious belief that everyone should be a painter was considered the most flashing and scintillating of *bons mots* at the high tables, while the favourable Pre-Raphaelite epithet of "stunner" became fashionable in Junior Common Rooms. A great deal of busy work was done in the debating hall, but then there were so many luncheons and dinners—while Morris and Burne-Jones found it very difficult to get out of bed in the mornings—that the work, which was supposed to have been finished in October, dragged on through November and December, and on through January; in February they were still painting, but it was never to be finished. And, owing to their complete innocence of all technical knowledge, Sir Tristram and Iseult, Sir Lancelot and the Chapel of the Holy Grail, the little figures of Morris in the angles of the roof, the sunflowers and the Australian Badger, all faded away till they became but pallid ghosts in the plaster.

In the diary of Cormell Price there is an entry dated 1st November 1857: "To Hill's where were Topsy, Ted, Swan, Hatch, Swinburne of Balliol (introduced, I think, by Hatch) and Faulkner." Without doubt this was Swinburne's first meeting with Morris and Burne-Jones. An introduction to Rossetti followed swiftly. To William Rossetti's statement that Swinburne had introduced himself to Gabriel in the debating hall of the Union, Swinburne replied in 1895

with outraged dignity: "I never (allow me to say) introduced
myself to anybody, and certainly should not have done so in
my nonage.  An Oxford friend, Hill, who knew Jones and
Morris and through them Gabriel, introduced me to them,
and Gabriel almost instantly asked me to sit (or stand) to
him—but the intended 'fresco' never was even begun."

Nevertheless he was made free of the debating hall, where
the artists, perched on ladders, painted in that peculiar
Pre-Raphaelite atmosphere of slangy, bawdy horseplay.
"What fun we had in that Union!" wrote Val Prinsep.
"What jokes! What roars of laughter!"  While Burne-
Jones was to remember: "It was blue summer then, and
always morning and the air sweet and full of bells."  Only
Pollen, some ten years older than the rest, complained to his
wife: "There is such a rattle of talk from surrounding
worthies that I fear my wits will fail; Topsy and Rossetti
giving vent to most startling opinions, with which I need not
trouble you.  I greatly feel the disadvantage of appearing
in such company."

By the three principals Swinburne was accepted at once.
If the relationship established with Rossetti was not immediately as intimate as with the other two, it was perhaps more
because he was frequently absent from Oxford at the bedside
of Elizabeth Siddall, whose illness was his constant anxiety,
rather than from any difference in age or any aura of *cher
maître*.  But Swinburne's attitude was one of immediate
and profound hero-worship.  It was the beginning of a
friendship that, reaching its apogee in 1861, was only to
terminate in 1872.  But if, as Burne-Jones said, "Rossetti
was the planet round which we revolved, we copied his ways
of speaking . . . we sank our own individuality in the strong
personality of our beloved Gabriel", it was more immediately
with the other two that Swinburne entered into the closest
friendship.  The recognition appears to have been immediate and mutual.  Burne-Jones said: "We are four where
we were only three."  And Morris, who, having met Jane
Burden, the daughter of an Oxford livery-stable keeper,
whom he later married, was to stay on in Oxford for a year,
wrote poetry which Swinburne received with rapture.  The
*Defence of Guinevere* was, no doubt, the inspiration for

Swinburne's *Queen Yseult*, the first canto of which, as we have seen, was published in *Undergraduate Papers*.

In the meantime there were excursions, dinners and entertainments to be enjoyed and the hospitable Dr. Acland, friend of Ruskin, and solemnly and pretentiously philanthropic, to be avoided. The "Rose of Brazil" they named him for some esoteric Pre-Raphaelite reason, and on one occasion they all took the train to London to avoid a tea-party to which he had invited them. "Acland's pulse," remarked Burne-Jones, "is only really quickened when osteologists are by, who compare their bones with his till the conversation rattles." And then when Dr. Acland, who always wished to share their "orgies and dare-devilries", was so kind as to read to them a paper on sewage, "there was a scene", remarks Gosse, "over which the Muse of History must draw a veil".

These winter and spring months of 1857–1858 were happy and profitable for Swinburne. In the Pre-Raphaelite Brotherhood he had found both inspiration and ideal companionship. Even his relationship with the college authorities appears to have been good at this time. Jowett was beginning to take an interest in this remarkable undergraduate. Moderations were successfully passed with a second class; a £25 bursary was won for studies in Italian and French; and had he not been honoured by Lord Tennyson in the Christmas vacation with an invitation to dine at Farringford and a reading from *Maud*?

It was too good to last. Till the long penumbra of The Pines closed about him, Swinburne's life was remarkable for its lack of even tenor. His nerves responded with exacerbation to any change in his surroundings. And now those friends who had made Oxford tolerable were disappearing one by one. It was, after all, to only a limited circle—the "Old Mortality", the Pre-Raphaelites and possibly Jowett—that he was really known or valued in the University. By the majority of dons and undergraduates he was considered mad and even, considering his political views, potentially dangerous. Now that the Pre-Raphaelites had gone, Nichol had gone, Hatch, Spencer Stanhope and others had taken their degrees, he was left very much alone. The "Old

Mortality" struggled on, but with an increasing aridity, a
more donnish intellectuality, which made less and less appeal
to him.   Even Jowett had not yet acquired the confidence
and respect which Swinburne was later to lavish upon him.
Though, for his part, with his unfailing intuition for future
eminence, though puzzled and irritated, Jowett was probably
more sympathetic than Swinburne realized.   But he was
not the man to excuse academic failure on the grounds
of extraneous reading or the composition of verses; and
towards the end of the year Swinburne was writing: "I have
myself been rather busy in working (unhappily too late) for
my first examination in classics — which turns out a failure."

Nevertheless he did not lose sight altogether of the Pre-
Raphaelites during these months.   There were occasional
visits to Blackfriars Bridge, where Rossetti was now living,
and there were letters from Burne-Jones which began:
"Dear little carrots . . ."   But he needed, as he was to need
throughout his life, sympathetic companionship, and this
was lacking.   The isolation, which he felt was in some way
*imposed* upon him, caused an outburst of that rebellion to
which he was prone at times of nervous irritation.   Not only
did it take the form of revolt against the liberal discipline
of the college but also—and this was perhaps even more
serious—wild, ecstatic and frequently not altogether lucid
speeches in the Union.   Dicey, President of the Union,
was friendly and amused.   Others were less tolerant.
The climax was perhaps reached with a violent if imprudent
defence of tyrannicide at the moment of the Prince of Wales'
visit to the University.   Gradually and with deliberation the
authorities became concerned.   There were, too, aggravating
circumstances: his landlady complained of "irregularities";
late hours and "alcoholic excesses".   Before matters came
to a head, Jowett, for fear that Balliol might make itself "as
ridiculous as University had made itself about Shelley",
arranged that he should temporarily quit the University at
the end of 1859 to cram history and law with the Reverend
William Stubbs, Vicar of Navestock.   It might be defined
as a merciful rustication; for Swinburne a change of air, for
Oxford a chance to forget.   All might yet, perhaps, come
right.   That it did not was no fault of Jowett's.

Though the reading for schools lacked system and application, the time had not been wasted. His general reading was wide and only less remarkable, because he was now older, than it had been at Eton. Amongst the moderns were Browning, Ruskin, Rossetti, the Brontës, Patmore, Arnold and even Emerson. Carlyle he read under the influence of Nichol, but repudiated as much on the grounds of natural antipathy as on the advice of Jowett. By Rossetti he was introduced to Meinhold, Charles Wells and Beddoes' *Death's Jest Book*. With Morris he read Chaucer and the medieval romances: the *Morte d'Arthur* and the Chronicles of Burchard, Brantôme, Froissart and Joinville. Perhaps, too, at this time, he had already heard the Pre-Raphaelites mention Blake with enthusiasm. He was certainly acquainted with the *Decameron* and had made an attempt to translate Dante into English verse. While in the register of the Taylorean Institute Swinburne appears to have borrowed from the library during the course of 1859 the works of Stendhal, Dumas, Ronsard, Balzac and Michelet amongst others. Hugo he read constantly, probably knew the novels of Georges Sand and Eugène Sue, and had approved of *Mademoiselle de Maupin*. With profound excitement he followed the developments of modern French literature in the *Revue des Deux Mondes*. This passion for France, its literature and civilization, was to have an enormous effect upon his own work. For years his writing, verse, prose and correspondence, was to be filled with French allusions, quotations, interjections and isolated words, till sometimes one wonders in which language his thoughts flowed the more easily, while the neurosis of French romantic literature, the erotic sensibility, was to find its English counterpart on the publication of *Poems and Ballads*.

But the full range of his reading, his intellectual preoccupations and the influence to which he was subject can best be realized by referring to the writings of these Oxford years. They may, roughly, be divided into three groups: political, Pre-Raphaelite, and dramatic. These are naturally no hard and fast divisions, but merely groupings of convenience. Political and medieval inspirations spilled over and are liable to be found fused and intermingled in any of the poems. It is remarkable that very little intrinsic literary merit is to be discovered in these early works—most of the output of this period was indeed not published in his lifetime, much of it even remaining unpublished to-day. He served perhaps a longer apprenticeship to his art than is the case with most major poets. Possibly one of the main reasons for this was his dangerous facility in *pastiche* which inhibited the development of a personal style. But the interest of these early poems lies in the light they throw upon his mental development. It is possible, for instance, to see in his preoccupation with revolutionary politics a searching for a means of attacking a society with which temperamentally he did not feel at one. In this sense it was a compensation for his unhappy eccentricity. It is to be remarked that from the moment he began to exploit his abnormality as the basis for inspiration, and began to build up the synthesis that culminated in *Atalanta*, the composition of political poems lapsed, only to be returned to with *Songs before Sunrise* when the algolagnic synthesis in its turn had failed him.

Of the political group, influenced by Saffi and the views of "Old Mortality", ("There was not one of us who would have questioned for a moment that sacred duty [of regicide]"), the earliest in time was the *Ode to Mazzini*, written in 1857, and found amongst his papers after his death in 1909. Of the technical influences in evidence Shelley's—of the *Ode to Liberty* and the *Ode to Naples*—is the most important. But it is instructive to compare the almost intimate form in which Mazzini is addressed with the idolatry of *Songs before Sunrise*. Despite the portrait hanging in Swinburne's rooms, Mazzini is rather the representative of a movement, a name in the newspapers, than a personal god.

> *And men despond around thee: and thy name*
> *The tyrant smiles at, and his priests look pale; . . .*
> *And hope dies out like a forgotten tale,*
> *O brother crowned among men . . .*

Never again was Mazzini to be addressed with this fraternal familiarity.

This first Italian political period was continued, under the fairly successful disguise of the ambiguous title set for the Newdigate in 1857, in *The Temple of Janus*. The MS. is in the British Museum and has never been published. The diction of Shelley shows through the heroic couplets which were a condition of the prize. But throughout the rather amorphous composition, by a sort of sleight of hand, the poet succeeds in introducing topical references to Liberty and modern Italy. Faithful to the doctrines of Mazzini and Landor—the first of whom had defended the principle of tyrannicide in *The Times* in 1856 and the second of whom had written to an Italian conspirator promising £95 sterling to the family of the "first patriot who asserts the dignity and fulfils the duty of tyrannicide"—he was, in reference to Brutus, able to speak of "The grand brows of the wan tyrannicide", while the "crowned snake of Naples" could be discerned amongst the melancholy crowd of royal criminals. Whether it was the too great respect for Liberty coupled with this too disrespectful reference to King Bomba which caused the judges to award the prize to a Mr. Worsley of Corpus we shall, alas, never know. With the metric form they could have found no fault, and though there is a certain callowness about the medley of discernible influences there are, too, moments of magnificence which were prophetic for the future:

> *I stood in thought among the buried years;*
> *I saw the daily veil of things undrawn*
> *And the grey gleam of immemorial dawn*
> *Upon the shoreless waters of the Past. . . .*

Though the Pre-Raphaelite influence intervened, there is one more poem of this period which may be linked to the "Italian primitives". *The Ride from Milan* is a description of Bazaine's obscure victory of Melegnano which took place on 8th June 1859, following closely upon the more important battle of Magenta. The metre, for Swinburne, is an extremely curious one:

> *Close our dear three colours drew; deeper all the battle grew;*
> *Face to face we smote and slew, man by man,*
> *And the sullen palpitation of a live and trampled nation*
> *On from station unto station throbbed and ran. . . .*

If the metre is reminiscent of Poe, the manner, though not the matter, is Kiplingesque!

In its earlier manifestations the Pre-Raphaelite influence was principally that of Morris, whose passion for the medieval and the use to which he put the monotonous rhythm of the ballads created a profound impression upon Swinburne. *Queen Yseult*, begun before Swinburne had actually met Morris, though he had had the opportunity of seeing some of his verse, was the first poem attempted in this manner. Other poems followed which must have required considerable reading, if not research, in the appropriate sources: *King Ban, Joyeuse Garde, Lancelot, Rudel in Paradise, The Queen's Tragedy* and others, some showing the influence of Rossetti, some of Morris. Many of these remained only fragmentary and none were published during his lifetime. They were nearly all illustrative of his fatal facility in *pastiche*—a facility which, when employed intentionally, could produce the most astonishing results. The Shakespeare sonnets, also written at this time, are a case in point. The accent is caught with an all too fluent precision:

> *I love thee; though my verse revolt and swear*
> *Thou are not worthy, I must love thee still;*
> *Some cruel planet full of wrath and feare*
> *Lowr'd on my birth, grim herald to this ill;*
> *I hate thy falsehood that is part of thee,*
> *I love the beauty that doth overpaint it;*
> *I love the brightness there and will not see*
> *For its rich sweetness what a curse doth taint it,*
> *Yet shall thy name live ripen'd in my song,*
> *And when thy limbs are dust, thy fault forgotten,*
> *My constant faith shall pale thee from the throng,*
> *Thy praise shall bloom, when envy's blame is rotten.*
> *The one shall live in glory, and to thee*
> *Lend of its praise; the other die with me.*

Side by side with these minor works Swinburne at Oxford was consistently engaged in an elaborate apprenticeship to the tragic drama. Following upon the enthusiastic schoolboy production of *The Unhappy Revenge* which demonstrated his admiration for the early English dramatists, came these fragments, deliberate exercises in *pastiche*: *The Laws of Corinth*, *Laugh and Lie Down* and *The Loyal Servant*. In a sense no doubt these may be considered to have been influenced by the Pre-Raphaelites for, though he had nothing to learn from Rossetti and Morris about his models, their enthusiasm for the archaic was undoubtedly a stimulus. With immense erudition and unassailable patience he sat down to learn his business. His general models were Beaumont, Fletcher and Marston. And in *The Loyal Servant* his complex archaisms become at times so pronounced, though so faithful, that Gosse was led to remark: "We could imagine that Beaumont and Fletcher improved upon Swinburne and wrote in an easier and more modern style of language." The plots of which these fragments are a part are of no particular interest. But there is a perfect *pastiche* of Marston from *The Loyal Servant*:

CESARIO: *Would'st then bring up a page?*
ANTHONIO: *I did once essay it; and thus, by goodly advice, I after much endurance whipped him into some kind of humanity, being indeed a beast fitt for a rod onlie and no other exercise, till his age be more riper. Marry, some are rotten already and will never be the better on't.*
PAGE: *Let me do battle with him good my lord.*
CESARIO: *What, for blaspheming thine estate, my boy?*
ANTHONIO: *I do accept the challenge, and for the armes nominate a hornbeck and a rod of birch; and I will appoint my seconds two builders of rawe youth, strippers and whippers by profession, who shall make thy pagehood a knight of the red rod and so good even to you.*

And Swinburne's preoccupation with whipped pages is not incidental. In *Laugh and Lie Down* can be traced the first steps towards the formation of his synthesis, the first milestone on the road to *Atalanta*. As he expressed it in *The Whippingham Papers*: "One of the great charms of birching lies in the sentiment that the floggee is the powerless victim of the furious rage of a beautiful woman." And out of this conception was gradually evolved his own particular version of the *femme fatale* which was to reach its ideal in the characterization of Mary Queen of Scots in *Chastelard*. The gradual evolution of this type in Swinburne can be traced without difficulty. Since he was never to have anything but the most perverse and limited experience of the opposite sex, his dominating female characters were but projections of his imagination and conformed to one type. The processes by which it gradually became established were merely the increasing mastery of his art and the various influences to which he became subjected. The earliest of these was undoubtedly Rossetti, whose interpretation of the Pre-Raphaelite ideal—unlike Hunt's and Millais'—found its highest expression in the depiction of beautiful women: those dolorous, romantic creatures moving amidst the cruel, blood-stained legends of the Middle Ages. Baudelaire and Sade were to follow and be assimilated, as had already the Old Testament, the Ate of Greek Tragedy and the crime-stained Renaissance of the Elizabethan dramatists.

In *Laugh and Lie Down* the algolagnia is for the first time definitely established on a masochistic basis. The character of Imperia, a famous Milanese courtesan, remains undeveloped, but the interest is centred on her relationship with her twin pages. This composite character, who for the sake of clarity may be called Frederick-Frank-Algernon, is a very curious conception. Beautiful, androgynous and flagellated—"Thou shalt be lashed so soundly, sweetly lashed, Frank!" exclaims Imperia—appearing dressed indiscriminately as boy or girl, capable of attracting either sex, he embodies the ambiguous dreams of adolescence and is the forerunner of the *Hermaphroditus* of 1863. But there is no ambiguity in the relationship of Frank and his mistress. His pains are offered up upon the altar of his love:

IMPERIA: *Come, come, you are not old enough.*

FRANK: *I have bled for your sake some twenty times a month.*
*Some twenty drops each time; are these no services?*

IMPERIA: *I tell you, if you use me lovingly,*
*I shall have you whipt again, most pitifully whipt,*
*You little piece of love.*

FRANK:                    *God knows I care not*
*So I may stand and play to you, and you kiss me*
*As you used to kiss me, tender little side-touches*
*Of your lip's edge i' the neck.*

IMPERIA:                    *By my hand's hope,*
*Which is the neck of my lord Galeas,*
*I'll love your beard one day; get you a beard, Frank;*
*I were as well now love a maid as you*
*With such child's cheeks.*

FRANK:                    *Madam, you have pleasant hands,*
*What sweet and kissing colour goes in them*
*Running like blood!*

IMPERIA:          *Ay, child, last year in Rome*
*I held the Pope six minutes kissing them*
*Before his eyes had grown up to my lips.*
*Alas!*

FRANK: *What makes you sigh still?   You are now*
*So kind the sweetness in you stabs mine eyes*
*With sharp tears through.   I would so fain be hurt,*
*But really hurt, hurt deadly, to do good*
*To your most sudden fancy.*

In a sense this fragment is the link between the dissipated
and generalized algolagnia of *The Unhappy Revenge* and the
crystallization of this emotion into the relationship and
interplay of character, the definite identification of it with
sexual pleasure. There is a revealing passage in the
*Chronicles of Tebaldeo Tebaldei*, written in 1861, which may
stand as the definition of the sensual theme in the dramas
that were immediately to follow:

"*Knowest thou not . . . that a nerve may quiver and be convulsed
with actual pain while the blood is dancing and singing for joy like
a nymph drunken? that to be pinched and torn by the lips and teeth
and fingers of love is a delight enduring when one is past kisses and
when caresses have no sting or savour left in them? that the ache
and smart of the fleshly senses are things common alike to pleasure
and to pain?*"

*Rosamond* was the first completed adult drama. Though
begun as early as 1857 it was successively changed, torn up,
revised, abandoned and rewritten till 1860. As eventually
published it probably contains no single complete passage
from the earlier draft. Swinburne was capable of composing
at enormous speed. Three acts of a drama in three days
was nothing to him, so, considering that he was working off
and on at *Rosamond* over a period of three years, the various

metamorphoses through which the play passed are beyond
calculation.  As it stands it is a not altogether unhappy combination of the Elizabethan drama and the Pre-Raphaelite
influence.

Rosamond was the unfortunate mistress of Henry II.  Her
tragic and horrible death had through centuries of chroniclers
and ballad-makers become a poetic myth.  It was a subject
likely to appeal to Swinburne and the Pre-Raphaelites.
Both Rossetti and Burne-Jones were inspired by the cruel
medieval story to paint pictures of the "Rosa mundi, non
Rosa munda"—their ideal of female beauty—while for
Swinburne it was the opportunity for the first essay in
the establishment of his prototype of the *femme fatale*.
Rosamond describes herself:

> *Yea, I am found the woman in all tales,*
> *The face caught always in the story's face ;*
> *I Helen, holding Paris by the lips,*
> *Smote Hector through the head; I Cressida*
> *So kissed men's mouths that they went sick or mad,*
> *Stung right at brain with me; I Guenevere*
> *Made my queen's eyes so precious and my hair*
> *Delicate with such gold in its soft ways*
> *And my mouth honied so for Launcelot . . .*

While upon men her supreme beauty has the effect of
physical pain infinitely desired, Henry addresses her:

> *God help ! your hair burns me to see like gold*
> *Burnt to pure heat; your colour seen turns in me*
> *To pain and plague upon the temple vein*
> *That aches as if the sun's heat snapt the blood*
> *In hot mid-measure; I could cry on you*
> *Like a maid weeping-wise, you are so fair*
> *It hurts me in the head, makes the life sick*
> *Here in my hands . . .*
> *Your beauty makes me blind and hot, I am*
> *Stabbed in the brows with it.*

*Rosamond* was to be published in 1860 together with *The
Queen Mother* as Swinburne's first book.  Upon *The Queen
Mother* he was also therefore engaged in 1859.  It appears
to have been written with greater certainty than *Rosamond*

and without the elaborate discardings and rewritings. The corrections in fact were comparatively superficial. The plot is concerned with the events which culminated in the Massacre of St. Bartholomew. Again, the chief influence discernible in the style is that of Fletcher, with the usual Elizabethan admixture of echoes of Shakespeare, Chapman, Marlowe and Webster, while the erudition and knowledge of sources is remarkable. Brantôme, the *Mémoires* of Marguerite de Valois, de Thou's. *Historia Mei Temporis* and the *Mémoires* of Gaspard de Saulx-Tavannes all appear, amongst others, to have been used. Here the algolagnic theme is impersonal and generalized, not with the innocence of *The Unhappy Revenge* but with the objectivity demanded by the dramatic theme. The centre of interest is neither in Catharine de Medicis nor in the King's mistress, Denise, but in Charles IX himself. He is drawn, not without the warrant of Brantôme —"Il prist fort grand plaisir de voir passer soubz ses fenêtres par la rivière plus de 4,000 corps ou se noyans ou tuez"— as a splendid and perverse monster, violent and weak-willed, given to fits of passionate and sadistic cruelty. His relationship with Denise, however, shows all the accustomed characteristics:

> And once in kissing me
> You bit me here above the shoulder, yet
> The mark looks red from it ; . . .

And again Denise says:

> Now I would kill you here between the eyes,
> Plant the steel's bare chill where I set my mouth,
> Or prick you somewhere under the left side . . .
> Yea I could search thy veins about with steel
> Till in no corner of thy crannied blood
> Were left to run red witness of a man . . .
> Sooner than lose this face to touch, this hair
> To twist new curls in; yea, prove me verily,
> Sift passion pure to the blind edge of pain,
> And see if I will.—

This cruel pleasure is the basis of their relationship; but where Denise revolts against the massacre, the King is intoxicated by the prospect of bloodshed. The Queen comments:

> *All's clear again; he smells about the blood*
> *That shall incense his madness to high strain.*

If too diffuse, lacking the precision of a sense of time which might confine the drama to the swift certainty of the actions of forty-eight hours, it has nevertheless something of the quality of inevitability which is reminiscent of classical tragedy. His imagination was fired by the tumult, the torchlight, the crimson horror of the night, the sadistic laughter of the court ladies, the King's bestial delirium. The presentation of the massacre has an almost Neronic complacency. When one remembers how he hated the wanton tyranny of despots, an almost schizophrenic attitude becomes evident. It is as if an opponent of capital punishment rejoiced in witnessing an execution.

When to the works mentioned here are added stories in imitation of Boccaccio, a proposed collection of *Ballads of the English Border*, at least the first act of *Chastelard*, as well as numerous poems some of which were to figure in *Poems and Ballads*, is it altogether surprising that, in spite of his astonishing powers of memory and assimilation, academic success eluded him? Indeed, Jowett, writing to the Reverend William Stubbs on the peculiarities, temperamental and other, of his pupil, remarked that he not only deplored the influence upon him of the Pre-Raphaelites—whose philosophy (if that it can be called) Jowett was constitutionally incapable of appreciating—but that "No good can be expected from him scholastically, unless he can be hindered from writing poetry". This, even the future Bishop of Oxford was unable to do, though he was to bring to bear all the sympathetic persuasion that Jowett recommended as the proper treatment for a young man who bore "an extreme and almost unintelligible unlikeness to ourselves". The measure of Mr. Stubbs' failure may be judged from his writing, shortly after Swinburne's arrival at Navestock in January 1860: "He is the most singular young man I have ever known; he certainly possesses genius. He has extraordinary powers of imitation in

writing and composes Latin Mediaeval hymns, French
Vaudevilles as well as endless poems with the greatest
facility." Gosse records that on reading a tragedy in blank
verse Mr. Stubbs "felt obliged to say that he thought the
tone of the amatory passages somewhat objectionable".
The criticism was met by a scream of rage and the burning
of the MS. The poet, however, sat up all night and rewrote
it from memory. The drama was probably *Rosamond*.

But perhaps Mr. Stubbs did not try very hard to dissuade
his strange pupil from his natural avocation. He appears,
indeed, to have given encouragement and advice over *The
Death of Sir John Franklin*, which Swinburne wrote as the
result of seeing a paragraph in *The Guardian*, of 8th February
1860, announcing that a special prize of £50 had been given
by "a non-resident member of the University much attached
to her interests" for a poem on that subject "with special
reference to the time, place and discovery of his death".
The judges were to be the Vice-Chancellor, the Dean of
Christ Church and Lord Ashburton. The poem is mainly
remarkable—though this was necessarily appropriate to the
subject—for a patriotism which had not hitherto been a
noticeable ingredient of Swinburne's verse. There are, too,
exquisite lyrical passages:

> Doubtless the backward thought and broad regard
> Was bitter to their souls, remembering
> How in soft England the warm lands were starred,
> And how the meadows in their sweet May sloth
> Grew thick with grass as soft as song or sleep . . .
> The bitter savour of remembered sweet
> No doubt did touch their lips in some sharp guise,
> No doubt the pain of thought and fever-heat
> Put passion in the patience of their eyes.

The prize, however, much to Swinburne's disappointment,
was to be awarded to a certain Mr. Vidal of Trinity College,
who, so far as is known, then retired once more into a
doubtless worthy obscurity. The taste of the judges was
deplorable.

Nevertheless, in spite of these poetic interludes, a great deal
of solid work was done at Navestock towards succeeding in

his final Schools. The position was this: the final Schools
were taken in two parts; in Swinburne's case the first was
Classics, the second Law and Modern History. He failed
in the first part in Michaelmas 1859 and had therefore to
take it again in May 1860. This he did with success. In
the meantime he was reading Law and History with Mr
Stubbs for the second part to be taken in June. Law,
unfortunately, he found intolerable. "The one really
awful piece of work . . . is now behind me. I have completed the analysis of Blackstone." History was, perhaps,
a little better. "That is the sort of history I like," he wrote
of the *Chronicles of Charlemagne*, "live biographical
chronicles." And so he went up to Oxford again for the
summer term of 1860 to take his Schools.

The quiet of the Essex vicarage had benefited him
considerably. Throughout his life he was to respond to
a regular routine with improved health and spirits. But
Oxford, as London was so often to do in the future, destroyed
in a few weeks all the good that the Stubbs' healthy regimen
had been able to achieve. He sat in his rooms in The Broad
writing verse instead of continuing his academic studies.
Those "irregularities", those "alcoholic excesses" which
had the previous autumn been noticed with so much dis-
favour by the authorities, began all over again. It was as
if there was something in the Oxford air which drove him
on to a contempt for its preoccupations, to a revolt against
its rules. But indeed this was part of the complexity of his
nature. An imposed routine, a hint of criticism, a sensation
of constraint, and he became a wild and implacable rebel.
While on the other hand, in the presence of those he loved
and respected—his grandfather, a Nichol, a Rossetti, even
towards the, as yet, rather nebulous figures of Mazzini and
Hugo—he showed a capacity for worship, a desire to serve
and obey, a submissiveness, a tendency even to humiliate
himself before them which, psychologically, is in perfect
accord with the characteristics discernible in his work—a
sensuality which may be gratified either in the inflicting or
the receiving of pain: dual yet compensatory manifestations.

Whether he would have succeeded in taking a degree had
it not been for an accident must remain uncertain. On 5th

June 1860 he wrote: "About the beginning of last week I had a bad fall from a horse in leaping a gate. It was in the end lucky that I alighted full on my chin and the lower part of my face—but as some teeth were splintered, the jaw sprained and the lips cut up it was not pleasant. For a week nearly I have been kept in bed and fed on liquids and still I can eat nothing but crumb of bread and such like. . . ." This was but a few days before Schools. Did he sit and fail? Or did he, fearing failure, not sit at all? When and how was the decision taken to "go down" without a degree? Was there some further disciplinary action taken by the college? We do not know. Disappointed of his degree, disappointed of the poetic prize, at odds with the authorities, he abandoned Oxford in disgust and mortification. He never forgave her. Nearly fifty years later, when Lord Curzon, the Chancellor, offered him an honorary degree he refused it with contemptuous courtesy. He himself said that he had been "rusticated and almost expelled" and, again, "my Oxonian career culminated in total and scandalous failure". But, somehow, it was all Oxford's fault. Was he to be like Shelley after all? Perhaps. But when he rejoined his family, and continued to work on *Chastelard*, the Admiral and Lady Jane must again have asked each other in bewilderment: What was to be done with Algernon?

## CHAPTER IV

## (1860–1862)

TOWARDS the end of June, Swinburne found his parents in London. They had just returned from a long stay at Pau. His reception, from the Admiral at least, was unlikely to have taken the form of the heartiest of welcomes. Swinburne's persistent scholastic failure could no longer be condoned or overlooked as the comparatively unimportant indiscipline of a schoolboy. It was more serious than that. The failure to achieve a degree appeared to close once and for all the door to the gentlemanly professions. But the tact of Lady Jane, the fact that Swinburne, smarting under the realization that Oxford had discarded him as scholar, man and poet, was himself prepared to admit that he was an "afflictive phenomenon", coupled with his temporary ill-health and the Admiral's own good sense, tended no doubt to diminish the acerbity of their relations. Undoubtedly there were long and inconclusive discussions as to the future. But since no one could think of anything constructive, a decision was deferred and the whole family went down to East Dene to allow themselves time for reflection. Nothing, obviously, would be gained by doing anything in a hurry. Algernon as a professional man of letters was not taken seriously by anyone but himself.

At East Dene in September Swinburne was working on *Chastelard*, impenitently maintaining his revolutionary politics, which exasperated the Tory-minded Admiral, and was nevertheless preparing to leave for Mentone, where the family proposed spending the winter.

This plan, however, had to be postponed. On 26th September Sir John Swinburne died at Capheaton in his ninety-ninth year. "We all naturally hoped to see him fill up his century, but the Fate said no," wrote Swinburne. His grandfather's death naturally took him to Northumberland and, after the funeral, he went to stay with the Trevelyans

at Wallington.    Sir George Otto Trevelyan recalled hearing
him recite his poems to the ladies in the Italian saloon.
"Unfortunately," remarks Gosse, "these symposia were
often more to the taste of the hostess than of the host."
Indeed, it appears that the latent antagonism between
Swinburne and Sir Walter Trevelyan came, during the
course of this visit, to the surface. Sir Walter's prudery
was outraged by finding a volume of the *Comédie Humaine*
in the drawing-room. French novels, it was well known,
were indecent. Algernon had introduced it into the chaste
household. With the tongs Sir Walter placed it upon the
fire. Swinburne left the house.

The breach, however, was not to be permanent. Lady
Trevelyan, who no doubt took his part, was too good a
friend for that. But, immediately, he went to stay in
Newcastle with William Bell Scott, who painted his portrait.
At this time Scott was nearly fifty and had been all his life
a serious, hard-working, but untalented artist. For thirty
years Swinburne was to be on terms of intimate friendship
with "old Scotus". Unfortunately, after his death in 1891,
his *Autobiographical Notes*, already referred to, were
published. They revealed a certain envy of the fame of
his younger friends, Rossetti and the rest. They contained,
too, a slighting reference to Swinburne's lack of success
at school and college. With tremulous rage Swinburne
seized his pen and wrote in the *Fortnightly Review* of "a
fair example of the writer's apparently habitual condition
of mind; a state of spiritual disease in which falsehood
is to the sufferer what alcohol is to a dipsomaniac, and
truth what water is to a patient afflicted with hydrophobia".
Scott became a "lying, backbiting, drivelling imbecile, a
doting, malignant, mangy, old son of a bitch". And he
composed an epitaph upon his old friend:

> *Here lies no envious man!   Refrain surprise;*
> *For in this grave incarnate envy lies.*

It was all very unfortunate.

While the journey to Mentone remained postponed—it
did not take place till the end of the year or even till January
1861, doubtless because the Admiral was engaged in settling

up his father's estate—Swinburne spent the intervening weeks, from about the middle of October onwards, in London, at 16 Grafton Street.   The question of a career had by no means been altogether shelved but the position was, no doubt, that a little literary success might cause the Admiral to view it differently.   Brandishing the manuscripts of *Rosamond* and *The Queen Mother* — were they not proofs of genius? — Swinburne persuaded his father that fame would follow upon their publication.   All that was lacking was the cost of printing.   This the Admiral guaranteed.   Swinburne immediately went to Pickering, the publisher and bookseller, from whom he had bought books since his Eton days, and the work was put in hand.

In the meantime he worked on *Chastelard*, which was still incomplete, on more poems for *Poems and Ballads*, and in the British Museum copying out Charles Wells' *Joseph and his Brethren*, which, though the author was still alive and living in Quimper, was so rare as to be attainable only in this way. Both Rossetti and Swinburne were enthusiastic for this forgotten drama, of which a new edition was eventually produced with a preface by Swinburne.   The dramatist himself remained disconcertingly indifferent to their rhapsodies.   During these weeks, too, he was able to renew and deepen his friendships with the Rossetti family—Gabriel, William and Christina— with Morris and Burne-Jones, who was now married, with Ford Madox Brown, who had visited Oxford at the time of the Pre-Raphaelite expedition to paint the Union, with Ruskin, with George Meredith and with Lord Houghton, whom he had first met the previous May on an introduction, probably, from Lady Trevelyan.   All these people were to play an important part in his life.

*The Queen Mother*, of which Pickering printed two hundred and fifty copies, was ready by Christmas.   Twenty review copies had already been sent out when Swinburne transferred the book from Pickering to Moxon, who was to remain his publisher till 1866.   The pages bearing the name of Pickering were destroyed and the volume reappeared with a new title-page and a new imprint.   The cause of this strange incident, which was to inaugurate Swinburne's fantastic difficulties with his publishers, remains obscure.

Did the Admiral take exception to Pickering's terms? The fact remains that Moxon, to whom Swinburne was probably introduced by Lord Houghton, took over the book.

"Of all the still-born books," Swinburne told Gosse, "*The Queen Mother* was the stillest." In 1862, two years later, he admitted that his publisher had, up to that date, sold seven copies. No one read it, no one heard of it, no one even reviewed it—except for *The Athenaeum*, who noticed it in the following terms: "We should have conceived it hardly possible to make the crimes of Catharine de Medici dull, however they were presented. Mr. Swinburne, however, has done so. There is more of real drama in Mr. Browning's short poem of the French poisoner in the laboratory than in the entire 150 pp. here wearily spun off. Having had such ill luck with one wicked Queen, we were unable to cope with a second one [*Rosamond*]; and thus the tragedy of Woodstock, once again told, though shorter as a play, is gladly handed over to others who are disposed to venture into the labyrinth." This was scarcely fame. Swinburne's friends did what they could to help—particularly Rossetti, to whom the volume was dedicated. But it was not until June 1865 that an appreciative notice appeared in *Fraser's Magazine*. By then *Atalanta* had been out some weeks and Swinburne was already famous.

In the meantime Swinburne went with his family to the Maison Laurenti, a villa leased by the Admiral at Mentone. The Mediterranean, "the tideless dolorous midland sea", made no appeal to him. It was too calm, too warm. As for the landscape: "How any professing Christian as has been in France and England can look at it, passes me," he wrote to Lady Trevelyan on 9th January 1861. "A calcined, scalped, rasped, scraped, flayed, broiled, powdered, leprous, blotched, mangy, grimy, parboiled country *without* trees, water, grass, fields—*with* blank, beastly, senseless olives and orange-trees like a mad cabbage gone indigestible; it is infinitely liker hell than earth, and one looks for tails among the people." Nor had the question of a profession been yet settled or permanently shelved. Evidently Lady Trevelyan had written him a letter of good advice, for he replied; "I wish I *had* anything to do besides my proper

work if I can't live by it. Which it's very well to pitch
into a party like brother Stockdolloger, but what *is* one to
do? I can't go to the bar: and much good I shd do if I
did. You know there is really no profession one can take
up with and go on working. Item—boetry (*sic*) is quite
work enough for any one man. Item—who is there that
is anything *besides* a poet at this day except Hugo? And
though his politics is excellent and his opinions is sound, he
does much better when he sticks to his work and makes
Ratbert and Ruy Blas. *I* don't want to sit in [a] room and
write, gracious knows. Do you think a small thing in the
stump-orater line wd do? or a Grace-Walker? Seriously
what is there you wd have one take to?"

Uncertain as yet as to the fate of *The Queen Mother*, he
hoped if it succeeded to publish a volume of poems. He had
a considerable number of completed manuscripts. The
MSS. included *Lord Soulis*, *Lord Scales*, *Broad Helen*, *The
Worm of Spindlestonheugh* amongst others which remained
unpublished till after his death. *Saint Dorothy* and *The Two
Dreams* were finished. There were a number of other poems,
some to be published in *Poems and Ballads*. There were
a number of stories in the manner of Boccaccio in process
of composition. He was working also at two longer MSS.,
*pastiches* of the medieval French and Italian chroniclers:
*The Chronicle of Queen Fredegond* imitated from Nicol Gille
and *The Chronicle of Tebaldeo Tebaldei*, a paraphrase of
Burchardus, the heroine being Lucrezia Borgia. He was
also writing a burlesque novel in French: *La Fille du
Policeman*. These were all the products of a feverish
industry. "Boetry" was indeed quite work enough for any
one man. Perhaps due to this manifest absorption, perhaps
to the difficulty of now finding a profession for Algernon,
the Admiral seems gradually to have been converted to the
idea that his son was perhaps already exercising one—though
with as yet little success. Nevertheless from this date
onwards he seems to have resigned himself to the fact that
Algernon would go his own way. To make this possible
he granted him an allowance of £200 a year. If fame should
prove reluctant, at least some sort of economic future was
assured.

Perhaps to celebrate his father's capitulation he decided on a tour of Northern Italy. He travelled by Ventimiglia, Genoa, Milan, Turin and Venice. There was much to attract him. Besides pictures and architecture, which he passed indefatigably in review in letters to Lady Trevelyan, there was his sympathy with the Italian national movement. He awaited hopefully the hanging of the Austrian Emperor and regarded Garibaldi as the greatest man since Adam—an appreciation which was to suffer some change when his hero quarrelled with Mazzini. Besides had he not made a story—"a big one about my blessedest pet which her initials is Lucrezia Estense Borgia"—and did he not hope to see "her hair as is kep at Milan 'in spirits in a bottle'"? He saw it, and some autograph letters into the bargain. He was fortunate, too, in other ways. "As to women I saw at Venice (14 years ago)," he wrote to Watts in 1875, "one of the three most beautiful I ever saw. The other two were at Genoa and Ventimiglia (Riviera). By her gaze I thought I might address her, but did not considering that we could not have understood each other (verbally at least); so caution and chastity, or *mauvaise honte* and sense of embarrassment prevailed." One wonders whether the woman's "gaze" was due to any feeling more profound than startled surprise at the strange little figure whose green eyes were so obviously admiring.

Italy was always to be for him "a true piece of heaven". He returned to London in the spring of 1861 filled with enthusiasm for the beauty of its land and the genius of its race.

Shortly after his return to London he went to stay with Lord Houghton at Fryston Hall in Yorkshire. Lord Houghton (at this date he was still Richard Monckton Milnes) was already fifty years of age. His complex and rather sinister personality requires some elaboration, since his influence upon Swinburne over a period of six years was to be both important and malign. A politician whose rather pompous eloquence in the House had failed to secure for him the Foreign Office which he considered to be his due, he was widely travelled, with an intimate knowledge of the capitals of Europe. An essayist and critic, editor of the posthumous works of Keats, he had, nevertheless, abandoned the hope of gaining recognition as a writer and become a bibliophile and patron of the arts. Personable and rich, with beautiful if rather elaborate manners, with an unrivalled knowledge of society and its scandals, he entertained largely both in London and at Fryston. His pleasure was to assist talent however obscure it might be, and by never refusing a letter of introduction bound many a struggling artist with the tendrils of gratitude.

And yet was there not something feline in his friendship, something of cynicism behind his kindness? Was it that, hospitable, he was insincere, that his kindness was a mask, that his guests were selected with a sardonic delight in their incompatibilities, or, possibly, in their even more startling affinities? He could extract the greatest pleasure from persuading Swinburne to recite *The Leper* and *Les Noyades* in the presence of the Archbishop of York. But his patronage was inconstant, forfeited by failure, regained by success. Jowett called him "the Barometer" and Burton once exclaimed: "Some good luck must be coming my way, Houghton has been so damned civil." He played upon the characters of his friends. Fascinated by their vices, without moral inhibitions, he encouraged them for his own almost scientific pleasure. "Oh! how wide is the diapason of my mind," he exclaimed, "from what a height to what a depth!"

Swinburne's character was one which was eminently suited to the play of Lord Houghton's talents. Not only was he prepared to recognize and assist his genius—he sent Swinburne's article on Charles Wells to Froude; he introduced him to the editor of *The Spectator*—but at the same time he recognized its abnormalities. With what almost sensuous pleasure might they not be developed! Down what vistas of perversity might he not lead the neophyte! At Fryston, Lord Houghton kept his collection of *erotica*. "He is," wrote Swinburne in 1869, "the Sadique collector of European fame. His erotic collections of books, engravings, etc., is unrivalled upon earth—unequalled, I should imagine, in heaven." And already, in October 1860, he had written to Lord Houghton: "Reserving always your corresponding promise that I am yet to live and look upon the

mystic pages of the martyred Marquis de Sade, ever since
which the vision of that illustrious and ill-requited benefactor
of humanity has hovered by night before my eyes." But now
the martyred Marquis had need to hover no longer. In an
illustrated edition of *Justine* Swinburne was able to discover
in grotesque and monstrous form the philosophy of his own
perverse desires. Nor was this all. Amongst the guests so
carefully selected, besides Carlyle, the Kingsleys and Froude,
was to be found Richard Burton. Swinburne and Burton!
Surely even for Lord Houghton this juxtaposition was a
masterpiece!

Burton was already celebrated. The journey to Mecca,
the expedition to discover the sources of the Nile had brought
him fame. But a grateful government had felt unable to
offer him a better appointment than consul at Fernando Po.
When in the Indian Army he had made, under the auspices
of Napier, expeditions, disguised as a native, amongst the
Sindians. His terms of reference had included the compiling
of a report on their sexual perversions. The report, no
doubt admirably complete—Burton had all the instincts of
a scientific anthropologist—was more than a prudish War
Office could stomach. They behaved towards him as if he
himself were responsible for the vices he had been sent to
investigate. It was, promotion being thus out of the
question, the end of his military career. He was to fare but
little better under the Foreign Office. All this, however,
was not known publicly at the time. He moved merely in
an aura of indefinable but sinister notoriety. His was a
reputation with an infallible appeal for Lord Houghton.

"I can shut my eyes," wrote Isabel Burton thirty years
later, "and mentally look around Lord Houghton's large
round table even now, which usually held twenty-five guests.
I can see Buckle, and Carlyle, and all the Kingsleys, and
Swinburne and Froude, and all the great men that were
and remember the conversation. I can remember the Duc
d'Aumale cheek by jowl with Louis Blanc. I can remember
Vambéry telling us Hungarian tales, and I can remember
Richard cross-legged on a cushion, reciting alternately in
Persian and English and chanting the call to prayer."

For Swinburne this dark, scarred, rather sinister adventurer

held all the romantic glow of the Elizabethans. Here was
Drake, Frobisher and Sir Walter Raleigh. He admired his
virility. He enjoyed his freedom from convention in the
matter of conversation. No doubt in Lord Houghton's *enfer*
of a library Burton was able to elaborate from his own
experience the nameless sins recorded in the pages of the
Divine Marquis. Swinburne confided to Arthur Symons
that he entertained for Burton a positive yearning; they had
instantly felt "a curious fancy, an absolute fascination, for
one another". He knew now, he said, what it was to have
an elder brother. Luke Ionides once saw Burton pick
Algernon up under one arm and carry him kicking downstairs—a familiarity which from anyone else would have
ended in screams of outraged dignity and a broken friendship.

This was only the first of many visits to Fryston. But
now Swinburne was able to make London his permanent
headquarters. Not that he was ever there for many months
together; there were innumerable visits to the country, to
East Dene, to Northumberland and to Lord Ashburnham at
Battle. But Grafton Street and his circle of London friends
were now his main interests. These friends were in the main
the Rossettis and their satellites. Gradually Swinburne got
to know the extensive connection. There was Ford Madox
Brown, now living with his second wife in Fortress Terrace,
Kentish Town. Madox Brown had in a sense an avuncular
relationship to the Pre-Raphaelites. Indeed, in the early
days, Rossetti had for a time taken lessons in painting from
him. But being older than the rest—he was now forty—he
had never actually joined the Brotherhood. While Rossetti
had found a generous patron in Ruskin, and Millais had
soared into the empyrean of success, Madox Brown still
struggled hopelessly to sell his pictures for any sort of
reasonable price. He had become rather aloof; gone,
partly through poverty, into retreat as it were, a retirement
which was soon to become even more profound due to the
death of his son, Oliver, the "marvellous boy". Swinburne
had a great affection for him and admired his art. "I never
knew till now," he wrote to Lady Trevelyan on the occasion
of an exhibition, "how great and various and consistent a
painter he is."

Then there was William Michael Rossetti, Gabriel's younger brother, who was to become Madox Brown's son-in-law. Swinburne probably met him for the first time towards the end of 1860. He worked as a civil servant in Somerset House, but his tastes were for the arts. He had been incorporated in the first Pre-Raphaelite Brotherhood as secretary, but wrote poems and criticisms, and had edited *The Germ*. There was in reality much more in common between Swinburne and William Michael than between Swinburne and Gabriel, and their friendship was to be more enduring. William Michael was a practical and trustworthy man of affairs and was always ready to help his friends over the difficulties in which they became involved with publishers and dealers. Besides, unlike Gabriel, he was interested in politics, a confirmed radical, an admirer of Mazzini and a detester of Napoleon III.

But Swinburne had also been introduced into the Rossetti family household. No greater incompatibility on the face of it could well be imagined than this vivid outspoken anti-theistical revolutionary in the presence of the elderly calm of Mrs. Rossetti, face to face with the cloistral asceticism of Christina. But perhaps there was something of iron behind the latter's melancholy and ill-health, something impressive in the dolorous black clothes that were the badge of severity and Christian renunciation. And was she not a poet? Did she not even read his own works with admiration, though her religious scruples were to compel her to paste a concealing strip of paper over the two blasphemous lines in the fourth chorus of *Atalanta*? Swinburne felt himself to be in touch with a strange *mystique*: an element of purity, of chastity—of deliberate and austere sterility—which was both fascinating and extraordinary. Here, he was always on his best behaviour. That aristocratic courtesy which he knew so well how to assume, that charm of the well-brought-up schoolboy, won Miss Rossetti's approval. And, furthermore, did he not read for hours tactfully selected works, sitting at her mother's feet? Never did he refer to her except in terms of affectionate respect and the affection, if not the respect, was reciprocated.

Then, too, there was the Red House, Upton, which

Morris, now married to Jane Burden, had built for himself
in accordance with Pre-Raphaelite conceptions. It consisted practically entirely of banqueting hall and monumental
staircase. Here, many of the old Oxford friends forgathered
—Faulkner, Webb, Burne-Jones. And early in 1861 there
took place a memorable evening in celebration of the birth
of Morris's first child. Rossetti, surrounded by his disciples,
sat in sovereign pomp eating raisins. Everyone was very
gay despite the lack of beds for the night. Such as
there were they disposed about the banqueting hall, while
some of the guests slept on the floor. Swinburne found
a sofa.

It was here, too, at the Red House that Elizabeth Siddall
had stayed for many months after her marriage to Rossetti
in 1860. She had been dying for many years. Even
marriage, after a ten years' engagement, had made no
alteration in that. She lived, no doubt on account of her
phthisis, a detached life, curiously devoid of intimacy even
with the Morrises. To Charles Ricketts she appeared "a
ghost in the house of the living". But now she was back
in Chatham Place: hardly suitable, as Rossetti himself
admitted, to her delicate health. After the birth of a still-
born child her health deteriorated still further. To the
phthisis was added insomnia and acute neuralgia. She
began to take laudanum, as Rossetti himself was later to take
chloral. Nevertheless, there was no noticeable difference in
the arrangement of their lives. They never got up till midday or even later. After a hurried luncheon Rossetti would
paint till evening, and then either friends would come in
to see them or they would go out to dine at a restaurant.
Swinburne saw more of them at this time perhaps than of
anyone else. William Hardman, a friend of Meredith's,
has left an account of an evening at Chatham Place in
December 1861: "Yesterday I went with G. Meredith to
see Rossetti, the celebrated Pre-Raphaelite painter. . . .
I am going on Friday to his place again, to a social reunion
of artists and literary men, short pipes and beer being, I am
given to understand, the order of the day." He furnishes
the following description: "Swinburne is a strange fellow,
young and beardless, with a shock of red hair; his parents

were of two nations, the father Welsh, the mother French, and this mixture of blood has produced a singular result. Swinburne is strongly sensual; although almost a boy, he upholds the Marquis de Sade as the acme and apostle of perfection, without (as he says) having read a word of his works. Now the Marquis de Sade was a most filthy, horrible and disgusting rascal, a disgrace to humanity—he wrote the most abominable bawdry books that ever were written. No one is fonder of good sound bawdry than I (or you), yet the Marquis completely bowled me over. I tried once to read him, but very soon stuck fast. S——y mixed with murder and hideous cruelty are the prevailing features of his writings. The assembled company evidently received Swinburne's tirades with ill-concealed disgust, but they behaved to him like a spoiled child. He has a curious kind of nervous twitching, resembling or approaching St. Vitus' Dance."

The errors of fact need not concern us. Those concerning Swinburne's parentage were probably Swinburne's own fault. That he had read *Justine* at least at this time we may feel reasonably sure. (Is there not a discernible satisfaction —despite the outraged modesty—in the fact that Hardman *himself* had read the master's works?) But this account is probably a reasonable indication of the effect produced by Swinburne on many of those outside the magic circle who did not know him.

Often in the evening Swinburne would join the Rossettis for dinner in a restaurant. On the 10th February 1862 they all three went to the Hôtel Sablonière in Leicester Square. It was a favourite of Gabriel's. Nothing unusual, apparently, occurred during dinner. Lizzie, indeed, was quite gay. After dinner Rossetti took her home at about eight o'clock and went out again, so it is supposed, to the Working Men's College. The next morning when Swinburne went round to Chatham Place, to sit as usual for the portrait Rossetti was painting, he discovered the house in turmoil. Coming home the previous night at half-past eleven Rossetti had found his wife unconscious. She had taken a whole phial of laudanum. Madox Brown had brought Doctor Marshall and two other doctors. Even the stomach pump had proved useless. She died shortly after seven o'clock in the morning.

"The anguish of her widower," Swinburne wrote twenty years later, "when next we met, under the roof of the mother with whom he had sought refuge, I cannot remember . . . without some recrudescence of emotion. With sobs and broken speech . . . he appealed to my friendship. . . ." His grief was evident but—had it no admixture of remorse? Had Rossetti in fact been to the Working Men's College? Or was Lizzie jealous of Fanny Schott—the "other woman"? Or did she suspect a yet grosser infidelity? Probably we shall never know. There is a tradition that Madox Brown found a note pinned to the bedclothes. It was not produced at the inquest. The verdict, which was Accidental Death, may well have been influenced by Swinburne's testimony to the effect that nothing but harmony and affection reigned over their marriage. He wrote to his family: "Till last week when I was laid up with a bad turn of influenza I have been almost always with Rossetti. . . . I would rather not write yet about what has happened—I suppose none of the papers gave a full report, so that I suppose you do not know that I was almost the last person who saw her (except her husband and a servant) and had to give evidence at the inquest. Happily there was no difficulty in proving that illness had quite deranged her mind so that the worst chance of all was escaped. I am only glad to have been able to keep him company and be of a little use during these weeks. Rossetti and I are going to live together as soon as we move— of course he could not stay in the old house and asked me to come with him—luckily I had put off deciding on a lodging as it would have been a great plague to change again. In the autumn we get into a house in Chelsea—in Cheyne Walk facing the trees and river—with an old garden. The house is taken (like every other nice one) for the Exhibition season, so we must make shift somewhere till then. . . ."

But this was not quite the end of the part Lizzie had to play. When lying in her coffin in Chatham Place, Rossetti had placed the book of his manuscript poems between her cheek and her hair while addressing her as if she still lived. Swinburne, it is said, was present—and strongly disapproving —at this romantic gesture. It was his astonishing memory that made the reconstruction of many of these poems possible during the next few years. But in 1869 Rossetti decided to recover his MSS. An exhumation order was obtained from the Home Office and poor Lizzie made her final appearance. Swinburne on this occasion wrote Rossetti a letter of encouragement and consolation.

While waiting to move into Cheyne Walk he took lodgings temporarily in the house of a music teacher at 77 Newman Street, Oxford Street. And in the spring of 1862 Swinburne found himself for the first time able to publish occasional poems and air his literary views. Through George Meredith *Once a Week* published in February *The Fratricide* (later reprinted as *The Bloody Son*) and later in the year the short story *Dead Love*. But more important than this were his relations with *The Spectator* which he owed to an introduction from Lord Houghton to the editor, R. H. Hutton. *A Song in Time of Order*, *Before Parting*, *After Death*, *Faustine*, *A Song in Time of Revolution*, *The Sundew*, and *August* all appeared between April and September. Amongst a number of articles of literary criticism there were five on Hugo's *Les Misérables*. It was due to these articles that there began the strange relationship between the two poets which over a period of twenty years consisted in the interchange of poems and effusive epistles of admiration on the one hand and brief messages of Olympian satisfaction on the other. Whether Swinburne actually sent the copies of *The Spectator* which contained the first anonymous articles or whether Hugo obtained them in some way is not now known. But he asked Hutton for the name and address of the author. As a result Swinburne wrote to Hugo himself and sent him the last two articles of the series, receiving from Guernsey in exchange the following letter: "J'ai connu seulement à mon retour en cette île vos deux excellents articles sur *Les Misérables*. Je suis heureux que ce livre ait appelé l'attention d'un esprit tel que le vôtre et que vous soyez vous aussi sollicité par les questions sociales, préoccupation suprême de notre siècle. Je vous félicite, Monsieur, et je vous offre avec tous mes remerciements, l'assurance de mes sentiments les plus distingués."

Swinburne immediately replied asking permission to dedicate to him *Chastelard*. The permission was gracefully accorded. Hugo sent his "sentiments affectueux" and thereafter joined Mazzini in the calendar of heroes.

Also through *The Spectator* Swinburne made another interesting contact. This was with Charles Baudelaire. *Les Fleurs du Mal* had been reprinted in 1861. Swinburne must have come across it on his way to Pau, where his parents had taken a villa, in the spring of 1862, for he is said to have composed his article upon it for *The Spectator* in a Turkish bath in Paris. He sent the article to Baudelaire, who is known to have received it, since he mentions it in a letter to his mother. They were never to meet, but messages must from time to time have passed between them and they had friends in common—Manet and Fantin-Latour, to whom Whistler introduced Swinburne in 1863. There was also Professor Alphonse Legros, who was constantly travelling between London and Paris and to whom Swinburne entrusted some of his French poems to be shown to Baudelaire. One cannot suppose that the French poet set much store by these, but on 10th October 1863 he wrote a letter to Swinburne, which he sent by the hand of a friend who, unfortunately, never delivered it. It was found many years later unopened in a drawer in Paris. It was the more unfortunate as it was calculated to give Swinburne the greatest pleasure.

"Un de mes plus vieux amis va à Londres, M. Nadar, que vous aurez sans doute quelque plaisir à connaître. Je vous prie de vouloir bien faire pour lui tout ce que vous auriez fait sans doute pour moi, si j'étais allé m'adresser au public de votre patrie. Indications, conseils, réclames, il a besoin de beaucoup de choses.

"Je suis infiniment de gré à Nadar de m'avoir demandé des lettres pour mes très rares accointances de Londres, car il m'a ainsi forcé de m'acquitter vis-à-vis de vous d'une grosse dette depuis longtemps non payée. . . . Je veux parler du merveilleux article (sur *Les Fleurs du Mal*) que vous avez produit en Sept. 1862 dans le *Spectateur*. Un jour M. Richard Wagner m'a sauté au cou pour me remercier d'une brochure que j'avais faite sur *Tannhäuser* et m'a dit: 'Je n'aurais jamais cru qu'un littérateur français pût aussi bien pénétrer la musique allemande.'

"N'étant pas exclusivement patriote, j'ai pris de son compliment tout ce qu'il avait de gracieux.

"Permettez-moi à mon tour, de vous dire: 'Je n'aurais jamais cru qu'un littérateur anglais pût si bien pénétrer la beauté française les intentions françaises et la prosodie française.' Mais après la lecture des vers imprimés dans le même numéro ('August') et pénétrés d'un sentiment à la fois si réel et si subtil, je n'ai pas été étonné du tout : il n'y a que les poètes pour bien comprendre les poètes.

"Permettez-mois cependant de vous dire que vous avez poussé un peu loin ma défense. Je ne suis pas si moraliste que vous feignez obligeamment de le croire. Je crois simplement, comme vous sans doute, que tout poème, tout objet d'art bien fait suggère naturellement et forcément une morale. C'est l'affaire du lecteur. J'ai même une haine très décidée contre toute intention morale et exclusive dans un poème.

"Ayez la bonté de m'envoyer ce que vous publiez ; j'y prendrai un grand plaisir. J'ai plusieurs livres à publier, je vous les expédierai successivement.

"Veuillez agréer, Monsieur, l'expression tres vive de ma gratitude et de ma sympathie."

This undelivered letter was followed by a copy of the pamphlet *Richard Wagner et Tannhäuser à Paris*, which was more fortunate. It bore the inscription: "M. Algernon C. Swinburne. Bon souvenir et mille remerciements. C.B." No doubt this called for another letter from Swinburne. In 1876 he wrote: "Charles Baudelaire and I had some friendly intercourse in the way of exchanging messages and review articles not long after I left college, which might have ended in close intimacy in spite of his being twice my age, but for his untimely illness and death." While on the 19th April 1866, on reading a false report in the newspapers of Baudelaire's death, he wrote: "The same day that your letter reached me I saw in the papers a notice of the death of a man whom I deeply admired and believed in—Charles Baudelaire. As you are now in Paris you may have heard more of the matter than has appeared in the English papers. I hope to write a little notice of his death, as I did before of his work, and I want to lay hold of any facts I can. My friend M. Fantin-Latour, the artist, whom you may know by name if not personally, was his friend also. But Fantin had not I think met him for some time back. It is a great loss to all men and great to me personally, who have had the honour to be coupled with Baudelaire as a fellow-labourer, and have exchanged with him messages and courtesies." It was on this occasion that Swinburne composed *Ave Atque Vale* which fortunately, on discovering that the report of Baudelaire's death was false, he did not destroy.

But the importance of Swinburne's article in *The Spectator* lies in this: that it was the first statement in England of the theory of Art for Art's sake—a theory that Swinburne was to elaborate still further in his *William Blake*. He had already met the argument for aesthetic self-sufficiency in Gautier's *Mademoiselle de Maupin* which he had read at Oxford. Gautier had maintained that Art was independent of all moral, political, or scientific ends, that it had no obligations towards civilization or progress, that "un drame n'est pas un chemin de fer". Edgar Allan Poe, on the other hand, in *The Poetic Principle*, had suggested that though Art was an end in itself—"There neither exists nor can exist any work more thoroughly dignified, more supremely noble than . . . this poem written solely for the poem's sake"— it might have subsidiary moral consequences. "It by no means follows that . . . the precepts of Duty, or even the lessons of Truth . . . may not be introduced into a poem, . . . for they may subserve incidentally the general purposes of the work . . . but the true artist will always contrive to tone them down in proper subjection to that Beauty which is the proper essence of the poem." In his *Notes Nouvelles sur Edgar Poe* and *L'Art Romantique* Baudelaire seized upon this theory of Poe's and attempted to systematize it. He maintained that in the first place the artist need and should have no concern with morals and, secondly, that the immorality of a work of Art was a contradiction in terms, since Art consisted by its very nature of Truth and Beauty and these were synonymous with the Good. It was inevitable that both Baudelaire and Swinburne should have accepted this theory owing to the nature of their poetic inspiration. It was their justification. Moreover, Swinburne felt for Baudelaire a particular affinity. *Les Fleurs du Mal* had been bowdlerized at the hands of the law; he felt that his own work might very well suffer the same fate when the moment came to publish it. By justifying Baudelaire he was, by anticipation, justifying himself. "Perfect workmanship," he

wrote, "makes every subject admirable and respectable."
He was the first English writer to attack on these grounds
the pervasive smugness of Victorian moralizing. But at
this first attempt even Baudelaire thought that he had
overstated his case, that the defence was misconceived, when
Swinburne wrote in his enthusiastic defence: "The writer
believes that there is not one poem of the *Fleurs du Mal*
which has not a vivid and distinct background of morality
to it." He disclaimed all moral intentions: that was the
reader's business.

Encouraged, perhaps, by the lack of reaction to his praise
of so notorious a work as *Les Fleurs du Mal*, Swinburne sent
to *The Spectator* two articles on books by entirely imaginary
authors: *Les Abîmes* by Ernest Clouet, which purported
to contain essays on such subjects as the relations between
Joan of Arc and Gilles de Rais, and on the Marquis de Sade;
and *Les Amours Étiques* by Félicien Cossu, a book of
profoundly immoral verses with titles such as *Spasme
d'Amour*, *Une Nuit de Sodome*, *Rictus* and *Coeur Eunuque*.
These curious works were quoted at length in the articles.
Swinburne's intention seems to have been—besides the fact
that it was quite a good joke—to give the critics, who at that
date were inclined to treat all modern French literature as
filthy and frivolous, something more worthy of their censure
than, for instance, *Madame Bovary*. If they thought French
literature was immoral and indecent, "drowned in the
beastly sinks of sensuality", he would do his best to see that
it lived up to its reputation.

Hutton, reading the proofs, was shocked: "*Les Abîmes*
(*i.e.* E. Clouet) are still in type," he wrote, "but I cannot
say I think they will appear. The subject seems to deserve
no more criticism than a Holywell Street publication, nor
could I speak of it in *The Spectator* without more real
disgust than your article expresses. There is a tone of
raillery about it which I think one should hardly use to
obscenity . . . such verses would blow the magazine off
the earth." It is probable that on reflection Hutton may
have suspected a hoax. In any case Swinburne was offended
by the non-publication of his articles. They quarrelled and
the columns of *The Spectator* were no longer at his disposal.

Indeed only a few years later, as we shall see, those same columns were to be consistently exploited by his detractors. But what was much more serious was that for three years, indeed until he acquired fame with the publication of *Atalanta*, he was unable to find anyone who would publish his work.

Besides *Les Fleurs du Mal* Swinburne had made two further important discoveries in modern literature during these years. It is surprising that he did not write about them in *The Spectator*. The first was FitzGerald's *The Rubáiyát of Omar Khayyám*. In January 1858 FitzGerald had offered the manuscript to *Fraser's Magazine* but, after some rather indefinite negotiations, publication had been abandoned. The next year Quaritch had published it, but it had suffered the same fate as Swinburne's *The Queen Mother*: its sale had been practically nil. Towards the end of 1861 Quaritch had remaindered the rest of the edition and exposed them for sale on a stall outside his shop at one penny each. Rossetti, with his usual astonishing perception, had found them, bought a copy and shown it to Swinburne. The effect was immediate; he suffered another "blinding flash" and went, excitedly declaiming, to the Burne-Joneses. They then all went off to Quaritch. "Thither we repaired," wrote Swinburne, "and expended a few pence on a few copies. Next day, when we were returned for more, the price was raised to the iniquitous and exorbitant sum of 2d. You should have heard, but you can imagine, the eloquent and impressive severity of Gabriel's humorous expostulations with the stall-keeper on behalf of a defrauded if limited public. But we were extravagant enough to invest in a few more copies even at that scandalous price. I think it was within the month that Quaritch was selling copies at a guinea—so at least we have heard and read." FitzGerald's poem certainly profoundly influenced Swinburne. George Meredith, whose evidence is not however altogether to be trusted, declared that, inspired by a re-reading of it, Swinburne composed the first verses of *Laus Veneris* when on a visit to Copsham in June 1862. The metre, if nothing else, is similar.

Another work to which an article in *The Spectator* might well have been devoted was Whitman's *Leaves of Grass*.

Though published in 1857 it was unknown in England till discovered by the Pre-Raphaelites. It was another example of their aesthetic intelligence system. Thomas Dixon, the cork-cutter, the "Working Man" of Ruskin's *Time and Tide by Wear and Tyne*, came across it in the stock of a book-pedlar who had been in the American Civil War. William Bell Scott was informed and through him Rossetti and Swinburne. Whistler recalled a dinner-party with Meredith and Rossetti at Tudor House when the opossum, a member of Rossetti's extensive menagerie, was placed on the table with the coffee and cigars and Swinburne declaimed his favourite passages from Whitman which, no doubt, included much of *Drum-taps*, for which he had a great admiration. Between 1867 and 1881 Whitman sent Swinburne no less than five volumes of his works with dedications and a signed photograph. But in 1887, under the influence of Watts-Dunton, Swinburne was to repudiate his youthful enthusiasm.

It was during the summer of 1862 that there took place another of those significant snatches at normality. He had been introduced some time before to the eminent pathologist Sir John Simon and his wife. They were interested in the Pre-Raphaelite movement and friends of Ruskin, Burne-Jones and Woolner. In their house Swinburne met Jane Faulkner, a niece whom they had adopted upon the death of her mother, Lady Simon's sister. With "Boo", as she was called, Swinburne proceeded to fall in love, an emotion which he manifested with all the proper procedure of the period. He gave her flowers, he attended her at the piano and turned the music while she played and sang; he wrote her tender and innocent little verses:

> You should love me a little my own love
>   One love for a week and a day,
> For either has hardly begun love,
>   For the space of a sickle-sweep, say—
> Suppose we should settle to try love,
>   It may be as sweet as its fame. . . .

After much heart-searching, led on, no doubt, in all innocence, he suddenly made up his mind to propose. One may imagine the sudden violence of his protestations, the dramatic form of his declaration. Surprised and nervous, "Boo" laughed in his face. After a furious scene Swinburne left the house for ever.

It may be questioned whether the marriage would have been a success. With Swinburne's curious temperament on the one hand, and the fact that "Boo", after an unhappy marriage, later became a dipsomaniac, it would appear unlikely that love could have proved "as sweet as its fame". But was there not in the violence of his chagrin, in the depths of his sorrow and despair, not only the pain of the rejected lover but something else—a tragically apprehended foreboding?

In *The Triumph of Time* he poured out his grief. This, one of the most sure and sustained of all his lyrics, is strictly autobiographical. Even the flowers and the music are there:

> *I shall never be friends again with roses . . .*
> *I shall hate sweet music my whole life long.*

Was there in fact a rival—or rivals? Imaginary or not, Swinburne stigmatized them as:

> *The lapdog loves that whine as they chew,*
> *The little lovers that curse and cry.*

He visualized the future as it might have been in heart-breaking stanzas:

> *We had stood as the sure stars stand, and moved*
> *    As the moon moves, loving the world; and seen*
> *Grief collapse as a thing disproved,*
> *    Death consume as a thing unclean,*
> *Twain halves of a perfect heart, made fast*
> *Soul to soul as the years fell past;*
> *    Had you loved me once as you have not loved;*
> *    Had the chance been with us that has not been.*

But the "chance" had not been with him. The chance of what? Not only of winning "Boo" but, it may be supposed, of leading a normal life. It was as if he realized that from now on there was no hope for him, no hope of intimate marital tendernesses. The looked-for support has been denied the drowning man. Now he was thrown back amid the sterile surges of the "raptures of vice". Henceforward:

> *I shall go my ways, tread out my measure,*
>   *Fill the days of my daily breath*
> *With fugitive things not good to treasure. . . .*

Denied "Boo", what was there left to him but Dolores?

# CHAPTER V

## (1862–1865)

ON the 24th October 1862 Swinburne and Rossetti took possession of 16 Cheyne Walk, Chelsea. Tudor House—called Queen's House to-day—was, indeed still is, a Queen Anne house built upon part of the site of an older mansion, once occupied by Queen Katherine Parr after the death of Henry VIII. It was spacious, grand and ramshackle, had an acre of garden, and the rent was £110 a year. Rossetti, who had a predilection for magnificence, proposed that besides Swinburne, William Michael and Meredith should take rooms there to help with the expense. A suggestion from Ruskin that he too should join them was turned down: it was more than Rossetti could bear. Ruskin was "The Great Prohibited". Had he not for years tried to control both his art and his life? "Keep your room clean and go to bed early," Ruskin had said. "If you do right I shall like it—if wrong, I shall not." Ruskin as an inmate of Tudor House was clearly impossible. A further suggestion that old Mrs. Rossetti and Gabriel's sisters should come to live there was also turned down. It was as well. Algernon and Christina beneath the same roof is not a juxtaposition that can be contemplated with equanimity.

The house itself consisted on the ground floor of a large hall with Swinburne's sitting-room to the right and Meredith's opposite. At the back, giving on to the garden, was Rossetti's studio. On the first floor was a long drawing-room with windows on to the river—this room was also used for dinner-parties—a smaller room in which Rossetti would breakfast during the course of the afternoon, and his immense and sombre bedroom with a four-poster bed. On the second floor were a number of smaller bedrooms.

Swinburne's stay at Tudor House was not in this first instance long. Indeed, during these years there seems always to have been an inner restlessness which drove him from place to place. Though they had only moved in on 24th

October, he was already writing on 3rd November that he proposed leaving London for Fryston at the end of the week. Concerning this visit we have some account. There were no ladies present, Lady Houghton being away. The guests were only four: Stirling of Keir, Laurence Oliphant and Henry Adams, who recorded in his autobiography: "The fourth was a boy or had the look of one. . . . He resembled in action . . . a tropical bird, high-crested, long-beaked, quick moving, with rapid utterance and screams of humor, quite unlike any English lark or nightingale. One could hardly call him a crimson macaw among owls, and yet no ordinary contrast availed. Milnes introduced him as Mr. Algernon Swinburne. The name suggested nothing. Milnes was always unearthing new coins and trying to give them currency . . . [he added] that Swinburne had written some poetry, not yet published, of really extraordinary merit. . . ."

The American attaché was to be amazed by this particular coin. After a few remarks by Oliphant about his novel *Piccadilly*, then in course of composition, Swinburne, it appears, held the stage. The American was, perhaps, slightly bewildered by the torrent of speech and declamation that followed. Stupefied by an astonishing flow of words, in which could be discerned whole passages of quotation from the works of Sophocles, Shakespeare, Dante, Villon and Victor Hugo, he was finally overwhelmed by the recitation of *Faustine*, *After Death* and *The Ballad of Burdens*. Stirling, who had been reading *Rosamond*, exclaimed in astonishment: "He is a cross between the Devil and the Duke of Argyll!" Lord Houghton was no doubt gratified at the effect of his protégé's performance.

Swinburne stayed at Fryston till the 8th December, talking, reciting, and deciphering the manuscripts of the Marquis de Sade. He was much pleased that his own handwriting, owing to a physiological weakness of the wrist, resembled in vileness that of the Marquis.

William Michael Rossetti must later have joined the party, for Swinburne wrote to Lady Trevelyan on 2nd December mentioning his presence in a letter headed: "Anniversary of the Treason of N. Buonaparte." He asked if he might stay at Wallington since Gabriel was at the Bell Scotts' at

Newcastle, where, presumably, there would not be room for him.   He also mentioned that he was going to Sussex to attend the funeral of his grandmother, Charlotte, Countess of Ashburnham.

Wallington was apparently full and he could not go there till later, for his next letter to Lady Trevelyan is from the Turf Hotel, Newcastle.   "I see," he wrote, "Destitution and Despair ahead of me. . . . If by any wild chance—say by offering the head waiter a post-obit, or a foreclosure, or a mortgage, or a bill payable at three months, or a Federal bond, or an African loan, or a voucher, or something equally practicable—I can stave off the period of my incarceration so as to get to Wallington on Wednesday, I shall take the train that leaves Morpeth at 2.15 and gets to Scotus's Gap [Scott's Gap—the station that serves Wallington] at 2.50. But I cannot disguise for myself, and will not for you, that this contingency is remote.   It is far more probable that posterity will appear, a weeping pilgrim, in the prison-yard of this city, to drop the tear of indignant sympathy on a humble stone affording scanty and dishonourable refuge To The Nameless Dust of A. C. S."

He went to Wallington and then returned unexpectedly to Newcastle.   William Bell Scott wrote: "It was close upon Christmas of 1862, when we . . . were preparing to change the scene by flitting to . . . Tynemouth for a holiday. . . . Swinburne suddenly appeared, having posted to Morpeth from Wallington early that morning.   Why so early? he could not well explain; just thought he had been long enough there! he wanted letters at the post, but had not given his address!   I could inquire no further; there appeared to be some mystery he did not wish to explain; we went by a later train, and he would accompany us.   So we had him to walk with us by the much resounding sea, when he declaimed the *Hymn to Proserpine* and *Laus Veneris*, two of the most lovely, perfect, and passionate among the triumphs of his best period of poetic performance, never to be forgotten when recited in his strange intonation, which truly represented the white heat of the enthusiasm that had produced them."

Thus the year 1862 came to an end.   It had been remarkable for the sudden soaring of his genius.   There was now but a little way to go till the full fruit would bloom in all its exotic maturity. *A Year's Letters* had been composed, *Chastelard* and a great part of *Poems and Ballads*. *Blake* had been begun.

In January 1863 he was summoned with the rest of his family to Bournemouth, where his sister Edith was alarmingly ill. She rallied, and in February he was back in Cheyne Walk.

This year was, like the previous one, to be a succession of journeys—to Cornwall, the Isle of Wight and France. But London was his headquarters, Cheyne Walk his home. It was also to be Rossetti's till the end of his life. Here, apparently recovered from the shock of Lizzie's death—were not Fanny Schott and Janey Morris supplying him with a sort of joint ideal of womanhood?—he upheld a princely if bohemian state. He appears to have been making up to about four thousand pounds a year, though he kept no accounts and would distribute handfuls of gold out of a drawer, meeting his expenses with the gesture of a medieval monarch bestowing largess. "Why is he not some great exiled king," the blind poet, Marston, was to exclaim in the declining years, "that we might give our lives to restore him to his kingdom?" But there was a laxness, an untidiness about life in Cheyne Walk that was far removed from the punctiliousness of a court. He collected quantities of curious and ornamental bric-à-brac, some of which appears quite inconsequently in his pictures; he collected china, of which the priceless plates could frequently be heard breaking in the pantry; he was the first in England to seek out blue-and-white Nanking. He stocked the house and garden with animals: at one time or another there was Wolf, the Irish wolfhound, there was Punch the Pomeranian, there were blue rabbits, dormice, hedgehogs, white mice, squirrels, chameleons, salamanders, an opossum, wombats, an armadillo, a racoon, a jackass, parrots, peacocks, a raven, owls and a Brahmini bull. This last he bought because it had eyes like Janey Morris, but it committed the solecism of chasing its master round the garden. Once acquired, the animals were left very much to their own devices. Indeed, the problem of preventing their eating each other was one that was never satisfactorily solved. They had a tendency, too, to disappear. A missing armadillo, much to the chagrin of the cook, returned through the floor of a neighbour's kitchen; while a much sought-for opossum was found dead in a cigar-box. A lion, which Rossetti coveted, was only not acquired by reason of the difficulty of installing suitable heating arrangements, and he often talked of purchasing an elephant which might be trained to clean the windows.

If in addition to all this there were the hopeless unpunctuality, if not the uncertainty, of the appearance of meals, and Swinburne's engaging habit of wandering about the house stark naked, it is not perhaps altogether surprising that the rather bourgeois Meredith's tenancy should not have endured long. Indeed, it is not thought to have lasted more than a fortnight. He was the same age as Rossetti and nine years older than Swinburne, and was, at that time, rather painfully acquiring a literary reputation. The Pre-Raphaelites had been impressed by his poems and particularly by *The Ordeal of Richard Feverel*, published in 1859. Swinburne had probably first met him through Rossetti in 1860. And now Meredith had reason to be grateful to him since in 1862, the year before, Swinburne had written a letter to *The Spectator* in defence of *Modern Love*, which was suffering at the hands of the critics. But a few days spent in company at Cheyne Walk was sufficient to dispel gratitude on the one hand and admiration on the other. Meredith was not destined to be an object of the Swinburnian worship. He was, they decided, a Philistine. Did he not demand meals at regular hours, preach abstemiousness to Swinburne and horse exercise to Rossetti? He was a brilliant and, on occasion, even Rabelaisian wit. But even this last trait, much admired in Pre-Raphaelite circles, was insufficient to compensate for his lack of tact. He ruthlessly criticized Swinburne's poems and, unforgivable sin, mocked Rossetti at the dinner-table before two possible patrons. Nor, apparently, was he punctual in paying his rent. His face, remarked William Michael, resembled the Emperor Hadrian's.

But Swinburne's relations with Meredith did not end with the latter's departure from Cheyne Walk. They assumed something of the nature of guerrilla warfare, punctuated by truces. Swinburne was particularly offended in 1864 by the character of Tracy Runningbrook in *Sandra Belloni*. But the final rupture was delayed till the winter of 1867. Morley, editor of *The Fortnightly Review*, had gone to America and Meredith was acting for him. Some sort of reconciliation had temporarily been established, and Swinburne and Meredith were dining together at the Garrick. Whistler recorded the following scene: "Meredith had recently sent Swinburne £10 for a poem. Meredith explained he was paying all contributors in Morley's absence. 'Yes,' said Swinburne, 'but why £10?' Meredith explained it was what he usually got for his own poems. 'Yes, for yours,' said Swinburne, 'but for mine?' Meredith tried to point out the justice of it; what was enough for him was enough for Swinburne. Swinburne got up, came over to him and slapped his face. That was the end of their friendship." There was to be, in later years, a partial reconciliation.

Exactly when Swinburne first met Whistler is uncertain. After having lived for some years in France he had come to London in 1859 and was living in Queen's Road. His painting had attracted the attention of the Pre-Raphaelites, but whether Rossetti first introduced him to Swinburne or Swinburne to Rossetti is not now known. Rossetti, Ruskin and Burne-Jones, though on the whole admiring his art, frequently disapproved of his technique, while Swinburne, on the other hand, defended him, and against all criticism admired *The Little White Girl*. He wrote verses in honour of this picture and in 1868, in his *Notes on Some Pictures*, consecrated to Whistler several pages of ardent praise.

Their friendship was due, no doubt, as much to the similarity of their aesthetic philosophy, the theory of Art for Art's sake, as to any real similarity of temperament.

Whistler must have been one of the few people in England who had approved Swinburne's article on *Les Fleurs du Mal*. And now, in 1863, Whistler in conversation was able to evoke for him the studios and the artistic life of Paris, which seems to have been, intellectually at least, as much a Mecca for the English writer and painter as it was to prove for the next generation—that of George Moore. They were the only representatives of the aesthetic movement in England. The Pre-Raphaelites were not interested. What more natural, then, that they should turn to Paris? Whistler talked of Baudelaire, Manet and Fantin-Latour; he promised to present Swinburne to them when occasion should offer. The opportunity came in March 1863. The date may be exactly marked since it is borne by the poem *Hermaphroditus*, which he composed on this occasion after a visit to the Louvre. With Whistler and Fantin-Latour he went to Manet's studio and twelve years later he mentioned this visit in a letter to Mallarmé: "Il y a maintenant 12 ans—c'était au printemps de 1863—que je fus conduit chez M. Manet par mes amis MM. Whistler et Fantin; lui sans doute ne s'en souvient pas, mais moi, alors très jeune et tout à fait inconnu (sinon de quelque amis intimes) comme poète ou du moins comme aspirant à ce nom, vous croyez bien que ce fut pour moi un souvenir qui ne s'envolerait pas facilement." Baudelaire, however, he did not meet.

The *Hermaphroditus* showed how well he had imbibed the doctrines of Gautier and this visit to the Parisian ateliers no doubt confirmed him in the theory of Art for Art's sake. Now it was that he started serious work on *William Blake* which he had considered, at Rossetti's invitation, taking over after the death of Gilchrist and which he was now to elaborate separately into something far different from the biographical study proposed either by its original author or Macmillan, its publisher, who feared the inclusion of an analysis of the Prophetic Books. Swinburne's study was not to be published until 1868, but the second part, that which enshrines his aesthetic theory, was written, or at least begun, at this time. It is curious to reflect that the originator of the aesthetic movement in England—that movement whose "hard gem-like flame" was, in a few years, to illumine with a sinister refulgence the sordid corners of dock and cabmen's shelter, to bathe in a ghastly and sallow light those self-torturing adherents whose *nostalgie de la boue* led so often to the criminal court or the morgue—should have been the first to abandon it. For in 1867, a year even before *William Blake* was published,

Swinburne was to accept with tears and protestations the overwhelming personal ascendancy of Mazzini and devote his art to utilitarian ends.

But this was not yet. "I spent days," he wrote, "in the Print Room of the British Museum scribbling in pencil the analysis of Blake's prophetic books, and hours at Lord Houghton's in the same labour in pen and ink." The result of his lucubrations was to impose upon his subject a theory which Blake would have been the first to question. "No one again," he wrote, "need be misled by the artist's eager incursions into grounds of faith or principle; his design being merely to readjust all questions of such a kind by the light of art." Or again: "To him, as to others of his kind, all faith, all virtue, all moral duty or religious necessity, was not so much abrogated or superseded as summed up, included and involved, by the one matter of art. . . . Again, as we have noted, he had a faith of his own made out of art for art's sake, and worked by means of art; and whatever made against this faith was as hateful to him as any heresy to any pietist."

This philosophy of art learned from Gautier—had he not written: "Je me suis toute ma vie inquiété de la forme du flacon, jamais de la qualité du contenu"?—Poe and Baudelaire was directed not only at the sententious critics of *The Saturday Review* and *The Spectator*, and other journals, who had said of *Salammbô* that it was "nothing else but a series of descriptions generally of the most revolting character", and that *Modern Love* should have been entitled *Modern Lust*, but also at such luminaries of art as Carlyle and Ruskin, of whom these reviewers were but so many scurrilous echoes. The fact was that no one in England had as yet been able to conceive of art except in terms of usefulness and moral purpose. The idea that it might be fulfilling itself merely by existing to be enjoyed was quite alien to the mid-Victorian mind. "The Fine Arts, too," Carlyle had written with no false humility, "like the coarse, and every art of Man's God-given faculty, are to understand that they are sent hither not to fib and dance, but to speak and work. . . ." While Ruskin had written in *Modern Painters*: "The choice of the high subject involves all conditions of right moral choice"

—which was in direct opposition to Gautier. By 1870 in *Lectures on Art* he had moved even further from the idea of enjoyment and stated categorically that the arts "have had and can have but three principal directions of purpose:— first, that of enforcing the religion of men; secondly, that of perfecting their ethical state; thirdly, that of doing them material service". To all of which Swinburne replied: "Art for art's sake first of all, and afterwards we may suppose all the rest shall be added to her (or if not she need hardly be overmuch concerned)."

The spring and early summer were spent at Cheyne Walk, working in the British Museum and enjoying the pleasures of society. It was about this time, too, that he made a new friend, Simeon Solomon. This was a young Jewish painter whose father was an importer of Leghorn hats and became the first Jewish Freeman of the City of London. All the three Solomon children, Abraham, Rebecca, and Simeon, became painters, but Simeon, the youngest and perhaps the most gifted, was the only one to fall a victim to the *maladie du siècle*. Falling successively under the influence first of Swinburne and then of Pater, lamps too brightly glowing for a moth so delicately winged, he was inevitably overtaken by disaster. But now at twenty-two, fair and handsome, with delicate features, more classical than Jewish, with a sensitive wit and a gift for facile paradox, a talent which, though weak in drawing, was yet much admired and in whose figures the initiated recognized something strange, androgynous and decadent, he appeared to Swinburne as he posed in Greek costume, laurel-wreathed and sandalled, to be the image of a pagan god. Under Swinburne's influence —and Swinburne's more formed genius and stronger personality held him all too soon in utter subjugation—he absorbed the theory of Art for Art's sake, the works of the Divine Marquis, and the more sinister pleasures that were their corollary. Was there for Swinburne perhaps the same fascinated pleasure in corrupting this youth as Lord Houghton had previously enjoyed on his behalf? But Solomon lacked even the tenuous moral restraints which preserved Swinburne from public scandal. He was to surrender himself whole-heartedly to the vices amongst which Swinburne was

never more than an ardent dilettante. And yet these first
months in London were childish enough. With Burne-Jones
as a somewhat surprising third they made a strange trio.
Laughing and screaming with high spirits, they would dance
through the house in Cheyne Walk, annoying Rossetti,
whose attitude was that of an indulgent uncle, and who
remarked that they were "like wild-cats". They wrote
letters to each other of the most monstrous yet infantile
indecency, illustrated with obscene drawings. Solomon
was to be the first English sacrifice upon the altar of post-
Baudelairean aesthetics.

At the same time there were respectable interludes.
Rossetti entertained with all the magnificence to which he
was addicted in his painting. The priceless china was
brought out into the big drawing-room and all that was
most influential in the arts came at one time or another to
dinner. Swinburne was part of the entertainment with
which he could supply his guests. He was perhaps a little
too inclined to get drunk, talk outrageously, become over-
excited and scream. But this was atoned for by the brilliance
of his conversation during the earlier part of the evening and
the very strangeness of his personality seemed in some sort
to minimize any possible offence. His was, as it were, an
established character, a licensed oddity, as it might be the
studiously ignored kleptomania of a duchess: her presence
atoning for the temporary absence of the spoons. In this
way he met Frederick Sandys, for many of whose pictures
he was to write verses; Frederick Leighton, who though
opposed to the P.R.B. was nevertheless on good terms with
them; Joseph Knight, dramatic critic to the *Literary Gazette*
and, later, to *The Athenaeum*, who was to introduce him to
Morley; J. W. Marston, who reviewed *Atalanta* in *The
Athenaeum*, and whose son, Philip Burke Marston, the blind
poet, was a year or two later, at the age of fifteen, to meet
Swinburne and develop a touching, almost idolatrous friendship which lasted throughout his short and tragic life;
George Augustus Sala; Thomas Purnell, who for Swinburne was to be haloed with the almost divine prescience
of introducing him to Mazzini; and J. W. Inchbold, the
landscape painter, whose calm and friendly temperament

was of great service to Swinburne on the many occasions when, taking refuge from the dissipations of London, he became his guest in the less inebriating airs of Cornwall.

But all this was not enough. Where was that literary fame which, three years ago, he had been so sanguine would be his upon the publication of *Rosamond* and *The Queen Mother*? Though he enjoyed a reputation as a poet of genius among his intimate friends, public acclaim had eluded him. Indeed, it had had but little opportunity of doing otherwise. And now, with a heap of manuscript poems, and *Chastelard* at last completed, it seemed that recognition was still to be unattained. His friends were averse from their publication. Rossetti and Meredith were apprehensive; Ruskin wrote that, if published, "they would win him a dark reputation".

Indeed, *Chastelard* would at that moment have been only less unsuitable than the poems as the preliminary fanfare to a great career. What Mr. Harold Nicolson has called "its pervading tone of sensuality" would have blinded the critics to its very considerable merits. For it is a rapid, readable play, dramatic and, at moments, tragic. For the last time we see that flamboyant Elizabethanism mingled with Pre - Raphaelitism in his style. But the affected archaisms have disappeared, the sudden descents into *pastiche* have been controlled. If influences can still be traced, the style is nevertheless his own, brilliant with the harmonies of his own inexhaustible technique and vivid with the colouring of his particular imagination.

His main sources for this historical drama were Brantôme's *Discours sur Marie Stuart* and Knox's *History of the Reformation*. From these, with one or two legitimate and comparatively minor alterations of historical fact—the date of Mary Stuart's marriage to Darnley for instance—he built up his intrigue and culminating tragedy.

However correct his historical detail may have been, the chief characters are largely his own invention. In the case of Chastelard, who is the central character of the piece, he had a completely free hand, since almost nothing is known of him. While Mary Stuart, though he has endowed her with an acute intellect and a practical folly of conduct—a paradox which seems to be upheld by the historians—is in her one important characteristic as far as the drama is concerned, as Lafourcade has pointed out, a projection of Chastelard's own mind; that is in her cruelty.   She is the apotheosis of the *femme fatale*, the source of those twin inseparable gifts, love and death:

> *I know not: men must love you in life's spite;*
> *For you will always kill them; man by man*
> *Your lips will bite them dead; yea, though you would,*
> *You shall not spare one; all will die of you. . . .*

And this sphinx-like, marmoreal cruelty—for which there is no warrant but Chastelard's last words on the scaffold as reported by Brantôme: "Adieu la plus belle et la plus cruelle princesse du monde"—is accepted by Chastelard with a perverse alacrity, a joyful self-immolation.   Condemned to death for compromising the Queen by being found under her bed when she is undressing—deliberately forcing her thereby to condemn him to death, since it is only thus that he can attain to the summit of pleasure—he refuses to escape and destroys the royal pardon.

> *I hear my blood sing, and my lifted heart*
> *Is like a springing water blown of wind*
> *For pleasure of this deed.   Now, in God's name,*
> *I swear if there be danger in delight*
> *I must die now: if joys have deadly teeth,*
> *I'll have them bite my soul to death, and end*
> *In the old asp's way, Egyptian-wise; be killed*
> *In a royal purple fashion.   Look, my love*
> *Would kill me if my body were past hurt*
> *Of any man's hand; and to die thereof,*
> *I say, is sweeter than all sorts of life.*
> *I would not have her love me now, for then*
> *I should die meanlier some time.   I am safe,*
> *Sure of her face, my life's end in her sight,*
> *My blood shed out about her feet—by God,*
> *My heart feels drunken when I think of it.*

And in the last interview in the prison, before the execution, there takes place a scene between Chastelard and Mary which for imaginative perversity surpasses anything even

in Swinburne's work.   The Queen is both his lover and his
executioner.   Chastelard addresses her:

> *Stretch your throat out that I may kiss all round*
> *Where mine shall be cut through: suppose my mouth*
> *The axe-edge to bite so sweet a throat in twain*
> *With bitter iron, should not it turn soft*
> *As lip is soft to lip?*

This is the most purely sensual, the most purely physical
of all his plays.   Chastelard is a sublimation of his own
desires and tendencies.   The whipped page of *Laugh and Lie
Down* has become a Queen's lover, ordered to the scaffold
by his mistress.   There is no doubt that this identification
of his own imagination with Chastelard's is the motive force
behind the dramatic and lyrical qualities of the play.   With
Chastelard's death the Queen loses her siren quality, survives
only as an intellectual reconstruction of an historical character
—possibly more accurate, certainly less interesting—which
accounts in fact for the failure of *Bothwell* and *Mary Stuart*,
which were to be written at a later date as the second and
third parts of a trilogy.   But with all its merits it must be
admitted that Ruskin had reason to view the possibility of its
publication in 1863 with concern.

It was, indeed, time that a masterpiece were written.   One,
moreover, that might be confidently placed before the public
without fear of gaining thereby that "dark reputation"
which was at the time so easy to acquire.   This masterpiece
was about to be begun.   In August 1863 Swinburne was
staying with his parents at East Dene and *Atalanta* was
already in his mind.   What suggested to him the particular
form this poem was to take—a form so much at variance
with his recent work?   It was probably Lord Houghton,
anxious that his patronage should be justified without
further delay, who suggested the classic form.   It would
have certain advantages.   The cruel myths of the Middle
Ages were obviously too dangerous, too exciting to Swinburne's temperament, whereas, in the convention of the
Greek drama, tragedy and its implicit cruelty gained a certain
impersonality, a saving lack of sensuality, from their supernatural origin.   No suggestion, oddly enough, could at this

juncture have been better suited to Swinburne's inspiration. The rebuff he had suffered from "Boo" had but confirmed the direction of his mind and the necessity for the poetical exploitation of his temperament. But now the *femme fatale*, as a projection of his imagination, was no longer sufficient. The study of Blake and Sade had caused him to rationalize those tendencies which she had hitherto been created to represent. A process of expansion was taking place in his mind, a synthesis was being formulated and its inclusiveness demanded that the *femme fatale* as the origin of pain should be replaced by God.

He seems to have stayed for some weeks at East Dene "half-living in the sea", and "swimming, riding and croquetting", and then, no doubt in company with his family, went to Bournemouth where Edith, his eldest sister, was ill of consumption. As in the previous year, there was a crisis in her disease. But this time she did not recover, her death taking place on 23rd September. She was his favourite sister and, no doubt, as he avowed to Lady Trevelyan, the shock of her death was partly responsible for the sombre tone of *Atalanta*. His grief persisted, for twelve years later he wrote to William Rossetti: "To me as to so many others Bournemouth is a place of as sad association as these of this day to your wife's family and their friends; several of the last hopeless months of my dear sister's illness were spent there by us all in weary expectation of the end."

Immediately after the funeral his family left for a change of scene on the Continent. Swinburne did not go with them. Instead, he went to stay with the Gordons at Northcourt. Here the calm and cheerful atmosphere and the presence of his favourite cousin, Mary Gordon (later Mrs. Disney Leith), not only assuaged his immediate sorrow, but provided surroundings free from the distractions of either London or Continental travel in which *Atalanta* might be composed. He was to remain there until February 1864.

It was here one day, when riding with Mary Gordon between Newport and Shorwell, that he recited to her the opening chorus, "When the hounds of spring are on winter's traces. . . ." And it was in the Northcourt library that much of the work was written out, the table strewn with the blue sheets of foolscap, while Mary played the organ. "My greatest pleasure just now," he wrote to a sister in Italy, "is when Mary practises Handel on the organ, but I can hardly *behave* for delight at some of the choruses. I care hardly more than I ever did for any minor music; but *that* is an enjoyment which wants special language to describe it, being so unlike all others. It crams and crowds me with old and new verses, half-remembered and half-made, which new ones will hardly come straight afterwards; but under their influence I have done some more of my *Atalanta* which will be among my great doings if it keeps up with its own last (*sic*) scenes throughout."

Here, too, he wrote *Ilicet* and *Anactoria*, continued writing his "running commentary" on Blake, supplied a *pastiche* of an Elizabethan morality play, *The Pilgrimage of Pleasure*, for a novel Mary Gordon was writing for children, which was published under the title of *The Children of the Chapel*, assisted her with the composition of another called *Trusty in Fight*, and by way of relaxation tutored her in Greek, indulged in endless *bouts-rimés*, and composed, with suitable propriety, numerous verses in the form known to-day as the Limerick.

Indeed, the stay at Northcourt, which originally had only been intended to last two or three weeks, had prolonged itself to four months. He had been unable to tear himself away in spite of the pleas of Rossetti, who took the somewhat peculiar view that his tenant should occupy his tenancy. Balked of his tenant he demanded his rent. Swinburne, whose practical affairs were never upon an altogether satisfactory basis — largely through negligence — till they became lodged in the almost too competent hands of Watts-Dunton, sent a cheque by return. "I have shrunk," he wrote, "from moving week after week, perhaps not wisely. . . . We must look up matters honestly when I come to London." But Rossetti was unappeased. Put, no doubt, to considerable inconvenience by what he probably considered Swinburne's irresponsibility, deprived of his tenant's company, uncertain of his rent—was there perhaps too some expressed disapproval from Swinburne, who remained loyal to Lizzie's memory, of Fanny Schott's position in the household?—Rossetti decided to make a break. Swinburne, many years later, in the manuscript note *A Record of Friendship*, gave his version of the incident: "It was not without surprise that after a separation of many months spent by me in the country I received from my friend a letter, couched in language as affectionate and cordial as had been the terms in which we parted when an impending domestic affliction had summoned me from London, but intimating with all possible apology that he wished to have the house at Chelsea to himself; for by this time the fourth original sharer in our undertaking had withdrawn from it, and Mr. W. M. Rossetti was now but an occasional inmate of the household. My reply was brief and clear, to the effect that I observed with his usual frankness and his usual rectitude that I had not understood our common agreement to be so terminable at the caprice of either party that one could desire the other to give place to him without further reason alleged than his own will and pleasure: but the ultimate result could only be an amicable separation." The separation was indeed amicable—fragments of *Atalanta* and *Blake* were submitted to Rossetti—but it was a separation nevertheless. Their friendship was never to be so warm as hitherto. This was perhaps the first rock of that shoal upon which it was ultimately to founder.

But at the moment this must have seemed to him but a trivial inconvenience. He was about to embark upon a pilgrimage. *Atalanta* was half finished, the first draft of the Greek dedication had been written, and in his pocket was a letter of introduction to Landor. It was another of Lord Houghton's beneficences. Now, at last, he was upon the point of meeting the venerable oracle face to face. On the last day of January he had written to William Michael: "Let them know at Chelsea that I may be expected by Saturday or Monday at latest." He stayed there a few days, no doubt packing his belongings, and then left for Italy.

He may have travelled part of the way with Lord Houghton. It is certain that they were together in Paris, where Swinburne was taken to tea with Charles MacCarthy, who suffered "quite a bad night", so haunted was he by

Swinburne's recitations. By the 1st of March he was in Florence.

Here, without delay, he "hunted out", as he wrote to Lord Houghton on 4th March, "the most ancient of the demigods at 93 Via della Chiesa". But "found him, owing I suspect to the violent weather, too much weakened and confused to realize the fact of the introduction without distress". It may, possibly, have been the weather. But when one considers Swinburne's capacity for hysterical excitement, the ardour of his hero-worship, the *empressement* with which he would have flung himself upon his knees, eyes gleaming, hair aflame, demanding a blessing, it would seem unnecessary to look to the inclemency of the climate in order to account for a nonagenarian's bewilderment. Swinburne was repulsed and "came away in a grievous state of disappointment and depression". But he was not to be so easily deprived of "the one thing I wanted with all my heart". He wrote "a line of apology and explanation . . . expressing (as far as was expressible) my immense admiration and reverence in the plainest and sincerest way I could manage". The result was a letter of invitation.

The second interview was more successful. "If both or either of us die to-morrow, at least to-day he has told me that my presence here has made him happy." Landor's poems Swinburne told him "had first given me inexplicable pleasure and a sort of blind relief when I was a small fellow of twelve". He then read him passages from *Atalanta* and the Greek verses of dedication, which were accepted. Soon Landor was calling him "dear friend" and pressed upon him several copies of his unpublished dialogue *Savonarola e Il Priore di San Marco*, which had been banned by the Tuscan Government. A parting gift, in spite of Swinburne's protestations, was a Correggio hanging on the poet's own wall. It turned out to be an incompetent fake. But what matter? Swinburne had received "the shock of adoration which one feels at thirteen towards great men"; his god was "indubitable and incarnate" before his eyes. Even Tennyson, he reflected, "into whose church we were all in my time born and baptized . . . is not a Greek nor a heathen, and I imagine does not want to be. I greatly fear he believes it possible to be something better; an absurdity which should be left to the Brownings and other blatant creatures begotten on the slime of the modern chaos". Landor had never been in danger of such heresy. For half an hour Swinburne had pierced the miasma of age in which the poet was now enveloped. He had "found him as alert, brilliant and altogether delicious as I suppose others may have found him twenty years since". But the strain had been too great. The next day he received a note: "So totally am I exhausted that I can hardly hold my pen to express my vexation that I shall be unable to converse with you again. Eyes and intellect fail me." Six months later the "demigod" was dead.

But Swinburne stayed on for some weeks in Florence, viewing the art galleries and being entertained by the English colony. Here he met John Temple Leader, and went sightseeing in his company, Mrs. Gaskell, Isa Blagden and the Barone Seymour Kirkup, to whom he had an introduction through the Rossettis. In his youth Kirkup had known Blake, talked with Shelley and been present at Keats' funeral. He was, besides, an old friend of Landor's. His memories were full of fascination for Swinburne, who profited by them for his study of Blake and made a friendship which was later to flower into correspondence concerning his *William Blake*. He disapproved, however, of Kirkup's experiments in spiritualism.

Leaving Florence, where he had done some work on the uncatalogued drawings in the Uffizi, he went to Fiesole, Siena, Pisa and San Gimignano. But the heat of the Tuscan spring was overpowering, "the weight of the violent sky" too heavy a burden for his Northumbrian soul. On 21st May he was in London, "beaten back by the Italian sun". And yet in the tenebrous years ahead his mind was often to revert with sharp nostalgia to this last visit to Italy, to the sun-warmed plains, to Florence and to Siena, "loveliest of my loves".

Back in London and no longer able to go to Cheyne Walk, he moved helplessly during the next two months from lodging to lodging: first to Bedford Street, then to Grosvenor Place, and in July to 124 Mount Street. He wrote to Nichol that he was "unpacking, blaspheming, arranging, etc., with my choicest books ruined and endless things lost." But in August he left London to stay with J. W. Inchbold at Tintagel. He was to remain in Cornwall till November. Here he swam "up the subterranean inlets of the sea—right into the dark, out of sight of daylight". Was it this summer that, as he recorded in a letter of 1890, he led the protesting Jowett—of whom he used to say, showing his dislike of Oxford, "that the Master of Balliol was officially a stranger to him, but Mr. Jowett an honoured and lifelong friend"— up the crag of Tintagel? He lived with Inchbold in the local schoolhouse, and by October, when the winter gales had begun, he was writing "the sea is very treacherous and tiring". So they hired horses and rode about the country-side, and on one occasion joined the local hunt, when "after 100,000,000 false starts the scent was lost after all, if indeed it ever existed. But we had some good gallops. . . ." The locals were "such a comic, boisterous set of people . . . clergymen, agents, farmers, all much alike, and also very hospitable". Then he cut his foot on a rock, escaping the tide, and was laid up for three weeks. His astonishing vitality could make the most ordinary days eventful.

But the company of Inchbold and the healthy country life was beneficial to the flow of his genius. He was again working upon *Atalanta* when the news of Landor's death reached him. It had taken place on 23rd September. Not only did it give him a vivid sensation of personal loss, but there was, too, the disappointment that the "demigod" would never now read the completed Greek tragedy, whose dedication he had accepted with so much condescension, could never now make known to his disciple his approval of its classic symmetry. To Lady Trevelyan he wrote on 15th March 1865: "It was begun last autumn twelvemonth, when we were all freshly unhappy, and finished just after I got the news in September last of Mr. Landor's death, which was a considerable trouble to me, as I had hoped against hope or reason that he who in the spring at Florence had accepted the dedication of an unfinished poem would live to receive and read it. . . . In spite of the funereal circumstances which I suspect have a little deepened the natural colours of Greek fatalism here and there, so as to have already incurred a charge of 'rebellious antagonism' and suchlike things, I never enjoyed anything more in my life than the composition of this poem, which though a work done by intervals was very rapid and pleasant. Allowing for a few after insertions, two or three in all, from p. 66 to 83 (as far as the Chorus) was the work of two afternoons, and from p. 83 to the end was the work of two other afternoons: so you will understand that I enjoyed my work. I think it is pure Greek. . . ."

Fortunately, perhaps, Swinburne's masterpiece was not "pure Greek". When later he attempted, under the eye of Jowett, the perfection of Aeschylean form in *Erechtheus*, though the classic shape was apparent, the poetic merit was less obvious. As he was later to say himself in the *Dedicatory Epistle* to the collected edition—having in the meantime digested the current criticism on this score: *The Spectator* said the choruses were "chaotic", Thirwell condemned the romantic element as anachronistic, and Jowett, who preserved a lifelong immunity to the aesthetic emotion, had no doubt said much in private—"*Atalanta*," wrote Swinburne, "was perhaps too exuberant and effusive in its dialogue, as it certainly was too irregular in the licence of its choral verse to accomplish the design or achieve the success which its author aimed at." This criticism is of course irrelevant, since *Atalanta* must be considered as an independent work of art and not as a *pastiche* of a Greek play. The restrictions of the Greek convention in so far as they were observed were only valuable in curbing his loose and facile fecundity—his besetting fault as an artist—while the manipulations of the classic outline permitted him a justly considered freedom. The result was a sustained magnificence which he was never able quite to achieve again upon a similar scale.

Indeed, it is difficult for the critic to approach *Atalanta* without enthusiasm. Here is the perfectly oriented work. However alien the implicit theme, it is expressed with a matchless perfection, a tact which never permits it to dominate the formal structure of the drama. The selection of the classical myth of the revenge of Artemis upon Calydon permitted him to work within a convention unhampered by the dictates of reality, absolved him from the necessity of creating characters, which was not a projection to which his genius lent itself with any facility. *Atalanta* is not in its essence a tragedy of blighted love and the death of youth: but rather a philosophic lament for this our earthly state. The main personages are symbols representing the forces of nature as he saw them in his Sadic pessimism: Althaea, the earth-mother, fecund and fatal; Atalanta, love, the origin of pleasure and pain; and Meleager, suffering humanity, the helpless victim, accepting his destiny with passive fatalism. His sources for the story, which is perfectly suited to the theme, were of the slightest: two allusions in the *Choephoroi* of Aeschylus and in the *Hymn to Artemis* of Callimachus probably attracted his more immediate attention. He had also read the fragments of the lost play of Euripides in the Dindorf collection *Poetarum Scenicorum Graecorum* which, on the authority of Sir George Young, had been given him as a "leaving book" on his departure from Eton. Apollodorus and the *Metamorphoses* of Ovid supplied him with proper names, local colour, and a description of the slaying of the boar. In a curious stilted prose he summarized the story in *The Argument*. Artemis in her fury against Calydon sends Atalanta, the virgin of Arcadia, to take part in the tragic boar hunt, causes Meleager, the King's son, to fall in love with her, to quarrel on her account with his mother's brothers, Toxeus and the "violent-souled" Plexippus, and to kill them. And then impels Althaea, Meleager's mother, to place upon the fire the magic brand on which his life depends. As it is consumed, so Meleager dies.

> *For all things else and all men may renew*
> *Yea, son for son, the gods may give and take*
> *But never a brother or sister any more. . . .*

The figures move in response to relentless and elemental stimuli. Their tragedy does not arise out of them but is arbitrarily imposed upon them. They are not of flesh and blood, but rather the inmates of a frieze whose ordered, tragic harmonies are fixed eternally by the unaccountable fury of the gods. And yet, as in the Greek drama, Swinburne permits his characters to comprehend the full horror

of their actions, even in their senseless performance.  Helpless, they are doomed to suffer twice, both in their actions and
in the consequences.

The Prologue opens quietly with the Chief Huntsman's
invocation to Aurora:

> *Maiden, and mistress of the months and stars*
> *Now folded in the flowerless fields of heaven . . .*

and a prayer to Artemis to

> *Help and give honour, and to mine hounds good speed,*
> *And edge to spears, and luck to each man's hand.*

Then follows the Parados: "When the hounds of spring
are on winter's traces . . ."  But the dulcet echoes of the
voices of the Aetolian virgins chanting the ode to Spring
are shattered by the entry of Althaea.  In the stichomythia
that follows the tragic note becomes immediately evident.
She is already the half-crazed instrument of the gods, already
the predestined tragedy is heavy upon her:

> ALTHAEA: *Look, ye say well, and know not what ye say;*
> *For all my sleep is turned into a fire,*
> *And all my dreams to stuff that kindles it.*
> CHORUS: *Yet one doth well being patient of the gods.*
> ALTHAEA: *Yea, lest they smite and with some four-foot plague.*
> CHORUS: *But when time spreads find not some herb for it.*
> ALTHAEA: *And with their healing herbs infect our blood.*
> CHORUS: *What ails thee to be jealous of their ways?*
> ALTHAEA: *What if they give us poisonous drinks for wine?*
> CHORUS: *They have their will; much talking mends it not.*
> ALTHAEA: *And gall for milk, and cursing for a prayer?*
> CHORUS: *Have they not given life, and the end of life?*
> ALTHAEA: *Lo, where they heal, they help not; thus they do,*
> *They mock us with a little piteousness,*
> *And we say prayers, and weep; but at the last,*
> *Sparing awhile, they smite and spare no whit.*

Althaea then states the complications of the tragedy, the
curse that Artemis has inflicted upon them in the love of
Meleager for Atalanta, for

> *Love is one thing, an evil thing, and turns*
> *Choice words and wisdom into fire and air.*

She tells the story of Meleager's birth, inveighs against the implacable gods, and ends on a note of hopeless resignation to the divine will.  The Stasimon that follows is a complaint against human destiny, against the cruelty of the gods who mingle pain with pleasure, permit no happiness to be unalloyed with sorrow, no life to be unabridged by death. Swinburne has discovered that the law of suffering which he had discerned in the passions has a universal application.

> Before the beginning of years
>    There came to the making of man
> Time, with a gift of tears;
>    Grief, with a glass that ran;
> Pleasure, with pain for leaven;
>    Summer, with flowers that fell;
> Remembrance fallen from heaven,
>    And madness risen from hell;
> Strength without hands to smite;
>    Love that endures for a breath;
> Night, the shadow of light,
>    And life, the shadow of death.

This is a recurrent theme throughout the drama, a philosophical undercurrent which caused Lafourcade to call *Atalanta* a "theological tragedy".  Instead of the fatalistic theology of the Greek drama, the acceptance of the divinely inspired tragedy with apathetic lamentation, Swinburne, largely through the media of the choruses, carries a critical warfare into, as it were, the divine camp, storming with blasphemy upon his lips Olympus itself.  If, he seems to be saying, there is a God—"the absurdest of all human figments" —then there is only one conception of Him possible.  For it is He who has "filled us full to the eyes and ears" with pain— the agony which is implicit in living, in the eternal contrasts of life and death, of love and sorrow, of war and peace.  It is thou, God, who hast laid

> Upon us with thy left hand life, and said,
> Live:  and again thou hast said, Yield up your breath,
> And with thy right hand laid upon us death. . . .

It is the gods who "mock us with a little piteousness", who "at the last, Sparing awhile, they smite and spare no whit".

But of what use is the agony of the world, of the groans and curses of suffering humanity, unless it is that they are of themselves pleasing to God, who savours them with a voluptuous and sadic cruelty?  "What shall be done with all these tears of ours? . . . A great well-head of lamentation Satiating the sad gods? . . ."

> *The gods guard over us*
> *With sword and with rod;*
> *Weaving shadow to cover us,*
> *Heaping the sod,*
> *That law may fulfil herself wholly, to darken man's face before God.*

Indeed, *Atalanta* is a demonstration of the tragedy—as well as the absurdity—of belief in this "human figment".  But where did he find his divine prototype?  In the *Essay on William Blake* he wrote: "Theism is . . . the source of all evil and error.  Grant . . . God his chance of existence, what reason has the theist to suppose or what right to assume his wisdom or his goodness?"  And Blake in the *Visions of the Daughters of Albion* has: "O Urizen, Creator of men! mistaken Demon of heaven! Thy joys are tears. . . ."  In the *Book of Ahania* God becomes "This abstract non-entity, This cloudy God, seated on waters, Now seen, now obscured, king of sorrow. . . ."  While for Swinburne in *William Blake* Urizen is "God of cloud and star, 'Father of Jealousy', clothed with a splendour of shadow, strong and sad and cruel; . . . sorrow is in all his works; he is the maker of mortal things, of the elements and sexes; in him are incarnate that jealousy which the Hebrews acknowledged and that envy which the Greeks recognized in the divine nature; in his worship faith remains one with fear".

It is round this conception of the divine will that the tragedy revolves.  With the dying cadences of Stasimon I, Meleager enters.  The air is already heavy with a foreboding which his youth and virility cannot altogether dispel.  And soon, indeed, in the episode that follows, with its dialogue on love and duty, with the presence of Toxeus and Plexippus, presentiment is reawakened in Althaea.  But with Stasimon II the chorus breaks into an ode to Venus Anadyomene:

*We have seen thee, O Love, thou art fair; thou art goodly, O Love;*
*Thy wings make light in the air as the wings of a dove.*

*Thy feet are as winds that divide the stream of the sea;*
*Earth is thy covering to hide thee, the garment of thee,*
*Thou art swift and subtle and blind as a flame of fire;*
*Before thee the laughter, behind thee the tears of desire;*
*And twain go forth beside thee, a man with a maid;*
*Her eyes are the eyes of a bride whom delight makes afraid;*
*As the breath in the buds that stir is her bridal breath;*
*But Fate is the name of her;  and his name is Death.*

With the entry of Atalanta, which leads to the first clash between Meleager and his uncles, the mechanism of the tragedy is set up.   The catastrophic and inevitable solution merely awaits the appointed hour.   But here the transition is marked by the choric ode of Stasimon III.   Forestalling the tragedy, in a sense irrelevantly at this point since the *dénouement* is still but obscurely seen and Oeneus has dismissed them all to the hunt with a suave farewell, the chorus nevertheless breaks out with the resounding and anarchic denunciation of God: "Yea, with thine hate, O God, thou hast covered us. . . ."   God, the "human figment", kills and tortures for his pleasure.   He is the supreme enemy:

> *When hast thou seen? or hast thou felt his breath*
> *    Touch, nor consume thine eyelids as the sun,*
> *Nor fill thee to the lips with fiery death?*
> *    None hath beheld him, none*
> *Seen above other gods and shapes of things,*
> *    Swift without feet and flying without wings,*
> *Intolerable, not clad with death or life,*
> *    Insatiable, not known of night or day,*
> *The lord of love and loathing and of strife*
> *    Who gives a star and takes a sun away;*
> *Who shapes the soul, and makes her a barren wife*
> *    To the earthly body and grievous growth of clay;*
> *Who turns the large limbs to a little flame*
> *    And binds the great sea with a little sand;*
> *Who makes desire, and slays desire with shame;*
> *    Who shakes the heaven as ashes in his hand;*
> *Who, seeing the light and shadow for the same,*
> *    Bids day waste night as fire devours a brand,*
> *Smites without sword, and scourges without rod;*
> *    The supreme evil, God.*

Though the conception of the person of the divinity may have been borrowed to some extent from Blake, the perverse and sinister pessimism that informed his "theory of the diabolic government of this world", as he terms it in a letter to Nichol in the September of this year, was derived from Sade. So much he admitted concerning the Chorus quoted above to Lord Houghton, who had alluded to it in his article on *Atalanta* in *The Edinburgh Review*: "I only regret that in justly attacking my *Charenton* you have wilfully misrepresented its source. I should have bowed to the judicial sentence if instead of 'Byron with a difference' you had said "De Sade with a difference'." Indeed, that algolagnic trait had here reached its ultimate level of sublimation. From the adolescent flagellation of *Laugh and Lie Down*, through the gradual development of the *femme fatale* in *Rosamond* and *Chastelard* to the Sadic synthesis of *Atalanta*, there can be traced a distinct and related development. As his genius matured, so the innate instinct, the acquired philosophy and the aesthetic imperative became integrated and fused. In *Atalanta*, the supreme example, the fusion is as complete as he was ever able to achieve, and the result a masterpiece.

"The poet, thinker and man of the world," he wrote, "from whom the theology of my poem is derived was a greater than Byron. *He*, indeed, fatalist or not, saw to the bottom of gods and men." And from Sade's tenebrous prose, which sets out to demonstrate the triumph of the "Prospérités du Vice" over the "Malheurs de la Vertu", he imbibed the general tone of his blasphemies. Sade had written in *Juliette*: "Je me dis: il existe un Dieu, une main a créé ce que je vois, mais pour le mal; elle ne se plait que dans le mal; le mal est son essence; tout celui qu'elle nous fait commettre est indispensable à ses plans. . . . Ce que je caractérise mal est vraisemblablement un très grand bien relativement à l'être qui m'a mis au monde. . . . Le mal est nécessaire à l'organisation vicieuse de ce triste univers. Dieu est très vindicatif, méchant, injuste. Les suites du mal sont éternelles; c'est dans le mal qu'il a créé le monde, c'est par le mal qu'il le soutient; c'est pour le mal qu'il le perpétue; c'est imprégnée de mal que la créature doit exister; c'est

dans le sein du mal qu'elle retourne après son existence. . . .
Comment le mal peut-il être tourmenté par le mal? C'est
qu'il s'augmente en retombant sur lui-même. Ce qui survit
de l'être naturellement mauvais . . . sera donc éternelle-
ment tourmenté par l'essence entière du mal à laquelle il sera
réuni. . . . Telle est la loi de l'Univers.

"'Pourquoi vous égarer dans les sentiers de la Vertu?'
dira l'Etre. 'Pourquoi ne détruisez-vous pas? Le mal
m'est nécessaire.'

"Je vois le mal éternel et universel dans le monde. Le
mal est un être moral non créé; éternel, non périssable; il
existait avant le monde, il constituait l'être monstrueux qui
put créer un monde aussi bizarre. L'auteur de l'univers est
le plus méchant, le plus féroce, le plus épouvantable de tous
les êtres. Il existera donc après les créatures qui peuplent
ce monde; et c'est dans lui qu'elles rentreront toutes, pour
recréer d'autres êtres plus méchants encore. . . ."

And it was in Sade, too, that he found the subtle excuse,
the intellectual equivocation, that admitted the reasonable-
ness of this paradoxical anathematizing of a "human
figment". With Sade he could declare "formellement,
authentiquement, publiquement, que je n'ai pas dans toi la
plus légère croyance", and yet because "les trois quarts de
l'Europe attachent des idées très religieuses à cette hostie . . .
à ce crucifix . . . j'aime a les profaner; je fronde l'opinion
publique, cela m'amuse; je foule aux pieds les préjugés
de mon enfance, je les anéantis; cela m'échauffe la
tête". Indeed, by blasphemy his instinct to rebel was
satisfied. In attacking God the myth he was attacking
society itself.

However sudden the shock of the fourth chorus may be in
reading the play, it nevertheless sets the tone for the second
half, the resolution of the tragedy. Atalanta is the instrument of Artemis who, though she has permitted the boar to
be slain, uses the Arcadian virgin as "a blast of the envy of
God" for a still more disastrous revenge upon Calydon,
while Althaea becomes a helpless robot in the hands of fate,
impelled by a supernatural power to the frenzied murder of
her own son. She passes into the house and burns the brand
upon which Meleager's life depends.

CHORUS: *I see a faint fire lightening from the hall.*

ALTHAEA: *Gaze, stretch your eyes, strain till the lids drop off.*

CHORUS: *Flushed pillars down the flickering vestibule.*

ALTHAEA: *Stretch with your necks like birds: cry, chirp as they.*

CHORUS: *And a long brand that blackens: and white dust.*

ALTHAEA: *O Children, what is this ye see? your eyes*
*Are blinder than night's face at fall of moon.*
*That is my son, my flesh, my fruit of life,*
*My travail, and the year's weight of my womb.*
*Meleager, a fire enkindled of mine hands*
*And of mine hands extinguished; this is he.*

CHORUS: *O gods, what word has flown out at thy mouth?*

ALTHAEA: *I did this and I say this and I die.*

And Meleager, true to his passive rôle, aware that it is a divine madness that has compelled the tragedy, blames fate alone, exonerating his mother. Neither does he evince any anger against the gods. His rage at the "diabolic government of this world" Swinburne reserved, as has already been indicated, for the choruses. Meleager's passive acceptance of suffering and death is—as, increasingly in Swinburne's view, is humanity's—almost contemptible.

> *I would thou hadst let me live; but gods averse,*
> *But fortune, and the fiery feet of change,*
> *And time, these would not, these tread out my life,*
> *These and not thou; me too thou hast loved, and I*
> *Thee; but this death was mixed with all my life,*
> *Mine end with my beginning: and this law,*
> *This only, slays me, and not my mother at all.*

But preluding the Exodos is the Kommos. Swinburne never surpassed the magnificence of this symphonic passage. The antiphonal voices answering each other in transcendent melody is overwhelming in its effect of pathos and horror. All the elusive rhythms of the tragedy are here knotted together into an exquisitely harmonic culmination. The heavy drum-beats of the first four lines in each stanza, the crying of the fifth, form a matchless metrical achievement.

MELEAGER

*Let your hands meet*
  *Round the weight of my head;*
*Lift ye my feet*
  *As the feet of the dead;*
*For the flesh of my body is molten, the limbs of it molten as lead.*


CHORUS

*O thy luminous face,*
  *Thine imperious eyes!*
*O the grief, O the grace,*
  *As of day when it dies!*
*Who is this bending over thee, lord, with tears and suppression of*
  *sighs?*

MELEAGER

*Is a bride so fair?*
  *Is a maid so meek?*
*With unchapleted hair,*
  *With unfilleted cheek,*
*Atalanta, the pure among women, whose name is as blessing to*
  *speak.*

ATALANTA

*I would that with feet*
  *Unsandalled, unshod,*
*Overbold, overfleet*
  *I had swum not nor trod*
*From Arcadia to Calydon northward, a blast of the envy of God.*


MELEAGER

*Unto each man his fate;*
  *Unto each as he saith*
*In whose fingers the weight*
  *Of the world is as breath;*
*Yet I would that in clamour of battle mine hands had laid hold*
  *upon death.*

CHORUS

*Not with cleaving of shields*
  *And their clash in thine ear,*
*When the lord of fought fields*
  *Breaketh spearshaft from spear,*
*Thou art broken, our lord, thou art broken, with travail and labour*
  *and fear.*

The strange echoing beauty of these sad and faultless stanzas merges into Meleager's dying speech. Atalanta embraces him for the first and last time as he goes "down to the empty weary house Where no flesh is nor beauty nor swift eyes". And in two lines oppressive with sorrow she bids him adieu:

*Hail thou: but I with heavy face and feet*
*Turn homeward and am gone out of thine eyes.*

The effect is cumulative, the impact overwhelming.

The MS. of *Atalanta* was completed in October 1864. Was it in truth the masterpiece that could be confidently placed before the public? Or was it just one more of those works which must join the rest in the limbo of a secret drawer? Swinburne had no doubts. It was now a case of publication or oblivion. Arrangements were made, under the paternal guarantee of expenses, with J. B. Payne on behalf of Moxon & Co. In November Rossetti wrote: "It is good news indeed to hear of *Atalanta's* approaching publication. I really believe on the whole that this is the best thing to bring out first. It is calculated to put people in better humour for the others, which when they do come will still make a few not even over-particular hairs to stand on end. . . . I tremble for the result of your reading Baudelaire's suppressed poems. . . . If . . . these new revelations are to be printed too, I warn you that the public will not be able to digest them, and that the paternal purse will have to stand the additional expense of an emetic presented gratis with each copy to relieve the outraged British Nation."

Payne, after his experience five years earlier with *The Queen Mother*, felt no particular enthusiasm over the prospects of the new work. If the verse itself were unsaleable, perhaps something might be achieved by impeccable presentation. It was ordered in such a manner as to be attractive to bibliophiles. The paper and type were of the most luxurious; the cream buckram cover was ornamented with a design in gold by Rossetti. In February 1865 Swinburne was correcting the final proofs. In March the book was published.

Its success was immediate. This was no doubt due in part to the influence of Lord Houghton, who thought it time

that his own reiterated faith in the genius of his young
protégé should be justified by public acclaim, in part, too,
to the efforts of Rossetti, but in the main to its own intrinsic
merit, which could not be denied.    Over the next few months
laudatory notices followed each other in rapid succession.
Typical of the tributes were:    *The Saturday Review*: "He
almost beguiles us into imagining that we are listening to one
of the great contemporaries of Euripides"; *The Athenaeum*:
"We yet know not to what poet since Keats we would turn
for a representation at once so large and so graphic"; *The
Sunday Times*: "He is permanently enrolled among our great
English poets: he possesses great tragic power."    Amongst
the general praise there were one or two more hostile
though fainter notes struck.    *The Spectator* in particular,
remembering the dispute with its erstwhile contributor, was
determined to be objective in its judgments.    It criticized
the choruses as "chaotic".    More remarkable was the
fact that none of the critics seemed to have been in the
least aware as to what the drama was about, if we exclude
Lord Houghton in *The Edinburgh Review*, who on the whole
rather dishonestly, considering his stable knowledge —
indeed there is a double dishonesty in his substitution of
Byron for Sade—criticized its "bitter angry anti-theism",
and *The Tablet*, which in duty bound mildly complained of
the author's lack of faith.    But Swinburne's justification
was in his public.    They read it with avidity.    For the
young, with little in contemporary literature to admire,
disappointed in what appeared to them as the "mildew"
of *Enoch Arden*, it was the first breath of a revolutionary
flame in modern letters—a flame that was to scorch and
consume with the publication of *Poems and Ballads*.    For
Marston *Atalanta* was "a well-head of delight".    Even
Ruskin could write of it as: "The grandest thing ever done
by a youth, though he is a demoniac youth."    A new edition
was called for.    Swinburne had, in the words of Gosse,
"shot like a rocket into celebrity"

# CHAPTER VI

## (1865–1866)

AFTER the long years of apprenticeship and hesitancy to publish, the overwhelming success of *Atalanta* could only be but the more grateful. Swinburne, now twenty-eight, was acknowledged to be the most interesting of the younger poets: a golden future seemed assured. The effect of public acclamation upon his character was, however, wholly deleterious. Those vices which he no doubt looked upon as inherent in his genius, as an integral part of his poetic personality, seemed somehow warranted by success. Fused by the sombre philosophizings of the Divine Marquis, they had now passed the test of publicity. For Swinburne there was too often no dichotomy between ratiocination and expression, between action and fantasy. Had it really escaped him that the success of *Atalanta* with the critics was only due to the superficial propriety of the work, the camouflage of a classical form which cloaked tragedy and its implicit cruelty with the impersonality, the saving lack of sensuality, of a supernatural and divine origin, and concealed the licentious and anarchic deeps only from the uninitiated? And from this unstable foundation he was, during the next few months, with the publication of *Chastelard* and *Poems and Ballads*, to make irretrievably clear what the critics had missed — the true basis of his aesthetic synthesis. There was in fact no better reason for publishing these volumes now than there had been hitherto—except perhaps that Payne was prepared to issue them without subsidies from the Admiral. Success added a new intransigence not only to his literary undertakings but to the waywardness of his life, to his excesses and his tendency to shock and rebel.

The spring of 1865 was spent in London. While the Admiral negotiated the disposal of East Dene and the acquiring of the lease of Holmwood, near Shiplake, the family were staying at 36 Wilton Crescent. Swinburne was with them and "all was innocence and purity". This, however, soon ceased to be the case upon his removal to 22A Dorset Street, which was to remain his lodging till the end of 1869.

It was at this point that his friendship with Charles Augustus Howell, whom he had probably first met during the course of the preceding year, became more intimate. With Simeon Solomon, Howell was now his chosen companion, prepared to abet and participate in any pleasure or, indeed, any vice. A remarkable character, sinister, vicious and dishonest, and yet with a pervasive gift of intimacy founded upon charm and wit, Howell's career was of a distinctive strangeness. Half Portuguese, the son of a drawing-master established at Lisbon, Howell had been sent to England at the age of seventeen to the guardianship of an uncle, who was Vicar of Darlington, owing, it was said, to the impossibility of his remaining in Lisbon after being detected cheating at cards. He had come to London, after working for some time in an office, and had established relations with the Pre-Raphaelites. In 1859 it is thought—though the truth, since Howell's imagination was in no sense bounded by it, is difficult to arrive at—that he was involved in the Orsini conspiracy, and was compelled for a time to leave London. But in 1864 he returned in triumph. Rossetti received him with delighted recognition. His posings, his lies, the red ribbon he wore across his breast—declaring it to be a Portuguese order—were a source of never-failing diversion. But perhaps—

> The Portuguese person named Howell
> Who lays on his lies with a trowel—

was a more dangerous character than Rossetti himself realized. De Castro in Watts-Dunton's novel *Aylwin* is a portrait of him. Whistler wrote: "He was of the greatest service to his friends. . . . He had the gift of intimacy. He introduced everybody to everybody, he entangled everybody with everybody, and it was easier to get involved with Howell than to get rid of him." He was the perfect parasite. He assisted Rossetti in the formation of his collections of bric-à-brac and blue and white china; he became a general artistic agent for the Pre-Raphaelites; he attended the "pulling" of Whistler's etchings. Nor was he slow to take advantage of his position. Many of the reported Rossetti drawings are almost certainly forgeries from the hand of Howell's wife, while after his death impressions of Whistler's etchings, surreptitiously abstracted, were found amongst his belongings. Swinburne was to have cause to regret this friendship. Fallen on hard days, Howell did not hesitate to blackmail by the threatened sale of letters which contained the customary puerile indecencies. His death was as mysterious and as unaccountable as many of the incidents of his life. He was found at dawn in a Soho street, his throat cut, a sovereign clenched between his teeth.

With his gift of intimacy, his charm and wit, with his peculiar and fascinating knowledge of the London demi-monde—"He was," wrote Whistler, "like a great Portuguese cock of the poultry-yard; hens were always clucking round him"—this picturesque character soon established an ascendancy over Swinburne, who came to rely upon him both as the companion of his wilder amusements and also to some extent as his literary agent.

Besides Solomon and Howell there was a further companion whose influence was not altogether beneficial. Richard Burton had returned on leave from Fernando Po. Indeed, he was about to be transferred—through the browbeating of the Foreign Office by his wife—to the Consulate at Santos, Sao Paulo, in Brazil. In the meantime, he was indulging in his own fantastic brand of learned debauchery. Vice-President of the Anthropological Society, which remained largely quiescent during his absences abroad, he now founded a special offshoot from it, to be known as the Cannibal Club. Anthropophagy—half in jest, half in earnest—was an article of faith with Burton.—"Without cannibalism how could the Zealander have preserved his fine physical development?"— As for Swinburne, who was now introduced to the club, if he lacked the scientific background for the faith, he could. at least meet Burton with a mutual admiration for Dolmancé. But this scientific fantasy — club dinners at Bartolini's, elaborately ghoulish, in the presence of a mace in the form of a Negro gnawing a thigh-bone ("Ecce Homo!")—

appealed not only to Burton and Swinburne, who was generally carried home insensible, but curiously enough to several distinguished scholars. Amongst these was Thomas Bendyshe, senior Fellow of King's College, editor of *The Reader* and translator of the Mahabharata, who was designated "chaplain" of the club and is reported to have exercised an influence over Swinburne's religious beliefs—though this is not clear, since the poet's paganism and atheism were already fully developed—and Charles Bradlaugh, for whom he wrote the *Cannibal Catechism*, a caricature of the writings of one of the Fathers of the Church, to be chanted at the club's reunions:

> *Preserve us from our enemies*
> *Thou who art Lord of suns and skies*
> *Whose food is human flesh in pies*
> *And blood in bowls!*
> *Of thy sweet mercy damn their eyes*
> *And damn their souls!*

Before the Burtons left England, Richard made a final round of the favourite haunts with Swinburne, and there was a farewell week-end with Lord Houghton at Fryston. It is possible that by now Houghton regretted having brought Burton and Swinburne together. He had, he felt, a proprietary interest in Swinburne's genius. Was Burton's influence altogether calculated to further it? Perhaps he was not sorry to see him depart for Brazil. Isabel Burton, that perennially blind and doting wife, felt that Swinburne was a bad influence upon her husband! She complained to Houghton, who passed the strictures on. We have Swinburne's answer: "As to anything you have fished (how I say not) out of Mrs. Burton to the discredit of my innocence, how can she who believes in the excellence of 'Richard' fail to disbelieve in the virtues of any other man? En moi vous voyez Les Malheurs de la Vertu; en lui Les Prospérités du Vice. In effect it is not given to all his juniors to tenir tête à Burton—but I deny that his hospitality ever succeeded in upsetting me—as he himself on the morrow of a latish séance admitted with approbation, allowing that he had thought to get me off my legs, but my native virtue and circumspection

were too much for him.   See now the consequences.   J'étais
vertueux—je devais souffrir.   Accomplis tes décrets, Etre
Suprême!"   One legacy, however, Burton left behind him—
the friendship of Dr. Bird.   This excellent and respectable
man was able to fulfil his literary aspirations vicariously by
tracking down and assisting to bed the all-too-frequently
intoxicated poet.

It was not only on behalf of Mrs. Burton that Houghton
had to complain of his protégé's behaviour.   "I will only
ask," wrote Swinburne, "Why?  When?  How?"  The
occasion was a meeting arranged with Tennyson who was
not this time to encounter the docile undergraduate who had
visited him at Farringford, but the famous young author of
*Atalanta*.   Swinburne, drunk or sober, preferred to Tennyson's company—did the Laureate know that his young
contemporary called *The Idylls of the King* the "Morte
d'Albert"?—that of Palgrave and Lewes.   Perhaps they dis-
cussed Blake and Flaxman, perhaps the talk was wilder and
the piercing voice was overheard.   Its echoes reached Lady
Trevelyan in Northumberland.   She wrote that he should
be "more guarded about what you say when men get
together and take alcoholic stimuli".   He should "deny
the talks attributed to him" and it was "horrid for your
friends to have to deny some things".

In the meantime, *Chastelard* had been published during
the autumn.   The success of *Atalanta*, the attitude of mind,
perhaps, of the new companions with whom he spent his
days and his nights in London, persuaded him that the sage
advice of his older friends need not be heeded.   He would
delay no longer.   In the brief interludes which he spent at
Holmwood and Ashburnham Place he corrected the proofs
of *Chastelard* and prepared new poems for the further book
he had in contemplation.   Success, the consciousness that
the synthesis was achieved, published and accepted, a certain
disquiet perhaps, after all, that its basis was now to be made
so flagrantly evident, induced in him an intellectual tension
which, with his physical irregularities, combined into a state
of nervous strain which culminated in the deliberately overt
*Dolores*.   He wrote to Howell from Ashburnham Place:
"Infâme Libertin, Write me a word according to promise.

I shall be up in town in a day or two on my way from an uncle's to a father's, and between domestic life, rural gallops with cousins, study of Art and Illuminated Manuscripts and Caxton print, and proofs of a new edition of the virginal poem *Atalanta, je m'enfonce dans des systèmes qui menent à tout—oui, chère fille, absolument à tout.*

"I have added yet four more jets of boiling and gushing infamy to the perennial and poisonous fountain of *Dolores.* *O mon ami! . . .*"

There followed a postscript: "Since writing the above I have added ten verses to *Dolores*—très-infâmes et très-bien tournés. 'Oh! Monsieur, peut-on prendre du plaisir à de telles horreurs?'"

In July the correction of the proofs was completed. Payne paid him £110. *Chastelard* was ready in August but Payne waited till the autumn to place it before the public. Nevertheless, Victor Hugo, who had accepted the dedication of the drama in 1862, received his copy at once. It was translated to him by his son. "Votre oeuvre," he wrote, "parle au coeur et à l'âme, au coeur par la passion, à l'âme par l'idéal." The souls of the English critics tended to be less receptive.

Here there was no question of wrapping up the teachings of Sade in the anti-theism masked by a classical formula. No longer was the perversity intellectualized, the passion universalized. In *Chastelard* the inspiration was plain for all to see. The hot and subtle sensuality was implicit in the characters, evident in every scene, demonstrably the mainspring of the tragedy. The critics began to understand. But the author of *Atalanta* could not as yet be lightly dismissed as a pornographer. "The picture has . . . undeniable grandeur," admitted *The Athenaeum.* "Many may dislike, no one can contemn," declared *Albion.* But others thought differently. *The London Review* feared "that Mr. Swinburne is wanting in the higher beauty of moral dignity and sweetness". *Atlas* decided that "The Poem . . . is morally repulsive". While *The Spectator*—the quarrel with Hutton had never been made up—denounced "the deformity of this poetry".

Indeed, in the diversity of opinion a note of puzzled

interrogation is discernible. The critics, each fearful of being the first to give himself away, of being the only one to recognize the perverse inclinations of the work, were neither frank nor clear as to the quality of the immorality or the attitude that should be taken towards it. And it must be remembered that criticism at that date was more concerned with ethics than aesthetics. Swinburne's genius very nearly succeeded in imposing his particular aspect of passion upon them. But not quite. Anxiety underlies the reception of *Chastelard*. Where was all this tending? The appearance of *Poems and Ballads* a few months later seemed to supply the answer.

The scandal that was to break with the publication of *Poems and Ballads* was already present in embryo. The disquiet displayed by the critics over *Chastelard*, the tone of the disapproval expressed here and there, was symptomatic of an attitude which was slowly gathering strength. "I have heard low mutterings already from the lion of British prudery," wrote Meredith. But the very strength of the forces that were gathering to crush Swinburne were the measure of his influence. Though much of the criticism, amounting to personal abuse, that was to be levelled at him was founded on envy and malice, there was an undercurrent of honest if misguided concern for the infrangible standards of nineteenth-century morality which the critics perceived were being so wantonly and, they had reason to fear, successfully attacked. A rival synthesis, particularly one so dangerous in its anti-theism, in its perverse passion, was, though perhaps its implications were not always clearly discerned, intolerable. Indeed, leaving on one side such uncomprehending but heartfelt enthusiasm as was to be sustained by the elderly ladies who mistook *Anactoria* for a Hymn to the Virgin Mary, there was a massive residue of excited approval which was to grow in the next year in proportion to the more vocal denunciations of the Press. Already, within six months, two masterpieces had come from the same hand. The one, though ill-comprehended, had brought a new music to English poetry. As wrote Professor Mackail: "The poetical atmosphere was exhausted and heavy, like that of a sultry afternoon darkening to thunder.

Out of the stagnation broke, as in a moment, the blaze and crash of *Atalanta in Calydon*. It was something quite new, quite unexampled. It revealed a new language in English, a new world, as it seemed, in Poetry." And the other, *Chastelard*, had glowed with a white-heat of passion, whatever its source, which had scarcely cast so searing a refulgence upon English letters since Shakespeare.

Among the tokens of admiration which Swinburne received after the publication of *Chastelard* was a letter from a young Welsh squire, George Powell, of Nant-Eôs, who asked him to accept the dedication of a collection of translated Irish ballads. Swinburne accepted, and a correspondence began between them which, after a visit to North Wales in 1866, ripened into a lasting friendship, a friendship, indeed, which endured till Powell's death in 1882. They had much in common. Powell, like Swinburne, was an Etonian, his tastes were aesthetic, he had a cult for the music of Wagner and, though this particular trait meant little to Swinburne, there was another with which he was in surpassing sympathy. Powell shared in the strange and esoteric worship of the Marquis de Sade. He was one of those rare mortals who could appreciate the majestic potency of his philosophy and, furthermore, was accustomed to honour his memory with peculiar and appropriate rites. The surprising intimacy which burgeoned so rapidly between them and endured so long was due in part to the fact that Swinburne had met at last someone who not only shared his tastes but was of the same age and similar social standing. Howell and Simeon Solomon were no doubt delicious companions, but would the Admiral entertain their presence at Holmwood? To these Powell was shortly introduced and to the Pre-Raphaelites and to Lord Houghton.

The year 1865 ended, appropriately enough, amidst a fevered activity which was to continue into 1866. Having spent October in Tunbridge Wells, he returned to Dorset Street till December. Payne on behalf of Moxon's was now to agree to publish his poems and his *William Blake*. For the same firm he was to write introductory essays for volumes of selections from Byron, Keats and Landor. There was even a scheme whereby he was to edit a literary review. But most of these plans were buried under the avalanche that followed the publication of *Poems and Ballads*.

The contents and date of publication of this last were now fixed. On the 4th of January 1866 he wrote to William Rossetti from Holmwood: "I have so much ready and so many projects in hand—my Poems first of all which must be got out in the spring." He was under no illusions as to the likely reception of his poems by the critics though he could not foresee the scandal that would ensue. His friends never ceased warning him. In December Lady Trevelyan wrote: "Now do, if only for the sake of living down evil reports, do be wise in which of your lyrics you publish. Do let it be a book . . . that can be on every one's table. . . . You have sailed near enough to the wind in all conscience in painting such a character for a hero as your Chastelard . . ., whose love has no element of purity in it."

Early in February Swinburne left Holmwood and returned to Dorset Street. He was feverishly busy. *William Blake* was in the press. The Byron volume, forming part of the series of Moxon's *Miniature Poets*, was to appear in the following month; he was making selections for the Keats volume; he tried to persuade Payne to publish *A Year's Letters*, which had been completed in 1862, but Payne, already extremely nervous, did not dare. It remained unpublished till 1877, when it appeared anonymously as a serial in *The Tatler* and, eventually, in book form in 1905. A large part of *Lesbia Brandon* had also by now been composed. The Byron volume passed practically unnoticed by the Press except for *The Spectator*. Hutton was unable to let go any opportunity of slating his late contributor. Swinburne was informed that his style was inflated and artificial, that he was in error in detecting any sincerity in Byron's verse, and Moxon's were recommended to dispense in any further edition with the "inflated piece of pseudo-criticism" which formed the preface. Lady Jane, however, was at last converted. "I find," she wrote from the country, "*Don Juan* (which I never read before) very beautiful." Byron was removed from the Index. It was a notable triumph.

Swinburne at this time was accustomed to frequent the Arts Club. He went there every day to converse with his friends and write his letters.  Unfortunately he carried the irregularities of his life within its portals.  He got into serious difficulties with the Committee.  He was accused of damaging the premises, insulting the waiters and generally provoking scandal.  There was talk of his being asked to resign, but he was saved temporarily by the intervention of William Rossetti.  But only temporarily: in 1870 another crisis culminated in his expulsion.  Whistler and some others of his friends resigned in sympathy.  His intemperate habits led also in this spring to what he called a "bilious attack".  These attacks, which were to grow more frequent whenever he was in London, were often accompanied by fainting fits.  Swinburne himself looked upon the "bilious attacks" as an Act of God, while the fainting fits are recorded by Gosse as being "epileptiform".  In fact they were both symptoms of alcoholic poisoning and attacked him only in London, never in the country.  The duality in his behaviour was noted by Henry Kingsley in 1871.  He was a neighbour of the Swinburnes.  "I believe Algy is very eccentric in London, but I never see him there.  Here he is a perfectly courteous little gentleman."  Alcohol, as Lady Trevelyan had noted, was the basic cause of most of Swinburne's social eccentricities.  Unfortunately, the stories to which these eccentricities gave rise, exaggerated and malicious as many of them were, only gave further cause for the public execration of which he was to become the object.

In the meantime, Lord Houghton, who on his own responsibility had offered the poems to Murray, who refused them in terms that infuriated Swinburne, was, nevertheless, determined that the publication of *Poems and Ballads* should be an important literary event.  Unwisely he mingled with his advance propaganda hints as to the indelicacy of much of the volume's contents.  No form of advertisement could have been more ill-judged.  He went further.  In his self-appointed campaign he dragged Swinburne to houses where he felt anything but at home, into a society where he was bored and ill at ease.  The results, as in the meeting with Tennyson, were not always happy.  His masterpiece was to foist a reluctant Swinburne upon an unenthusiastic committee to reply for "Literature" at the annual dinner of the

Royal Literary Fund, of which he himself was Chairman. "I got a note yesterday about the dinner," wrote Swinburne, "and will say my say as I can." He proposed to speak of the mutual influence of contemporary French and English literature. This he did in the presence of Dean Stanley, Anthony Trollope, Leslie Stephen, Charles Kingsley and others. They do not appear to have been unduly perturbed by the literary faith that was expounded to them. But Venables, in proposing "The Historical and Imaginative Literature of England", said he had no doubt "that in the long career which is probably before him, Mr. Swinburne will take many easier and many pleasanter subjects [than *Chastelard*]. . . ." Venables felt sure that Mr. Swinburne would feel "that as a representative of the future in English poetry he has a great responsibility upon him". Was he in fact so sure? Charles Kingsley endorsed "every word that Mr. Venables had said". This was the only speech that Swinburne ever made after leaving Oxford, if we except the occasion of another public dinner to which Dr. Bird introduced him in 1873. There were a number of journalists present. Being invited to propose the toast of "The Press", Swinburne leapt to his feet and shrieked: "The Press is a damnable institution, a horrible institution, a beastly institution!" and then relapsed into his chair and closed his eyes. The critics by then had done their work.

Meanwhile, the publication of the poems was delayed. He was still subject to the gratuitous advice of his friends as to what should be excluded. In the previous December he had written to Lady Trevelyan: "As to my poems, my perplexity is this; that no two friends have ever given me the same advice. . . . I have been advised to suppress *Atalanta*, to cancel *Chastelard*, and so on till not a line of my work would have been left. Two days ago Ruskin called on me and stayed for a long evening, during which he heard a great part of my forthcoming volume of poems, selected with a view to secure his advice as to publication and the verdict of the world of readers and writers. . . . I can only say that I was sincerely surprised by the enjoyment he seemed to derive from my work, and the frankness with which he accepted it."

The process continued. And now new delays were caused in the proof-reading. The type had been badly set up and it is, too, more than likely that Swinburne wished to make alterations and additions on his own account at the last moment. Some of the poems had indeed only just been composed and the process of polishing hurried. Nevertheless, by the beginning of July the first copies were ready. A presentation copy was sent to Hugo—"J'ai toujours désiré voir deux hommes: vous et Mazzini";—review copies were distributed.

On the 4th of August, Swinburne and Payne were walking down Dover Street. The book was about to be placed on sale; reviews were due to appear. As they walked, Swinburne bought a copy of *The Saturday Review*. The shock of John Morley's article was instantaneous. As he read the searing paragraphs his fury mounted till he was uncontrollably dancing with rage about the pavement, screaming abuse at the top of his piercing voice. Payne took him into a tea-shop and endeavoured to calm him. The abuse flowed on. The waiters fled. Payne begged him to give vent to his feelings in French. Obligingly Swinburne obeyed, without in the least diminishing the violence of his expressions. The following day Payne, on behalf of Moxon & Co., told him that the book had been withdrawn from circulation.

This was a serious blow to Swinburne. He felt himself betrayed. "My hound of a publisher," he wrote to Powell, "has actually withdrawn from circulation my volume of poems—refuses to issue any more copies—through fear of consequences to himself!—I shall take out *Atalanta*, etc. . . . But then to whom (as Catullus says) shall I give them? C'est embêtant!" But there was much more behind Payne's action then the tone of Morley's review. Rossetti and Sandys went to interview Payne on behalf of the author. They found him, writes Gosse, "distracted with terror of the Public Prosecutor and desired nothing so much as to be rid of the poet and his friends". There was some excuse for him. The fact that some thirty years before the firm had been prosecuted for reprinting Shelley's poems was very present to his consciousness. And now, according to Hardman, he had been warned that Dallas "had written a

crushing review for *The Times*, in which both poet and
publisher were held up to the execration of all decent people".
Their prosecution was demanded. The article was in type,
though in the event was never published. Superimposed
upon honest and outraged morality were jealousy and spite.
A faction were after Swinburne, though how deliberate was
the attempt to suppress his work it is now impossible to say.
Other reviews followed Morley's attack. They were only
less telling because less intelligent. They served to reinforce
Morley's judgment that Swinburne was "an unclean fiery
imp from the pit", that he was "the libidinous laureate of a
pack of satyrs", that the spirit of the "fevered folly" of many
of the poems is akin to "the feverish carnality of a schoolboy
over the dirtiest passages in Lemprière". Mr. Morley was
at pains to point out to the public what in their innocence
they might otherwise have missed.

What was Swinburne to do now? The position was
peculiar. The Press was overflowing with venomous attacks
upon a book which the public was unable to buy. Its author
was condemned unheard. Worse still, Swinburne's more
respectable and influential friends were not available. Lady
Trevelyan, to his great grief, had died in May at Neuchâtel,
Lord Houghton was circumspectly absent for his health in
Vichy, Whistler was in Valparaiso. At this juncture Lord
Lytton, who had been an early admirer of *Atalanta*, offered
to help. "You will see," wrote Swinburne on 10th August,
"that it [your last letter] came at a time when I wanted
something of the kind, when I tell you that in consequence of
the abusive reviews of my book, the publisher (without con-
sulting me, without warning, and without compensation) had
actually withdrawn it from circulation. I have no right to
trouble you with my affairs, but I cannot resist the tempta-
tion to trespass so far upon your kindness as to ask what
course you would recommend me to take in such a case. I
am resolved to cancel nothing, and (of course) to transfer
my books to any other publisher I can find." On the 13th
he wrote to Lord Lytton again: "I did, rather against my
own impulse [withdraw or alter passages in two instances],
which is a fair proof that I am not too headstrong or conceited
to listen to friendly counsel. But *now* to alter my course or

mutilate my published work seems to me somewhat like deserting one's colours. One may or may not repent having enlisted, but to lay down one's arms, except under compulsion, remains intolerable." On the 18th he went to Knebworth for a week. While there he received an offer from John Camden Hotten to publish the book immediately. This was probably arranged by Howell, who acted throughout as a go-between. Hotten was not the most reputable of publishers and was not above issuing what were then known as "Holywell Street publications", from the street in which such pruriencies were sold. But it was not an offer that could be turned down. At all costs the book must be published and the terms were fair. Hotten was to take over all Payne's interests, not only in *Poems and Ballads* but in all Swinburne's work published or in the press. Lord Lytton advised acceptance, so did Lord Houghton from Vichy.

Even Hotten, however, now that the book was already notorious, did not make up his mind to bring it out till he had obtained, confidentially, from a police magistrate a letter of reassurance to the effect that it was neither "seizable nor indictable". Nevertheless, it was agreed that it would be better not to republish till Swinburne's reply to the critics, an ironical, impassioned, if disingenuous defence—*Notes on Poems and Reviews*—had been published. This took place at the end of October, and in the following month *Poems and Ballads* appeared once more on the bookstalls; so did criticism in the reviews. But Swinburne was able to write some years later: "There is not one piece, there is not one line, there is not one word, there is not one syllable in any one copy ever printed of that book which has ever been changed or cancelled since the day of publication." So far he had won his battle: the book was published. All too soon he was to abandon the positions gained.

Judged as a whole, in so far as any comparison can be made, *Poems and Ballads* must take second place to *Atalanta* as a work of art. The inspiration is uneven and the order apparently haphazard. But to Swinburne himself, to his critics and, indeed, to his admirers it had a peculiar importance. Here, for those who could see, were laid bare the mechanics that had produced the philosophy of *Atalanta*,

the passion of *Chastelard*. It was the revelation of the
growth of a talent, of the process of the integration of a
synthesis. All that had been obscure was here made clear
and the vision, whatever the reaction, overwhelming.

The poems contained in the volume were all those he
wished to preserve written between 1858 and 1865. From
various sources, including watermarks, the approximate
dates of composition of most of them are known. From
a letter to Chatto, written in 1876, upon the question of
separate publication for his early poems, and from the fact
that certain of these began appearing in *The Spectator* from
April 1862 onwards, we can be fairly certain of those
composed before that date.

It is easy in these early poems to distinguish the first bloom
of an undirected talent, the pristine inspirations passing
across his mind like clouds across the sun, the early undergraduate enthusiasms without system and without consequence. At this stage he was a dilettante of the emotions
but with an innate and unregulated desire to revolt, while his
retentive mind was stored with a wide historical reading and
his imagination was fired by the influence of the Pre-Raphaelites into a sumptuous, flaming magnificence. In these early
poems he evokes the Queens of Antiquity: Aholibah whose

> . . . *mouth's heat was the heat of flame*
> *For lust towards the kings that came* . . .

Hesione with all summer in her hair, Ahola whose "words
were soft like dulcimers", Atarah anointed with myrrh and
spikenard, Semiramis greater than "the strength of love in
the blood's beat", and Chrysothemis whose face was as
a rose. He describes the martyrdom of St. Dorothy, and
the conversion of Theophilus; from Boccaccio he takes the
story of Girolamo's dream and Andrevola's despair in the
garden of love. With Villon he writes rondels. The
Border ballads echo in his memory from the nurseries of
Capheaton and find expression in *The Bloody Son* or *The
Sea-Swallows*; the medieval chronicles inspire *A Christmas
Carol*. His delight in scholarly mystification is evident in *The
Leper*, where the historical note is pure *pastiche*. Sappho,
Landor, and Gautier mingle their influences with Morris,

while incipient revolt, thus far limited to political expression, is evident in *A Song in Time of Order*:

> *When the devil's riddle is mastered*
> *And the galley-bench creaks with a Pope,*
> *We shall see Buonaparte the bastard*
> *Kick heels with his throat in a rope.*

Indeed, here, in these early poems is the bright panoply of forming genius; under the Pre-Raphaelite cloak, covering a multiplicity of inspirations, there is a charged and personal emotion. Taken in conjunction with the early dramatic fragments, with *Rosamond* and *The Queen Mother*, there is a difference, felt as yet but obscurely, between his aspirations and those of the literature of the period. His sensitivity is unquestioned: but what form was its expression to take?

> *I sang these things long since and knew them not;*
> *"Lo, here is love, or there is love, God wot,*
> *This man and that finds favour in his eyes,"*
> *I said, "but I, what guerdon have I got?"*

Sappho and Faustine, "the sterile growths of sexless root", the cruel infecundities of the love to which he was condemned formed the intolerable basis of his fantasies. Their expression necessitated the theory of Art for Art's sake. How could desires so innate be wrong? The perfection of their expression, the beauty of their form was, indeed *must* be, a substitute for morality, was, surely, morality itself? In *A Ballad of Life* and *A Ballad of Death*, written in 1862, he pursued this theory to its farthest limits. With them he opened *Poems and Ballads*. It was an explanation of the contents of the volume, the propounding of its pervasive attitude.

> *Ah! in the days when God did good to me,*
> *Each part about her was a righteous thing;*
> *Her mouth an almsgiving,*
> *The glory of her garments charity,*
> *The beauty of her bosom a good deed,*
> *In the good days when God kept sight of us;*
> *Love lay upon her eyes,*
> *And on that hair whereof the world takes heed;*
> *And all her body was more virtuous*
> *Than souls of women fashioned otherwise.*

And yet in the first rhapsodies of his love for "Boo",

Faustine and her disquieting allurements were abandoned. New possibilities opened before him, new hopes and aspirations dawned in him with an unparalleled violence of emotion:

> *In the change of years, in the coil of things,*
>   *In the clamour and rumour of life to be,*
> *We, drinking love at the furthest springs,*
>   *Covered with love as a covering tree,*
> *We had grown as gods, as the gods above,*
> *Filled from the heart to the lips with love,*
> *Held fast in his hands, clothed warm with his wings,*
>   *O love, my love, had you loved but me!*

It is in the denial of this sane and normal love, in his rejection by the one being that had the power to deliver him from the clutches of Dolores, that lie both the tragedy of his life and the tragic core of *Poems and Ballads*. Half-consciously he knew now that it was for ever beyond his grasp, that he was condemned to be "a barren stock", that his last chance had gone. In accents of despair he wrote:

> *But love lacks might to redeem or undo me;*
>   *As I have been, I know I shall surely be;*
> *"What should such fellows as I do?" Nay,*
> *My part were worse if I chose to play;*
> *For the worst is this after all; if they knew me,*
>   *Not a soul upon earth would pity me.*

The reaction was exactly what might have been expected. Having expressed his anger, his despair and his suffering in *The Triumph of Time*, he turned back "to the violent delights which have violent ends". *Anactoria* is the fierce symbol of that reaction:

> *I would find grievous ways to have thee slain,*
> *Intense device and superflux of pain;*
> *Vex thee with amorous agonies, and shake*
> *Life at thy lips, and leave it there to ache;*
> *Strain out thy soul with pangs too soft to kill,*
> *Intolerable interludes, and infinite ill;*
> *Relapse and reluctation of the breath,*
> *Dumb tunes and shuddering semitones of death.*

Side by side with the note of personal tragedy, though

reinforced by it, the synthesis that culminated in *Atalanta* was in process of development. Throughout *Poems and Ballads* the idea of beauty is never pure: with it both pleasure and pain are inextricably confounded.

> *Ah, ah, thy beauty! like a beast it bites,*
> *Stings like an adder, like an arrow smites.*

He set himself to analyse and develop this esoteric fusion. Cruelty becomes an essential attribute of the loved one. The desire to inflict it must be there, and the craving to lie passive beneath its onslaught is ever present:

> *—O Sweet,*
> *Had you felt, lying under the palms of your feet,*
> *The heart of my heart, beating harder with pleasure*
> *To feel you tread it to dust and death.*

But this passivity is capable of a delicate transition. If the desire to suffer at the hands of the loved one is a manifestation of love, it must be common to all lovers. Necessarily, therefore, the infliction of pain must also be one of love's attributes:

> *Cruel?    But love makes all that loves him well*
> *As wise as heaven and crueller than hell.*

This active sadism is expressed over and over again throughout *Poems and Ballads*. One quotation will suffice to make the point. Here the algolagnia is carried to the last extreme. In the link which may be traced with the mock solemnities of the Cannibal Club—as so often with Swinburne upon a different level of seriousness—the perva.. ness of the emotion in his consciousness becomes clear:

> *Ah that my lips were tuneless lips, but pressed*
> *To the bruised blossom of thy scourged white breast!*
> *Ah that my mouth for Muses' milk were fed*
> *On the sweet blood thy sweet small wounds had bled!*
> *That with my tongue I felt them and could taste*
> *The faint flakes from thy bosom to the waist!*
> *That I could drink thy veins as wine, and eat*
> *Thy breasts like honey! that from face to feet*
> *Thy body were abolished and consumed,*
> *And in my flesh thy very flesh entombed!*

And in *Dolores*, one of the last poems to be written before

the publication of *Poems and Ballads*, he announces once
and for all this strange duality. The fundamental mixture
of joy and suffering:

> *For the lords in whose keeping the door is*
> *That opens on all who draw breath*
> *Gave the cypress to love, my Dolores,*
> *The myrtle to death.*
>
> *And they laughed, changing hands in the measure,*
> *And they mixed and made peace after strife;*
> *Pain melted in tears and was pleasure;*
> *Death tingled with blood, and was life.*
> *Like lovers they melted and tingled,*
> *In the dusk of thine innermost fane;*
> *In the darkness they murmured and mingled,*
> *Our Lady of Pain.*

But this strange paradox was not limited for Swinburne
to a mere theory of love. The anguished sensibility with
which he responded to the beautiful, of which the passions
were only one manifestation, and the sympathetic study of
Sade drove him on to discover a universal law of suffering
applicable to all nature. Ruin and destruction are the great
principles upon which the universe is founded: to create is
to destroy, to live is to suffer.

> *For who shall change with prayers or thanksgivings*
> *The mystery of the cruelty of things?*
> *Or say what God above all gods and years*
> *With offering and blood-sacrifice of tears,*
> *With lamentation from strange lands, from graves*
> *Where the snake pastures, from scarred mouths of slaves,*
> *From prison, and from plunging prows of ships*
> *Through flamelike foam of the sea's closing lips—*
> *With thwartings of strange signs, and wind-blown hair*
> *Of comets, desolating the dim air,*
> *When darkness is made fast with seals and bars,*
> *And fierce reluctance of disastrous stars,*
> *Eclipse, and sound of shaken hills, and wings*
> *Darkening, and blind inexpiable things—*
> *With sorrow of labouring moons, and altering light*
> *And travail of the planets of the night,*
> *And weeping of the weary Pleiads seven,*
> *Feeds the mute melancholy lust of heaven?*

This surely is the ultimate expression of a cosmic pessimism. And this "vision of ghastly glory" had certain consequences for the Swinburnian synthesis. If the universe is based upon a principle of suffering and death, these must be the attributes of its creator. God must be essentially evil and cruel.

> *Is not his incense bitterness, his meat*
> *Murder? his hidden face and iron feet*
> *Hath not man known, and felt them on their way*
> *Threaten and trample all things and every day?*
> *Hath he not sent us hunger? who hath cursed*
> *Spirit and flesh with longing? filled with thirst*
> *Their lips who cried unto him? who bade exceed*
> *The fervid will, fall short the feeble deed,*
> *Bade sink the spirit and the flesh aspire,*
> *Pain animate the dust of dead desire,*
> *And life yield up her flower to violent fate?*
> *Him would I reach, him smite, him desecrate,*
> *Pierce the cold lips of God with human breath,*
> *And mix his immortality with death.*
> *Why hath he made us? what had all we done*
> *That we should live and loathe the sterile sun,*
> *And with the moon wax paler as she wanes,*
> *And pulse by pulse feel time grow through our veins?*

The accents of revolt are reminiscent of the Fourth Chorus of *Atalanta*—with which, indeed, they are contemporary. And in them, at the very moment of the completion of the synthesis, may be detected the seeds of its disintegration. No synthesis, no philosophy, is perfectly inclusive. The mere fact of triumphantly roofing a structure of thought establishes a new foundation, a basis for further building. That the new structure may prove too heavy for its supports is a philosophical commonplace. In Swinburne, as in Sade, the contradictions are obvious. How revolt against a "human figment"? Sade's admission of disbelief and his reasons for reviling, nevertheless, a non-existent deity amount to no more than a desire to *épater les bourgeois*. The fundamental anarchy of "les Prospérités du Vice" and "les Malheurs de la Vertu" was not one that in the long run could appeal to an intelligence so infinitely superior to his

master's.   Beside the Sadian rejection of Virtue and exaltation of Vice—"Come down and redeem us from virtue Our
Lady of Pain"—and the cry for yet rarer and still more
delicate sins—"Shall no new sin be born for men's trouble,
no dream of impossible pangs?"—there is discernible the
beginnings of a stoicism in face of the surrounding chaos.
Anarchy is no solution; complaint, if there is no God,
useless.

> Can ye beat off one wave with prayer,
>     Can ye move mountains?

Here and there he sounds a note of resignation and death
is "The end of all, the poppied sleep".
    Nevertheless there are compensations, the contemplation
of nature, the majesty of the elements, to which, as we have
seen, he responded so sensitively in childhood, were not to be
denied.   They at least are enduring.   Insensibly he passes
from anti-theism to pantheism.

> Wilt thou yet take all, Galilean? but these thou shalt not take,
> The laurel, the palms and the paean, the breasts of the nymphs in
>     the brake.

He identified himself with the great forces of nature.
The pantheistic ecstasy, which was to find its intellectual
expression in *Hertha*, is present in *Poems and Ballads*, as
it is, indeed, in the more or less contemporary *Lesbia
Brandon*:

> I shall sleep, and move with the moving ships,
>     Change as the winds change, veer in the tide;
> My lips will feast on the foam of thy lips,
>     I shall rise with thy rising, with thee subside.

And by a natural extension he recognizes that there is
in man an aspect of the divine.   His human pride, his
courage, his latent need for action impels him to revolt.
Man, being divine, is worthy of freedom.   In the love of
liberty, in the battle for political emancipation he will find a
new inspiration for his art.   Indeed, in *Poems and Ballads*,

in some of the last poems composed for it, may be found the foreshadowing of the next phase of his life. In *Félise* he proclaims the power to freedom that is latent in man:

> *Why should ye bear with hopes and fears*
> *Till all these things be drawn in one,*
> *The sound of iron-footed years,*
> *And all the oppression that is done*
> *Under the sun?*

And with, perhaps, a more political accent in *To Victor Hugo*:

> *One thing we can; to be*
> *Awhile, as men may, free. . . .*

Thus, chronologically speaking, the forgotten fury of *A Song in Time of Order* and *A Song in Time of Revolution* was reawakened after an arduous and perilous excursion into the eccentric philosophy of Dolmancé. The synthesis was shattered, the structure had collapsed. The reverberations, unremarkable as yet, were to be extensive in their effect.

Neither to his critics nor to his admirers were the signs of this incipient change of heart visible. For them a position had been taken up, a platform established, and *Dolores* was its significant manifestation. The Philistines were in the ascendant. Not only was England the most powerful country in the world, but to them it was also an article of faith that she was the most moral and the most pure. They reacted with an extraordinary sensitivity to anything which might rob them of this assurance. Browning had been attacked; Tennyson's *Maud*, inconceivably, had caused shivers in prudish spines; the Pre-Raphaelites were generally condemned as moral decadents. This must be remembered if the shock of Swinburne's advent is to be properly understood. His immorality was clear and, worse still, did it not smack of France, whose literature was so rightly banned from middle-class drawing-rooms? As the better-informed did not hesitate to make clear, Swinburne had adopted "the indecent garbage of the French Baudelaire". Obviously every respectable household was in peril of infection. National hypocrisy, conscious or not, could not well have gone farther, as Stead's *The Maiden Tribute of Modern Babylon* was to reveal a few years later. Indeed, one is painfully impressed by the campaign of vilification. Sincere indignation is acceptable but it was by no means general. Besides John Morley's famous article in *The Saturday Review*, which has already been noted, there were many others of equal violence if less sincere and intelligent. Lush in *The Athenaeum* denounced Swinburne as "unclean for the sake of uncleanness". *The Pall Mall Gazette* entitled its review *Swinburne's Folly* and attacked his "mean and miserable indecency". *The Spectator*, now in full cry, published a satirical poem by Buchanan, *The Session of the Poets*, and called Swinburne "unmanly" and "effeminate" *The Saturday Review* produced a second article on the volume's republication. It condemned the "wailings of the frenzied Bagpipes". *The Globe* complained of "excessive carnality". *Punch*, forgetting his manners, satirized him as "Mr. Swineborn".

This wave of indignation, which was not indeed limited to the Press but obscured the judgment of whole classes of the nation, gave rise to a number of revealing incidents during the next few years. It was only necessary for Swinburne to praise in a picture the painting of a cat, for the owner to have the "splendid animal" painted out. In the proceedings Buchanan *v.* Taylor in 1876, when *The Examiner* had to pay £150 damages to Buchanan because he was held to have been insulted by Swinburne's *The Devil's Due*, Mr. Justice Archibald remarked from the Bench, with reference to Swinburne's works, that if they "had not been written at all, or had been committed to the flames it would have been much better". In sermons and religious articles, too, Swinburne became a sort of antichrist: Prebendary Thorold wrote in *The Guardian*: "While Renan with his treacherous praise said, 'Master, Master,' and kissed our Lord, Swinburne insulted him as he hung on the bitter cross." While more immediately he was overwhelmed with threatening and insulting letters. "I wish," he wrote to Burton in Brazil, "you had been at hand or within reach this year, to see the missives I get from nameless quarters. One anonymous letter from Dublin threatened me, if I did not suppress my book within six weeks of that date, with castration. The writer, 'when I least expected, would waylay me, slip my head in a bag, and remove the obnoxious organs; he had seen his gamekeeper do it with cats'. . . . I beg to add that my unoffending person is as yet no worse than it was."

Burton had been one of the few people who, when consulted upon the possible reception of *Poems and Ballads* by the public, had prophesied disaster. It has been pointed out that he was probably the only one who understood what they were about. But however that may be, he was one of the few friends that Swinburne felt was sympathetic to him in this crisis. Surrounded by a family whose propriety was overwhelmed by the scandal, by friends whose attitude could at best be described as neutral—even the Rossettis made reservations ("poet nascitur, non fit . . . for publication")—and acquaintances who were careful not to greet him in the street, he felt himself ostracized. Even his relations with Whistler never altogether recovered from his failure to write sympathy and encouragement from Valparaiso, while his feelings towards Lord Houghton he described to Burton: "I am still the centre of such a moral chaos that our excellent Houghton maintains a discreet and consistent neutrality. . . . I have not set eyes on his revered form for months. Your impending opulence, and my immediate infamy, will too evidently cut us from the shelter of his bosom. . . ."

There were, however, fortunately, certain sections of the Press that voiced a timid and discreet approval. Even John Morley had noted that the stanzas of *Dolores* were "admirable for their sustained power if so hateful on other grounds". Bendyshe in *The Reader* at least forbore to condemn; *Fraser's Magazine*, *The Westminster Review* and *The Sunday Times* praised; while Professor Henry Morley in *The Examiner* wrote a courageous and enthusiastic article. He noted the "music of strength in this book, outspoken honesty, a sturdy love of freedom, earnestness, poetic insight beyond anything attained to by others of the young poets of the day. The withdrawal of the volume is an act of weakness". He discerned the "terrible earnestness" of the book. And the enthusiasm amongst the younger generation was much

wider and more profound than might have been suspected.
At Cambridge, after an impassioned debate, the Union placed
the volume upon its library list; at Oxford undergraduates
might have been heard chanting *Dolores* in the Turl; the
young Thomas Hardy walked the streets of London with the
volume in his hand.   The unfettered, liberating romanticism
of *Poems and Ballads* fulfilled a need of the period.   *Maud*
had awakened Victorian susceptibilities; the Pre-Raphaelites,
Morris and Rossetti, had romanticized the flesh under a
medieval cloak; but it had required the urgent passion, the
melodious strength, the genius of Swinburne to endow a
generation with new sensibilities and perceptions.   "Teachers
like yourself," an admirer wrote, "will infuse strength into
the English mind and kill the Philistine."   Nor was it only
amongst the young and irresponsible that Swinburne aroused
enthusiasm.   Mill and Lytton defended him; Ruskin wrote:
"I like them—there are redundancies to prune—not in
*Faustine*! which made me all hot, like pies with the devil's
fingers in them.   It's glorious."   And Froude, who himself
disliked Swinburne but wrote, nevertheless, "He convinces
me in fact for the first time that he has real stuff in him. . . .
I am very unwilling to follow the crew of Philistines and bite
his heels like the rest of them," was recorded as recounting
—perhaps with dubious veracity—an occasion upon which
Ruskin, after a recitation, seized Swinburne in his arms
exclaiming: "How beautiful, how divinely beautiful!"
However that may be, it is certain that Ruskin refused to
attack Swinburne with the words "he sweeps me away as a
torrent does a pebble . . . I am *righter* than he is, so are the
lambs and swallows, but they are not his match", while to
Swinburne himself he wrote: "I should as soon think of
finding fault with you as with a thunder cloud or a night-shade
blossom.   All I can say of you or them—is that God made
you, and that you are very wonderful and beautiful."   It is
impossible to forget that Ruskin had passed the poems for
publication but, leaving on one side any natural impulsion
this might have given him to approve of them once published,
one cannot but be surprised, with Swinburne, that anyone
who could be swept "away as a torrent does a pebble"
should have combined "philanthropic morality with such

exquisite sense of what is right and good in things higher. R. actually intimates," wrote Swinburne, "that 'genius ought to devote itself' to the behalf of humanity and 'to overthrow its idols', in a word to justify the ways of Urizen to the sons of Enitharmon. Quelle horreur!" Curiously enough this was exactly what Swinburne was about to do.

# CHAPTER VII

## (1866–1872)

A FORMAL analysis of Swinburne's thought cannot with any facility be derived from a contemplation of *Poems and Ballads*—nor was that thought itself in any sense formal. It is too diverse in temper, reflecting often from moment to moment, from stanza to stanza, the poet's mood. It is crossed by the furrows of immediate enthusiasms and temporary despairs. To look for a precise structure of thought in a romantic poet is invidious. Nevertheless, an attitude, based on innate disposition, became formalized with his intellectual development and the semi-conscious process of selection amongst the influences to which he was subject into what may, for want of a better term, be described as a "synthesis". In the preceding pages an attempt has been made to show the development of this process both in his dramas and in *Poems and Ballads*. Clearly it was no prim, logical process. Founded upon emotion rather than upon ratiocination, the paradox that the seeds of its dissolution should be discernible at the moment of integration in no way invalidates the thesis that algolagnia was the dominant basis from which his inspiration sprang during the period in which he was most fecund of great poetry. During the years 1863 to 1865— the period of *Atalanta* and the best of *Poems and Ballads* — he reached, under the aegis of Art for Art's sake, the uttermost peak in the expression of erotic sensibility. Such passion and such music had scarce been heard in English poetry since the reign of Elizabeth. But the peak attained, there began the first gentle movements of a glissade which, gathering speed, was only to be arrested in the conciliating arms of the Philistines.

After the nervous strain and the excitement of the publication of *Poems and Ballads* the lassitude of exhaustion overcame him. He went to stay with Powell at Nant-Eôs and then to Holmwood, returning to Dorset Street in the last days of November. Almost immediately he succumbed to "one of those damned bilious attacks which prove the malevolence of the deity" and in December, deprived of the brandy bottle, was recovering at Holmwood. And these calm periods, away from London, provided the opportunity for reflection. When he analysed the experience he had undergone he found much in it to support a strategic retreat from the position he had taken up. There were practical arguments to reinforce the intellectual doubts which had been hinted at in *Poems and Ballads*. He had won his battle; the volume had been published unaltered. No one could accuse him of cowardice if he now found a new basis for his inspiration. His friends, Woolner, Palgrave, Houghton, even Whistler, had, he persuaded himself, betrayed him; he had been held up to public execration in the Press; ostracized by his acquaintances; the butt of indecent epigrams in the clubs. Half in disgust, half by a process of natural evolution, he divorced himself from the ideas of the last few years. As early as October 1866 he wrote to W. M. Rossetti: "I have begun verse again after many months of enforced inaction through worry and weariness. I am writing a little song of gratulation for Venice with the due reserves and anticipations; and hope to wind up the scheme of the poem by some not quite inadequate expression of reverence towards Mazzini. I have already touched on most others of the later patriots and martyrs—I am half afraid and half desirous to touch on him—*i.e.* to lay my lips on his feet. . . . After all, in spite of jokes and perversities— malgré ce cher Marquis et ces foutus journaux—it is *nice* to have something to love and believe in as I do in Italy. It was only Gabriel and his followers in art . . . who for a time frightened me from speaking out; for ever since I was fifteen I have been equally and unalterably mad—tête montée —as my mother says—about *this* article of faith; you may ask any tutor or schoolfellow. I know the result will be a poem more declamatory than imaginative; but I'd rather be an Italian stump-orator than an English prophet; and I meant to make it acceptable to you and a few others of our sort. As far as I can judge, I think it contains already some

of my best verses.   Only, just as one hears that intense desire has made men impotent at the right (or wrong) minute,
my passionate wish to express myself in part, for a little,
about this matter, has twice and thrice left me exhausted
and incompetent; unable to write, or to decide if what has
been written is or is not good.   I never felt this about my
poems on other subjects; and I'd give a year of my life to
accomplish the writing of a really great song on this one."

Though the full implications of abandoning Art for Art's
sake had perhaps not been as yet completely realized—it
was to need Mazzini's influence to eradicate it altogether—
the process had already begun.   The poem was *A Song of
Italy*.   At the same time he was composing a pamphlet
entitled *Liberty and Loyalty*.   He had taken refuge from the
fantasies of fleshly beauty in politics.   It had at least the
advantage of giving full scope to his need for revolt.   The
compensating necessity of his nature—submission—was soon
to find a corresponding satisfaction at Mazzini's feet.

In January 1867 William Rossetti went to stay with
Swinburne at Holmwood.

"*Saturday* 12*th January*: Visited Swinburne's father at
Holmwood.   Old gentleman kindly, conversible—has seen
and observed.   Lady Jane has an attaching air and manner
and seems very agreeable in home life—simple, dignified and
clever.   There are three daughters at home, all sensible and
agreeable; the second with a handsome sprightly face, and the
youngest evidently talented.   The younger son was unwell
and has not shown.   Swinburne shows well at home, being
affectionate in his manner with all the family and ready in
conversing.

"*Sunday* 13*th January*: Stayed at Holmwood all day.
Swinburne read me at night his poem approaching completion on Italy; and yesterday one which he has written
for the Candiote refugees to give them the profits."

Indeed, some Greek friends had written to him appealing
for "the co-operation of that spirit which poets breathe to be
welded in the strength of the strong.   The very gods stretch
their hands imploringly for sympathy.   Do all you can with
your pen and influence."   And Madox Brown wrote: "Do
go in for it and your stanzas will roar like tongues of flame."

If they did not quite do that they had, nevertheless, certain interesting, if more intimate, consequences.

*The Ode on the Insurrection in Candia* was published on 1st March in *The Fortnightly Review*, where a few weeks earlier *A Child's Song in Winter* had already appeared. Through a mutual friend, Joseph Knight, Swinburne had been introduced to John Morley, who never knew that his authorship of the attack on *Poems and Ballads*, since it was unsigned, was known to the poet. Swinburne was to become a valued contributor. The poem published—and £20 contributed to the fund for Greek refugees—Swinburne sent a copy to Mazzini. Though they had never met, there were already certain points of contact between them. They had mutual friends and Mazzini had been sent a copy of *Atalanta* in 1865. Now, perhaps at the instigation of these friends or in the realization that Swinburne was a potentially valuable propagandist, he replied from the Fulham Road at length and in his most elevated style: "I have still to thank you for the gift of your beautiful *Atalanta*. I was, when it came, overworked and unable to read it for a while; then I had no clue to your address; and, while delaying, sad yet imperative, and, in my mind, sacred work fell again upon me and took the thought of thanking you away. But now, arising, with the most admiring and communing impression, from the reading of your masterly Ode on Greece, I cannot help writing a few words to tell you how grateful I felt at the time and how hopeful I feel now: hopeful that the power which is in you has found out its true direction and that, instead of compelling us merely to admire *you*, you will endeavour to transform *us*, to rouse the sleeping, to compel thought to embody itself into Action. That is the mission of Art; and yours.

"Whilst the immense heroic Titanic battle is fought, christened on every spot by the tears of the loving ones and the blood of the brave, between Right and Wrong, Freedom and Tyranny, Truth and Lie, God and the Devil—with a new conception of Life, a new Religious Synthesis, a new European World struggling to emerge from the graves of Rome, Athens, Byzantium and Warsaw, kept back by a few crowned unbelievers and a handful of hired soldiers—the

poet ought to be the apostle of a crusade, his word the
watchword of the fighting nations and the dirge of the op-
pressors. Don't lull us to sleep with songs of egotistical
love and idolatry of physical beauty: shake us, reproach,
encourage, insult, brand the cowards, hail the Martyrs, tell
us all that we have a great Duty to fulfil, and that, before
it is fulfilled, Love is an undeserved blessing, Happiness a
blasphemy, belief in God a Lie. Give us a series of 'Lyrics
for the Crusade'. Have not our praise but our blessing.
You *can* if you choose."

No communication could have been better calculated to
inspire Swinburne's new-found enthusiasm. It was a voice
from Olympus. And now, the ice broken, it but remained
to meet "The Chief" in the flesh. Had he not the delicate
duty of asking him to accept the dedication of *A Song of
Italy*? But, curiously, they both shrank from a meeting.
Was it possible that Swinburne feared his new divinity might,
on inspection, lack a halo after all? Did Mazzini fear that
his physical presence might fail to realize his disciple's
exaggerated ideal, or was it that the poet's psychology was
too alien and too unsympathetic? In spite of its wording
there is an evident reluctance underlying the letter to Karl
Blind: "Quant à Swinburne, dont je sais tout, je ne comprend
rien au désir d'être introduit, etc. Il a déjà une lettre de moi
qui lui donne mon addresse et le droit de venir chez moi
quand bon lui semble. Etes-vous sûr que le désir exprimé
à Mr. Purnell soit d'une date récente?" They hesitated
and the meeting did not take place till the 30th March.

Mazzini, who was now sixty-one, had found refuge in
England, like so many political exiles, as long ago as 1837.
He was well known to the public through his indefatigable
journalism. As a young man his natural bias had been
towards literature rather than politics. But was it possible
to have great art without a country and without liberty?
This to Mazzini was a self-evident proposition. He devoted
his life to acquiring both: the country by the unification
of Italy, liberty by the establishment of a republican government. "If we were successful," he wrote, "the art of Italy
would bloom and flourish over our graves." His tragedy
was that the unification of Italy was to take place at the

hands of a monarchy. This by March 1867 was almost complete. Western Venetia had, by plebiscite, united with Italy in the previous October. Rome, however, still remained under the temporal dominion of the Pope. The question for the next three years would be: Could the "Universal Republican Alliance", which had been founded by Mazzini, succeed in arousing sufficient revolutionary spirit on the banks of the Tiber to set up a democratic republic which might then spread throughout unified Italy, or would "that satellite of a dead dog Victor Emmanuel" be successful in moving his capital from Florence to Rome? "I shall be furious," wrote Swinburne, "and would kiss the toes of a priest who would poison him in a wafer." Indeed, at this time, there appeared still to be a chance for Mazzini and the Republic. The Italian populace, exasperated by the humiliation of Villafranca and the defeats of 1866, were turning from Victor Emmanuel towards the illustrious exile. Messina constantly re-elected him; a petition of amnesty was signed by forty thousand names; in England he was more popular than ever. It seemed possible that he might yet succeed at the expense of the "Savoyard". Whatever his personal feelings about Swinburne, whom he seems to have regarded as a sick mind in need of a spiritual doctor, such genius—if only it could be used aright—would be an asset to the cause. But *could* it be used aright? The Candiote Ode was but little to set against *Atalanta* or *Poems and Ballads*. And was Art for Art's sake susceptible of furthering a revolution?

Swinburne, however, had already prepared himself for total submission on that evening when, the manuscript of *A Song of Italy* under his arm, Thomas Purnell by his side, he set out for Karl Blind's lodging at 2 Winchester Road. They were shown into a crowded room, into an atmosphere redolent of conspiracy. Swinburne was nervous. Suppose the Chief spurned his adoration, refused the dedication, excluded him from his confidence? The hands fluttered unduly. Suddenly Mazzini entered, pale, bald, white-bearded. The piercing black eyes lit on Swinburne—who could fail to distinguish him once described?—and "I know *you*," he said. And next day Swinburne wrote to his mother: "I did as I always thought I should and really meant not to do if I could help—went down on my knees and kissed his hand." And as Swinburne intoned *A Song of Italy*, "He held mine between his for some time while I was reading, and now and then, gave it a great pressure. He says he will take me to Rome when the revolution comes, and crown me with his own hands in the Capitol." And to George Powell, with whom he had broken an engagement for the meeting, he wrote: "I unworthy spent much of last night sitting at my beloved Chief's feet. He was angelically good to me. I read him my Italian poem all through and he accepted it in words I can't trust myself to try to write down . . . to-day I am rather exhausted and out of sorts. Il y a bien de quoi. There's a tradition in the Talmud that when Moses came down from Sinai 'he was drunken with the kisses of the lips of God'."

The first meeting had passed off perfectly. Mazzini had given Swinburne permission to come and see him whenever he liked. During the course of April there were two long interviews with the Chief and another on 5th May. "He is divine the more one sees of him. We are quite on familiar terms now, and what a delight this is to me I need not tell you." What transpired at these meetings? "He said things to me and told me stories I can't write about." Secrecy, even in the simplest matters, had become a habit with the old conspirator. For Swinburne it added the subtle delights of mystery to his communings with the Chief whose "immense magnetic power" he felt operating upon him. "I know, now I have seen him, what I guessed before: whenever he has said to anyone 'Go and be killed because I tell you', they have gone and been killed because he told them. Who wouldn't I should like to know?" But from Swinburne something perhaps even more difficult was to be demanded. "I wish very much," Mazzini wrote, "that he would write something . . . giving up the absurd immoral French art for art's sake's system." Was not the composition of that book of "Lyrics of the Crusade" bound to be in opposition to his aesthetic tenets? The way to surrender had been prepared but the garrison still struggled. "All Mazzini wants is that I should dedicate and consecrate my writing power to do good and serve others exclusively; which I can't.   If I tried I should lose my faculty of verse even."   But the pressure was relentless, the tact sure.   If Mazzini was not "born king and chief and leader of men", at least Swinburne thought he was.   Subjection was assured.   *Songs before Sunrise* was begun.

Even then submission was not immediately complete. Swinburne was still engaged upon his "aesthetic" novel *Lesbia Brandon*.   At first he attempted a compromise between the past from which it had sprung and the present to which it was eminently unsuited.   Two new and fortuitous characters were introduced: Attilo Mariani, an Italian patriot, for whom it is "an inconceivable honour to die for Italy", and the other, a French exile, Pierre Sadier, who was very likely modelled on Louis Blanc as Mariani, who had "broken his soul at the feet of Italy", was, no doubt, a modified portrait of Mazzini.   But the Chief's spiritual leadership, the constantly reiterated necessity for whole-hearted service to the cause, for "aesthetic" abnegation, triumphed even in this.   *Lesbia Brandon* was abandoned, never to be completed.

During these years Mazzini was much abroad.   In the summer of 1867 he went to Zürich and Lugano and returned to London only in January 1868.   He returned to Switzerland from which he was exiled in 1869 and in August 1870 he was arrested and imprisoned in Gaëta.   In 1871 he was active in Switzerland and at Pisa.   But amidst all these vicissitudes he was always careful to give Swinburne the impression that his eyes were upon him.   Though, so he suggested, it was too dangerous to write direct, there were communications through Emilia Venturi, oral messages and "bulletins from headquarters".   Mazzini, too, insisted upon having reports sent him by Dr. Bird as to the state of the poet's health.

The constant pressure exercised on Swinburne by Mazzini to write the "Lyrics of the Crusade" was in part due to his fear that the poet would die—"he will not last more than one or two years".   Indeed, it seemed perfectly clear that he was drinking himself to death.   "I wish," wrote Mazzini, "very much that he would, before vanishing, write something." Though he was able profoundly to influence the poet's inspiration, he evidently did not feel himself capable of reforming the poet's life. Would he not lose all in the revolt that might ensue? He had, nevertheless, the intuition to realize what it was the poet needed and what, ultimately, he was to find. "He might be transformed but only by some man or woman—better a woman of course—who would like him very much and assert at the same time a moral superiority on him." Would Emilia Venturi do? "I should like," he wrote to her, "a certain degree of intercourse between you and him: it might do good, in your sense, to him." Other friends, as we shall see, had a similar idea. Their selection was Adah Menken. But the moment was not yet ripe for reform. In the end it was not to be a woman but a man who was to exercise the "moral superiority".

Historically, however, the moment was not one of great stimulation to a Republican muse. *A Song of Italy* had, in view of the defeats at Custozza and Lissa, the poor showing of Italian arms in the Seven Weeks' War, not unnaturally failed to sound a clarion note of triumph. It had all been a little apologetic, a little vague, and very long. Published, too, at a time when Lord Derby and Disraeli, who were not altogether in favour of Italian unity, had just taken office, it was not a success. Reviews were brief; Mazzini complained of "la conspiration du silence". The edition was not sold out till the end of the century. And now the spring and summer of 1867 were no better. Revolution was quiescent, nothing happened. Mazzini's plots in the Papal States seemed doomed to failure. The Conference of London appeared to have established the *status quo*. Disappointed of revolutionary subject matter, Swinburne turned his attention to the past rather than the present. "I am writing . . . a poem on Siena of a discursive sort." *Siena*, serene and exquisite in its cadences, is no revolutionary banner. Garibaldi, however, was about to reach another milestone in his perennial march on Rome. In September he went to Geneva as President of the Peace Congress. There he pronounced the inspiring words: "It is our duty to go to Rome and we shall soon go." He endeavoured to do so, but Rattazzi had him arrested and sent to Caprera.

It was not a particularly inspiring occasion but Swinburne, refusing to be defrauded of his opportunity, hurriedly composed *The Halt before Rome* and sent it to *The Fortnightly Review*. Unfortunately he was too early for, almost coinciding with its publication, Garibaldi escaped from Caprera, crossed the frontier and seized Monterotondo on 29th October. But a French corps, hastily sent from Toulon, landed at Civita Vecchia and defeated and captured him at Mentana. For Swinburne it was an opportunity missed. He had applied his poem to the wrong occasion. Three anniversaries of Mentana were to be commemorated but not the event itself.

Nevertheless, he was now definitely committed to writing the volume that Mazzini desired. In October he wrote to William Rossetti: "I may tell you between ourselves that I have now done enough to enable me to speak with some hope of a design which must come either to nothing or to much— much (that is) for me, if I may so speak of my own aims and achievements. I think I may some time accomplish a book of political and national poems as complete and coherent in its way as the *Châtiments* or *Drum Taps*. This, as you know, Mazzini asked me to attempt—'for us', as he said. Phantoms and skeletons of national songs I have for some time seen floating in the future before me in plenty, but now I have also done one or two in words and so embodied them that I think they will turn out in good marching order—des soldats viables! This week I have worked off one on the news of Garibaldi's arrest which I am tempted to think my best lyric ever written. . . . I am hopeful that it will seriously please Mazzini—rather confident that it must. . . . There is I think room for a book of songs of the European revolution, and, if sung as thoroughly as Hugo or as Whitman would sing them, they ought to ring for some time to some distance of echo."

During the last months of 1867 and in the course of the next year he composed a number of the poems that were to take their place in the eventual volume: *A Watch in the Night*, *The Litany of Nations*, *Mentana: first anniversary*, *The Song of the Standard* and *Blessed Among Women*. In March 1869 the *Dedication* of the unfinished volume was sent to Mazzini.

SWINBURNE IN 1868

In it he acknowledged the debt his inspiration owed to the Patriot:

> *Take, since you bade it should bear,*
> *These, of the seed of your sowing,*
> *Blossom or berry or weed.*
> *Sweet though they be not, or fair,*
> *That the dew of your word kept growing,*
> *Sweet at least was the seed.*

Swinburne was now "his poet". Perhaps in failing health and failing hope the knowledge that he had inspired so exquisite a body of verse was to be some consolation to his declining years.

Several more poems were composed during the course of 1869: *A New Year's Message* and *Super Flumina Babylonis* amongst them. Mostly, however, Swinburne refrained from immediate publication. And in December he was searching for a title. "I must," he wrote to William Rossetti, "settle on a name for my progressing book; 'Songs of the Republic' is generally liked, and seems to myself presumptuous for any man but Hugo to take by way of title; 'Songs of the Crusade', Mazzini's proposed name, is ambiguous and suggests by derivation Galilean gallows. I think of calling them 'Songs before Sunrise' — will you tell me how you like that or 'Before Dawn' or 'Morning'?"

In estimating the poems contained in *Songs before Sunrise* it is necessary to make a distinction between those that were inspired by the literal facts—or personalities—of political revolution and those, more philosophical, which belong to the *Hertha* group. Of these the most important in any attempted analysis are *Genesis* and the *Hymn of Man*. The purely political group suffer from the fact that the events of 1867–1870 were not susceptible to an afflatus which might indeed have been all very well in 1848, and that Swinburne himself had no direct experience of the events involved. A further disqualification, which was not altogether Swinburne's fault, was that, when eventually published, in 1871, the sun had very definitely set upon Mazzini's hopes with the entry into Rome of the Royal troops in September of the previous

year. The clarion of revolution sounded but mutely in a
Savoyard desert. Swinburne's verses, for all his assurance,
were hardly "art and part" of the revolution. But these
considerations, fortunately, do not apply to the central core
of the book. Here that pantheism which had already been
disclosed in *Poems and Ballads*, and which had led to the
conception of the divinity of man and to his right to liberty,
is carried a stage further. It is notable that from the first
impassioned but unintegrated revolutionary ardours of 1867
it took him three years to develop the full significance of his
thought which was to culminate in 1870 in the composition
of *Hertha*.

Swinburne starts from the typically nineteenth-century
Mazzinian doctrine "Humanity is not an aggregation of
individuals but a collective Being". Mankind has a collective
soul and its indestructible prerogative is Liberty.

> Are ye so strong, O kings, O strong men? Nay,
> Waste all ye will and gather all ye may,
> Yet one thing is there that ye shall not slay,
>   Even thought, that fire nor iron can affright.
>
> The woundless and invisible thought that goes
> Free throughout time as north or south wind blows,
> Far throughout space as east or west sea flows,
>   And all dark things before it are made bright.
>
> Thy thought, thy word, O soul republican,
> O spirit of life, O God whose name is man:
> What sea of sorrows but thy sight shall span?
>   Cry wellaway, but well befall the right.

This philosophy of Liberty is made clear in a manifesto
which, with William Rossetti, he composed in November
1869 for Ricciardi's anti-Catholic Council. This Council
was being held at Naples as a counterblast to the famous
Oecumenical Council which adopted the dogma of in-
fallibility and the notorious *syllabus* condemning liberal
doctrines. "The Liberty we believe in," it ran, "is one and
indivisible: without free thought there can be no free life.
That democracy of the spirit without which the body,
personal or social, can enjoy but a false freedom, must, by

the very law of its being, confront a man-made theocracy to
destroy it.   Ideal or actual, the Church or priests, and the
Republic, are natural and internecine enemies.   Freedom,
which comes by the law of the life of man — flame of his
spirit, root and heart and blood and muscle of his manhood—
can make no truce with the creeds or miscreeds which inflict,
not (as some kings of our past) upon the flesh, but upon the
souls of men, the hideous and twofold penalty of blindness
and eviration.   She expects no non-natural message from
above or from without; but only that which comes from
within — faith, born of man, in man, which passes in
contagious revelation from spirit again to spirit without
authority and without sign — Truth, Right, Freedom are
self-sufficing, and claim service from the soul that suffices to
itself."

Having vainly tried to get the manifesto printed in England,
he proceeded with the composition of the *Hymn of Man*
which expressed the same viewpoint.   "I have in my head a
sort of Hymn for the Congress—as it were a 'Te Hominem
Laudamus' to sing the human triumph over 'things'—the
opposing forces of life and nature—and over the God of
his own creation, till he attains truth, self-sufficience and
freedom."

Indeed, Swinburne saw in the conception of God
as a supreme being one of the main barriers to the
development of the freedom of the soul.   In *Christmas
Antiphones* and *Before a Crucifix* he attacks the God of the
Churches:

> *It was for this, that men should make*
> *Thy name a fetter on men's necks,*
> *Poor men's made poorer for thy sake,*
> *And women's withered out of sex?*
> *It was for this, that slaves should be,*
> *Thy word was passed to set men free?*

And in *Genesis* he endeavours to show the origin of this
"human figment", that God was created from human fear
of the pervasive reality, the necessity even, of the co-existence
of good and evil.

*The very darkness that time knew not of,*
  *Nor God laid hand on, nor was man found there,*
*Ceased, and was cloven in several shapes; above*
  *Light, and night under, and fire, earth, water, and air.*

*Sunbeams and starbeams, and all coloured things,*
  *All forms and all similitudes began;*
*And death, the shadow cast by life's wide wings,*
  *And God, the shade cast by the soul of man.*

God being the invention of man, man necessarily remains his superior. Thus he was able to hymn "the human triumph over . . . the God of his own creation". The Collective Soul of Man is, indeed, the real, the only God:

*Therefore the God that ye make you is grievous, and gives not aid,*
*Because it is but for your sake that the God of your making is made.*
*Thou and I and he are not gods made men for a span,*
*But God, if a God there be, is the substance of men which is man.*
*Our lives are as pulses or pores of his manifold body and breath;*
*As waves of his sea on the shores where birth is the beacon of death.*
*We men, the multiform features of man, whatsoever we be,*
*Recreate him of whom we are creatures, and all we only are he.*
*Not each man of all men is God, but God is the fruit of the whole;*
*Indivisible spirit and blood, indiscernible body from soul.*
*Not men's but man's is the glory of godhead, the kingdom of*
  *time, . . .*

In *Hertha* these conceptions are still further universalized. Against the background of his wide reading and the new Darwinian theories of evolution he evolved the idea of Hertha, representing the principle of growth. "Of all I have done," he wrote, "I rate *Hertha* highest as a single piece, finding in it the most of lyric force and music combined with the most of condensed and clarified thought." Indeed, here the Collective Soul of Man is coextensive with God and Liberty.

*Freedom we call it, for holier*
*Name of the soul there is none.*

This is the essence of man's evolution, the principle upon which depends the attainment of his full stature. The soul is infinite and finite, objective and subjective, supreme and subservient, the essence, the all-inclusive.

> *I am that which began;*
> *Out of me the years roll;*
> *Out of me God and man;*
> *I am equal and whole;*
> *God changes, and man, and the form of them bodily; I am the soul.*

*    *    *

> *First life on my sources*
> *First drifted and swam;*
> *Out of me are the forces*
> *That save it or damn;*
> *Out of me man and woman, and wild-beast and bird; before God was, I am.*

> *Beside or above me*
> *Nought is there to go;*
> *Love or unlove me,*
> *Unknow me or know,*
> *I am that which unloves me and loves; I am stricken, and I am the blow.*

Man having abandoned the false Gods—"O my sons, O too dutiful toward Gods not of me"—will at last be able to attain to his full personality, be able to develop and grow in truth and freedom to unimaginable heights. Already "God trembles in heaven, and his angels are white with the terror of God". But this tremendous anti-theism is followed by the promise that man will arise from the ashes of a false creed knowing himself, aware of the magnificence of his destiny:

> *Thought made him and breaks him,*
> *Truth slays and forgives;*
> *But to you, as time takes him,*
> *This new thing it gives,*
> *Even love, the beloved Republic, that feeds upon freedom and lives.*

> *For truth only is living,*
> *Truth only is whole,*
> *And the love of his giving*
> *Man's polestar and pole;*
> *Man, pulse of my centre, and fruit of my body, and seed of my soul.*

*One birth of my bosom;*
*One beam of mine eye;*
*One topmost blossom*
*That scales the sky;*
*Man, equal and one with me, man that is made of me, man that is I.*

It is impossible on reading *Hertha* to acquit Swinburne of "the (to me) most hateful charge of optimism". It is clear that he viewed the "false God" as being in a state of decline and that the liberation of man from these figments would place him in a true relation to "the vital principle of matter", and that this process in his opinion was already taking place. How could it be otherwise when men were holding anti-Catholic Councils in Naples and dying for the cause of freedom? It was natural to suppose—and Mazzini's failure was not yet apparent—that these very proper sentiments would spread. Indeed, was it not possible that man was almost on the point of manumission? The belief has always been dear to revolutionaries that their particular success is the spark that will send a mighty flame of freedom flaring across the world. Indeed if the synthesis implicit in *Atalanta* and the central poems of *Poems and Ballads* is one founded upon a profound pessimism, that of the central poems of *Songs before Sunrise* is founded upon an optimism only proportionately more qualified. *Hertha* is necessarily, as a result, more philosophically constructive. But what promise did it hold of further poetic development? At first sight it would appear that a considerable advance had been made both in intellectual power and the control of emotion; a new and rare perfection of form had been attained; but the synthesis was exclusive. In it there was no room for the esoteric passion which until now had been the mainspring of his inspiration. And it was too violent an emotion, too important an ingredient of his sensibility, to admit of neglect in the long run if his inspiration were to maintain the quality of white heat—"pies with the devil's fingers in them"— which was so essential an element of his genius. The love of liberty and freedom was all very well, but as the inspiration of great poetry in Swinburne it seems that it required certain particular conditions. Without these conditions it was all too apt to degenerate at best into invective, at worst into irritability. And the circumstances in which *Songs before Sunrise* was composed were never to recur: the participation —Swinburne felt it to be that—in the actuality of revolution; the close communion with, and hero-worship for, that revolution's leader; and, perhaps psychologically most important of all, the temporary stilling of his erotic fantasies in the first overwhelming release provided by the "fair friend who keeps a maison de supplices à la Rodin" in the Euston Road and which there is reason to believe Swinburne only began to frequent at this time. It is possible that "Mrs. A." was as much responsible for the form of *Songs before Sunrise* as was Mazzini himself. But the fact remains that when Swinburne followed Ruskin's precept to devote himself "to the behalf of humanity, . . . 'to overthrowing its idols'," and Mazzini's command to abandon Art for Art's sake, he was, in his own way, compromising with society, attacking its tenets, not for art's sake but for its own good. And compromise was to be fatal to his art. That his conception of Liberty as a goddess who, unrestrained and cruel in the exaction of human sacrifices, was merely a sublimation of the *femme fatale*, is irrelevant. He was not aware of it. Whereas in *Prelude* he made it quite clear that he was abandoning one basis of inspiration for another. It is therefore no paradox incapable of resolution to say that Swinburne ceased to be a revolutionary upon committing himself to a volume of revolutionary poems. It is in this sense that *Songs before Sunrise* was prophetic of a decline in his genius.

Capitulate as he might in his art, there were, as has already been indicated, no signs of capitulation to society as yet in the conduct of his life. There were to be no more of those ardent snatches at normality, or at least none that can with confidence be placed in the same classification, as had taken place in the past—the desire to become a soldier, the proposal to "Boo"—till the final surrender of 1879. "Mrs. A." and the brandy bottle were dominant features in his existence during the period of the composition of *Songs before Sunrise*. In 1866 he had written to William Rossetti: "As to your screed of friendly counsel concerning Bacchus . . . I own the soft impeachment—now and then—notamment when we

met last. . . . 'L'ivresse, mes amis, est un vice vraiment dé-
licieux et dont le véritable philosophe ne saurait se passer'."
But the "now and then" was, whenever he was in London,
becoming more and more frequent.  It is astonishing how
a physique so frail, at any rate in appearance, was able to
withstand the strain to which it was subjected for as many
years as it did.

And in the spring of 1867 he was back in London again
for one of those periods of frenzied activity which ended in
the inevitable collapse and period of recuperation at Holmwood.  His portrait was being painted by Watts, a process
which Swinburne found almost intolerable and, on 10th
April, Dr. Westland Marston brought his son, the blind
poet, Philip Burke Marston, to see him.  Swinburne behaved
with all the astonishing charm and kindness of which he was
capable.  He made up his mind to "make him as happy as
he could".  He was successful.  Years later the boy was to
write: "I remember so well the first evening I came to see
you in Dorset Street. . . . I testified of it in a sonnet called
*To a Day*. . . . I had no sleep the night before, and I recited
in my room choruses from *Atalanta*.  The servants thought
I was in prayer."  Swinburne was touched by the evidences
of hero-worship for himself—an emotion which so often he
had lavished upon others.  A friendship developed which
was only terminated by Marston's death after a short and
tragic life.  "I was actually," wrote Swinburne in 1887,
"going to write 'poor Philip's death'—but, thank God, it
isn't 'poor' Philip any more now."  It is right to insist
upon Swinburne's quality of tenderness which, side by side
with a sometimes passionate cantankerousness, was constantly displayed towards his family and his friends.  But
in July, while breakfasting at Lord Houghton's, he was
overcome by one of his fainting fits.  The Admiral was
telegraphed for and the next day removed his son to Holmwood.  The doctors, so Swinburne wrote to Lord Houghton,
"have together prescribed for me a course of diet and tonic
medicine, and advise country air".  He was, he said, "rather
tired and weakened".  The diet, one may suspect, was the
exclusion of brandy though, apparently, champagne was not
altogether forbidden.  Nevertheless, he found "things were

awfully slow"; but it was not till the end of September that
he was allowed to spend a week-end at Etretat with Powell
on the condition that he promised to be as "regular as here".

After over three months' absence he was back in his
lodgings in Dorset Street by the end of October. A month
later he was again ill. But in spite of this, and in spite of the
fact that he had cut his face in a hansom accident, he determined to remain in London. And there, unusually for him,
he remained practically throughout the year 1868. The
cause of this extended sojourn was to be discovered, strapped
to a circus-horse, waving—if the number of her husbands
was any criterion — an irresistibly seductive sword, at
Astley's in a spectacle entitled *Mazeppa*.

Rossetti has generally been credited with being the author
of this baroque entanglement. Indeed, it is said that Adah
Menken returned to Rossetti as unearned the ten pounds he
is supposed to have given her for the conquering of Swinburne's affections. It is nevertheless certain that Swinburne's
friends were much concerned about him and were prepared
to go to some lengths in the hope of canalizing into a more
placid course his wilder irregularities. Was this one of the
results of the—again possibly apocryphal—meeting held to
decide "what could be done *with* and *for* Algernon"? It is
only with reluctance that the vision of Mr. Jowett weighing
the respective merits of Mazzini's intellectual and the
Menken's physical guardianship is abandoned. Abandoned,
however, it must probably be.

Adah Isaac Menken was at this time thirty-two, being
two years older than Swinburne. She had had a varied
career of some notoriety. She had been married five times—
the prizefighter, John Heenan, figured upon the list of her
husbands—while her *liaison* with the elder Dumas had not
passed without remark. *Mazeppa*, a melodrama adapted
from Byron, in which she rode about the stage bareback on
a white horse, was the basis of her fame, and the cause of her
coming to Europe for the first time in 1864. So successful
was it that she was able to revive it at intervals both in Paris
and London. Whether Swinburne had seen her on her
previous visits is not clear, but it is certain that the first
advances came on this occasion from her side. In December

1867 Swinburne was writing to Purnell that he was shy of being seen by Dolores (she had, happily, been christened Dolores Adios McCord at her birth in New Orleans) "sick and disfigured" after being spilt out of the hansom. Burne-Jones produced a set of cartoons of the Ancient Dame weeping and writing anxious notes of inquiry on being refused admittance to the poet's lodging. And Purnell was informing the poet, "She fears you are ill; she is unable to think of anything but you. . . . She concludes: 'Tell him all —say out my despairing nature to him. . . . Write at once; believe in me and my holy love for him.'"

Swinburne rapidly succumbed to these blandishments. He assisted her to correct the proofs of her volume of Whitmanesque poems, *Infelicia*, and persuaded Hotten to publish them. He arranged for them to be photographed together. To Nichol he wrote: "I must send you in a day or two a photograph of my present possessor—known to Britannia as Miss Menken, to me as Dolores (her real Christian name)—and myself taken together. . . . Of course it's private." Unfortunately it was not to remain so. Friends circulated the photographs, partly no doubt as a joke, partly perhaps in denial of the current scandal as to Swinburne's habits. They were all too successful. By March the photographs were displayed in the shop-windows and the *liaison* had become notorious. The rumour was even seriously credited that Swinburne was to play Cupid to Menken's Psyche on the stage. His latest extravagance became known to Mazzini, the Admiral and Lady Jane. His family no doubt protested. "There has been a *damned* row about the photographs," he wrote to Powell, "paper after paper has flung pellets of dirt at me." But what was the real truth of their relationship? It is impossible to say. A letter from George Moore on this subject, once in T. J. Wise's library, has unfortunately gone astray. Though he had no particular means of knowing the truth his speculations might well have proved of interest. Francis Burnand recorded finding her terrorizing a man who had slighted her: "She had closed the door with a bang, and was standing in front of it barring the way with a shining dagger in her hand. . . . Her eyes flashed more brilliantly than her dagger,

they gleamed murderously." She was "like an angry
tigress". Perhaps here is a clue to this grotesque *liaison*.
With her magnificently athletic physique, with her fiery
temperament, she was a type who might well have appealed
to the author of *Grausame Frauen*.

Nevertheless, it was all ended in a few months. At the
end of May Menken went to Paris and there, in August,
she died. A few days later Swinburne wrote: "I am
sure you were sorry on my account to hear of the death of
my poor dear Menken; it was a great shock to me and a real
grief. I was ill for some days. She was most lovable as a
friend as well as a mistress."

The Menken *liaison* was unfortunately but very imper-
manently effective in producing the reform his friends had
hoped for. Even before her departure for Paris he had
succumbed to another of his fainting fits. This time he fell
while carrying a lamp in his lodging and injured his head.
On 15th May Dr. Bird was able to inform Mazzini that
"for five days past Mr. Swinburne has avoided 'the perilous
stuff' . . .", but only a few weeks later Gosse saw him being
carried, his head bloody, from the Reading Room of the
British Museum. His friends were in a perpetual state of
alarm. Jowett wrote a "kindly and friendly letter on the
hypothesis that I have been injuring my natural health by
intemperate and irregular ways and offering even pecuniary
help if needed to set me straight". No wonder that he was
unable to get much work done hindered as he was by what,
euphemistically, he referred to as "London, business and
society". His two most important publications in 1868
were his *William Blake* and *Ave Atque Vale*, both of which
had now been completed for some time and were published
in the same month of January, the latter in *The Fortnightly
Review*. For the same paper he revised his *Old Masters at
Florence*, written in 1864, which were to draw from Pater
the acknowledgement, upon being congratulated by Swinburne upon his *Studies in the History of the Renaissance*,
that "he [Pater] considered them as owing their inspiration
entirely to the example of my own work in the same line".
It was a just tribute. To establish its truth it is only necessary
to compare Pater's famous passage on the Gioconda with

Swinburne's description of Michelangelo's studies of female heads. But of new work there was little: certain poems for *Songs before Sunrise*; rough notes for *Bothwell* and *Tristram and Iseult*, both of which were lost in a cab; and *Notes on the Royal Academy*, most of the work for which was done by William Rossetti.

In the autumn he was staying with George Powell at Etretat in "the sweetest little old farmhouse fitted up inside with music, books, drawings, etc. There is a wild garden all uphill, and avenues of trees". The sea-bathing was, as ever with Swinburne, the chief attraction of the place. And thus in early October he was very nearly drowned, being carried out to sea through a rocky archway. The "guetteur au sémaphore" raised the alarm on the cliffs above, while Powell ran down the beach and sent off some boats to the rescue. In the meantime, however, the poet had been picked up by a fishing boat commanded by the "Patron Vallin". He was carried to Yport but refused to return in the carriage Powell had provided and came back by sea.

The incident, in itself of but relative importance, was to have a curious effect upon decadent French literature. Amongst those present on the beach was the young Maupassant, then aged eighteen. Without hesitation he added his cries to the pandemonium and in later years was easily able to persuade himself that he had been instrumental in saving the drowning poet. More immediately, he introduced himself to the two friends and was invited to dine at the farmhouse. This, he discovered with an agreeable *frisson*, was named Chaumière Dolmancé, while the avenue of trees was known as the Avenue de Sade. Many years later, in a preface to a French translation of *Poems and Ballads*, he described some of the peculiar contents of the house. The two friends shared a taste for the *macabre* which had no doubt been stimulated by a reading of Meinhold and Borel. Among other knick-knacks "des ossements traînaient sur des tables" and "parmi eux une main d'écorché, celle d'un parricide, parait-il, dont le sang et les muscles séchés restaient callés sur les os blancs". Swinburne, himself, he described thus: "Le front était très grand sous des cheveux longs, et la figure se rétrécissant vers un menton mince ombré d'une

maigre touffe de barbe. Une très légère moustache glissait
sur les lèvres extraordinairement fines et serrées, et le cou qui
semblait sans fin unissait cette tête, vivante par les yeux clairs
chercheurs et fixes, à un corps sans épaules, car le haut de la
poitrine paraissait à peine plus large que le front. Tout
ce personnage presque surnaturel était agité de secousses
nerveuses." And "les opinions de ces deux amis jetaient
sur les choses une espèce de lueur troublante, macabre,
car ils avaient une manière de voir et de comprendre qui me
les montrait comme deux visionnaires malades, ivres de
poésie perverse et magique." Imaginative though the master
of realism's account no doubt was, it sufficiently impressed
Goncourt—to whom he reported this meeting in presumably
similar terms—to lend Swinburne's physical characteristics to
the sadist he depicted in his novel *La Faustin*. This character
has "un tic nerveux" and goes to a "petite maison sur les
côtes de la Bretagne, la Chaumière de Dolmancé". His
name was George Selwyn, and thus Swinburne was blended
with the famous sadistic contemporary of Horace Walpole
into a prototype that became not uncommon throughout
the French decadent *fin du siècle* novel. Even before the
publication of *The Maiden Tribute of Modern Babylon* in *The
Pall Mall Gazette* in 1885, the French showed an inclina-
tion to attribute to the English a particular partiality for this
vice, but with the translation of these articles as *Les Scandales
de Londres* there could be no further hesitation. Sadism
became *le vice anglais*. And green eyes, a nervous trembling,
murmured passages from *Anactoria* and English nationality
were the hall-marks of its amateurs.

By the end of October Swinburne was back in England.
November was spent at Holmwood; December in London;
and Christmas with Bendyshe at Cambridge, where some
excitement was caused by the attendance at divine service
of two such notorious atheists. His sense of irony was
particularly gratified at sitting in a bishop's seat and at being
preceded on leaving "by a man with a silver poker"! The
early months of 1869 were spent at Holmwood and in April,
after a visit to Jowett at Balliol, he returned to Dorset Street,
where he remained till July.

In the meantime the Burtons had returned from Brazil.

Before taking up the new appointment in Damascus, which
the indefatigable Isabel Burton had at last succeeded in
extracting from a reluctant Foreign Office, Richard had
been recommended by his doctor to take the waters at
Vichy, while Isabel returned to pack in London.   Swinburne
joined him and they travelled together.   Amongst those
gathered for the cure were Sir Frederick Leighton and
Adelaide Kemble Sartoris.   Leighton, according to Augustus
Hare, introduced the two "young men" (Richard was forty-
eight) to Mrs. Sartoris.   At coffee in the gardens they began
to air their opinions with the obvious intention to shock.
Mrs. Sartoris looked at Burton and said: "You believe, I
think, in *Juggernaut*, therefore with regard to *Juggernaut*, I
shall be very careful not to hurt your feelings.   And you,
Mr. Swinburne, believe, I think, in *nothing*, but if anything
is mentioned in which you *do* believe, I shall be very careful
not to hurt your feelings either, by abusing it: now I expect
that you will show the same courtesy to me."   The reproof
only had to be administered once more during their stay,
when Mrs. Sartoris began: "You believe, Mr. Burton, I
think in *Juggernaut* . . ."   Amid mutual laughter they
succeeded in remaining friends.   Indeed, Swinburne enjoyed
Mrs. Sartoris' music: "She plays and sings to me by the
hour, and her touch and her voice are like a young woman's.
*But*—they have sent her here to get down her *fat*—and—!"
   In August Mrs. Burton, who "did not see why I could not
have the month with him there too", arrived.   They went for
carriage drives to Clermont-Ferrand and Le Puy-en-Velay.
Mrs. Sartoris sang; Swinburne recited.   He was particularly
gratified to visit what, in the face of all evidence, he insisted
was the home of his ancestors—the castle of the Polignacs.
In September, after a few days in Paris and a short stay at
Etretat, he returned to London, while the Burtons headed
for Damascus.
   Till March 1870 he remained at Holmwood.   He was
busy upon *Tristram and Iseult* and the writing of articles for
*The Fortnightly Review*.   Amongst these last was a review of
Rossetti's poems which had now been exhumed.   The article
appeared in May.   *Songs before Sunrise*, too, was now
nearing completion.   His friends were anxious that it should

appear before its political *raison d'être* should have lapsed.
They counselled haste. The volume was due to appear in
the summer but it was delayed, as so often with Swinburne,
by difficulties with his publishers. Dissatisfied with Hotten,
he had made arrangements with Ellis to bring out the book.
Hotten immediately argued that in August 1866, while at
Lord Lytton's, Swinburne had sent him a document giving
him the right to publish all his works, past, present and
future, and on this basis threatened legal proceedings. He
was, however, unable to produce the document. Nevertheless, both Swinburne and Ellis were afraid of legal complications. Though the proofs had been corrected by
September, Ellis postponed publication. Through Howell
and the Rossettis some sort of agreement with Hotten was
arrived at and the book was eventually published in April
1871. It was too late. The revolution was dead. The
book, in spite of its magnificent poetry, attracted little
attention and was but briefly reviewed. Instead of being
the prelude to a revolution it was the epitaph to a period.
Napoleon III, Rattazzi, Guarini had but a few months to
live. "Our work," said Victor Emmanuel on opening the
first Roman Parliament, "is done." It was indeed. Mazzini,
tired, sick and disappointed, succumbed in March 1872
and, with his death, Swinburne was left rudderless upon
the sombre and chaotic seas of his own perverse and fluid
temperament.

# CHAPTER VIII

## (1872–1879)

THE years immediately following the publication of *Songs before Sunrise* and Mazzini's death are marked by a tragic lack of direction. There was no possibility of a return to the aesthetic theory which had alone given him an independent inspiration, a personal poetic core. And now, with the collapse of the revolution and the removal of the Chief, his particular ideal of Liberty, the philosophy of Hertha, seemed no longer capable of poetic development. They had, in a sense, been an extension of Mazzini's personality, and the bright white light of Liberty had been fused with the Chief's conception of an ideal Republic and conditioned by the ecstasy of submission which was the tropic atmosphere in which Swinburne's hero-worship thrived. And now that there could be no more "bulletins from headquarters", no more delicious, secret, personal interviews, the lyric impulse lapsed—never again to be recaptured with its pristine fire. A dramatist, a critic, an historian, a pamphleteer emerges. And because Swinburne's genius was a lyric genius, his most memorable work had now been done. Had Swinburne died in 1872—or, indeed, in 1879—we should have been deprived of much admirable verse, much acute and learned criticism, but one may hazard that his reputation would have stood higher to-day. But unlike Nelson—through no fault of his own, be it said—he failed to make the immortal gesture of dying triumphantly at the height of his powers and chose instead the protracted senility of a Wellington, whose long declining years dangerously obscured in popular esteem the lineaments of the victor of Waterloo. And so it was with Swinburne. The thirty-odd volumes of his last thirty-seven years add little to an estimate of his genius. They, with the fact that he lived into a new generation from which his early biographers with all their necessary reticences were drawn, served merely to obscure the true proportions of his art.

160

His life, too, in this period became increasingly clouded.
Though Mazzini, himself, had not tried to exercise any
direct influence upon Swinburne's manner of living, the mere
feeling that the Chief was there to disapprove must have
caused him to endeavour, not altogether successfully, to curb
his worst excesses.   But with the Chief's disappearance all
restraint went too.   Even in the last year of Mazzini's life,
when Swinburne had not seen him for many months, the
deterioration had noticeably set in.

Early in 1871 his family was thrown into great con-
sternation by Swinburne's temporary disappearance.   The
Admiral came up from Holmwood and applied for assistance
to Dr. Bird.   It was on this occasion that he is reported as
saying to the doctor's sister: "God has endowed my son
with genius, but He has not vouchsafed to grant him self-
control."   Dr. Bird succeeded in tracking down the errant
poet and he was restored to his family.   From May to July
he stayed at Holmwood.   His parents were by now well
aware of the situation, as is shown by a letter of Lady Jane's:
"He must not take lodgings in town.   He should stay here
to overcome his fearful propensity: his health is better, he
is happy."   But they were incapable of keeping him away
from London for long.   Lady Jane might recognize that
"books are not sufficient, he should have intellectual society",
but where was that society to be found in the country?   So
in July he escaped once more and once more fell ill and was
fetched home by the Admiral.   He was, he wrote, "ashamed
to think of my friends knowing it was my own fault".
These events were to be constantly repeated during the years
1872–1879, till at last the dying poet was carried to safety
in the competent arms of Walter Theodore Watts.

Indeed, these were sad years of loneliness and self-induced
ill-health.   Without the support of an overwhelming inspiration, without the comfort of an idolized leader, he
languished in the aftermath of persecution.   The cooling
of old friendships distressed him for all his superficial
truculence, and his enforced resignation from the Arts'
Club, now that he had leisure to consider it, induced in him
a mistrust of society—or was it of himself?—which found
expression in an uncharacteristic solitariness.   "Your letter,"

he wrote to Churton Collins in March 1876, "gave me great pleasure and a sense of something in the rather dull monotonous puppet-show of my life, which often strikes me as too barren of action or enjoyment to be much worth holding to, better than nothingness, or at least seeming better for a minute." And in contemplating the work, the letters, the politics of these years one becomes aware of the presence of an implicit though unacknowledged sense of insufficiency; something was lacking. The afflatus which had buoyed him up had withdrawn its support. Could it be that in recapitulating the past he might recapture the fire, the urgency of direction, the consciousness of significance, which had invested his life with so radiant a nimbus? He plunged into *Bothwell*. "The fusion of lyric with dramatic form," he wrote, "gives the highest type of poetry." But where was the passion that had informed *Chastelard*? For three years he wrestled with it. The detail of history usurped the place of inspiration. "It is," he wrote, "necessary to omit no detail, drop no link in the chain, if the work is to be either dramatically coherent or historically intelligible." "Mon drame épique" became "my chronicle play", and when, in 1874, the five hundred odd pages were published, it was no error to describe the immense drama as an "ambitious, conscientious, comprehensive piece of work". That it was well received by the critics and the public says much for the leisure and the powers of concentration of that monumental age.

In *Erechtheus* alone, perhaps, of the productions of these years is to be found some echo of the white-heat of authentic inspiration. Written during a comparatively happy interlude in 1874, it at least achieves a splendour of diction and an unusually sustained control. Critics have been unable to agree as to its merits. To some it has seemed to be the passionate and dramatic expression of the philosophy of *Hertha*, to contain an elevated and transcendent morality. The sacrifice of a young girl, at the behest of the gods and to ensure the safety of the State, has appeared to them a proper, indeed a lofty, contribution to the concept of the ideal human Republic. Ever since the anonymous writer in the *Edinburgh Review* of 1876, who likened the sacrifice of Chthonia to the Atonement on Calvary, this view has had its adherents. T. Earle Welby, for instance, while admitting that "*Atalanta* issues from the totality of Swinburne's genius; *Erechtheus* from what was specialized in it", goes on to say that "it is not the poet, majestically at home in this rarefied atmosphere, but we who are to be condemned if the ideal is too foreign to us for complete appreciation". This may well be so: but while not denying that the play, if it is to be intelligible, must be approached from the standpoint of *Songs before Sunrise*, it is not always easy to be convinced that its "rarefied atmosphere" arises entirely from the elevation of its idealism. There would seem, indeed, to have been a certain degeneration in Swinburne's philosophy of the ideal Republic and the divinity of man: have not the autochthonous gods returned with a more ruthless, a more meaningless, a more catastrophic cruelty even than before? It is possible to discern in this mingling of Sade and Mazzini a manifestation of the lack of direction which afflicted these years. But what impact does the play make upon the reader? Beyond the immediate verbal effects of its poetry, its "marmoreal uniformity of diction", it cannot be considered altogether successful. To quote Mr. Harold Nicolson: "It is never wholly clear whether Athens is to be destroyed by the Thracians or by the sea; it is never wholly clear whether the central theme is the sacrifice of Chthonia or the heroism of her mother; and the final holocaust of Erechtheus and his remaining daughters is treated in a manner wholly unconvincing and almost incidental." And, indeed, planned under Jowett's eye, with a too-conscious regard to exact conformity with the principles of the Aeschylean drama, with a too-disciplined, a too-impeccably hellenic symmetry, the play moves in a serene, remote empyrean, in an atmosphere too rarefied for the breath of human tragedy or the quickening of the heart's beat.

In his politics, too, there was a similar uncertainty, a similar attempt to echo the past. Who now could lead him in the Crusade? And where, indeed, *was* the Crusade? Alas, there was now no one to distinguish for him the bastions from the windmills. Hugo renounced so thankless a rôle with flattering phrases: "Bravo, O mon poète," and

"Je suis fier de vous." The banners of revolution flapped,
so it seemed, but sluggishly on the breeze. Even the death
of Napoleon III, tired, sick and exiled, drew no valedictory
thunder from Hugo. Was the death of the arch-fiend to
pass unmarked? Regardless of taste and propriety Swinburne composed *The Descent into Hell*, rejoicing "That we
have lived to say, The dog is dead." It cannot be considered
one of his happier compositions. But denied the political
leadership of Hugo, disappointed by the conservatism of the
new French Republic, he turned, in spite of his "loyalty as
a Frenchman (partly by blood and wholly in heart and
sympathy and inherited duty)", to the contemplation of
what, in his eager anticipation of a universal republic, he
had so far largely ignored—English politics. He was, of
course, committed to the Liberal side. Did not his writings
prove it? And had he not been invited (an invitation which
Mazzini had permitted him to decline) to a seat in Parliament
by the Reform League in 1868? But now a new difficulty
presented itself. Foreign revolutionaries were all very well:
Karl Blind, Louis Blanc, Mazzini were leaders, heroes,
martyrs to a cause. But could the same thing be said of
Mr. Gladstone and John Bright? Could the aristocratic
descendant of countless Swinburnes, Ashburnhams and
Polignacs be expected to collaborate with manufacturers
and business men? What would Shelley and Byron have
said? Obviously they would have been "utterly opposed
to the current of English Radicalism". By 1877 Disraeli
had so far advanced in favour that he "has the merit (1) that
he is not Gladstone, (2) that he keeps Gladstone out". No
doubt the controversy over Bosnia and Herzegovina, which
began in 1875, had helped to bring about this curious
political *volte face*. The Turkish massacres in Bulgaria in
1876 caused a wave of indignation, led by Mr. Gladstone,
to sweep the country, and a campaign in the Liberal Press
against Disraeli's pro-Turk policy. Russia sent an ultimatum
to the Sultan; Disraeli criticized it. In December a conference opened in Constantinople to settle their mutual
disagreements. Swinburne wrote his *Note on the Muscovite
Crusade*. For him the Sultan was a "waning evil", while
the Czar was a "waxing" one. Besides, had he not always

detested Russia and even climbed Culver Cliff as a substitute to leading a charge at Balaclava, the glory of which had been denied him? There was, too, another reason: Carlyle had been enlisted by the Liberals for their propaganda. And had not Carlyle made unflattering comments about him in the Press? With matchless vituperation he attacked in his *Note* the "most foul-mouthed man of genius since the death of Swift". He lashed this "crusade which has Alexander of Russia for its Godfrey de Bouillon, and Thomas Carlyle for its Peter the Hermit". As a supplement to the *Note* he composed the *Ballad of Bulgarie*, to whose satire no publication dared open its columns. But in the war of 1877–1878 the Sultan was defeated and Swinburne in his fury composed *The White Czar*, which again no one would print till, upon the suggestion of Nichol, it appeared in the *Glasgow University Magazine*. Nevertheless, a doubt assailed him. Could he be sure, in the heat of these personal polemics, with no mentor at his elbow, that he had not departed from his principles? Was he, indeed, any longer quite sure what these principles were? Nervously he wrote for reassurance to Karl Blind. All was well. He received a "most kind letter". "It is," he replied, "a very great honour to be accepted as a fellow-soldier (tho' but a humble private and good only as a trumpet or flag-bearer to some small regiment) in the great and noble army of which you are one of the generals." The blazon on the flag might be uncertain, the trumpet sound a strange new note, but the army, so he persuaded himself, still numbered in its ranks Mazzini's veterans as in the days that were.

But in this state of unsatisfactory retrospection, exacerbated by the natural irritability of the alcoholic, it was unlikely that these controversies would be limited to the field of politics. Nor was it the case. Criticism had become with him a main literary activity and in the practice of it there were, for Swinburne, no half-measures: only the dead, Shakespeare for instance, might be the subject of rational appraisal and analysis: for the living there was black and there was white, while to disagree with the Swinburnian verdict was to be guilty not only of intellectual error but of moral turpitude. He was ever prepared to say so in withering

phrases and at the top of his voice.   His opponents were by
no means always guiltless, but his own attitude was a fan to
the slumbering fires of obloquy which had been undermining
his name since 1866.   And, indeed, it was in that year, with
the opportunity afforded by the publication of *Poems and
Ballads*, that Robert Buchanan first manifested his peculiar
hostility towards Swinburne.   It was due to the transference
by Moxon's of the volume of Keats' selections from Buchanan
to Swinburne.   Buchanan's retort was *The Session of the
Poets* published over the name of Caliban in the ever-hostile
columns of *The Spectator*.   In 1871 he renewed the attack
in *The Contemporary Review*, with an article which though
superficially a denunciation of "The Fleshly School of
Poetry" through history was in fact an attack on Swinburne
and Rossetti.   It was spiteful sensationalism, and the article
was signed "Thomas Maitland", which Swinburne considered to be an act of cowardice.   Swinburne, resilient as
Rossetti could not be, replied with *Under the Microscope*.   It
is an entertaining piece of invective.   Buchanan had been
unwise enough to allude to Swinburne's "falsetto" and to
announce that "a training in Grecian literature must tend
to emasculate the student so trained".   "And well,"
Swinburne wrote, "may we congratulate ourselves that no
such process as robbed of all strength and manhood the
intelligence of Milton, has had power to impair the virility of
Mr. Buchanan's virile and masculine genius.   To that strong
and severe figure we turn from the sexless and nerveless
company of shrill-voiced singers who share with Milton the
curse of enforced effeminacy; from the pitiful soprano notes
of such dubious creatures as Marlowe, Jonson, Chapman,
Gray, Coleridge, Shelley, Landor, 'cum semiviro comitatu',
we avert our ears to catch the higher and manlier harmonies
of a poet with all his natural parts and powers complete.
For truly if love or knowledge of ancient art and wisdom be
the sure mark of 'emasculation', and the absence of any
taint of such love and any tincture of such knowledge (as
then in consistency it must be) the supreme sign of perfect
manhood, Mr. Robert Buchanan should be amply competent
to renew the thirteenth labour of Hercules."
The controversy was not to end there.   After, it must be

admitted, further considerable provocation Swinburne in
1875 wrote a letter to *The Examiner* which was held to be
libellous and which cost that paper £150 damages. It was
on this occasion that Mr. Justice Archibald made certain
remarks from the Bench concerning Swinburne's work
which have already been quoted.

But there were, indeed, innumerable literary quarrels
which engaged his attention and his time. No doubt they
acted as a stimulus in his incipient melancholy, they filled
his life with action which, he strove to persuade himself,
was significant. He attacked George Eliot ("an Amazon
thrown sprawling over the crupper of her spavined and spur-
galled Pegasus"); he attacked Zola; over Rabelais he
attacked the Society for the Suppression of Vice; he publicly
insulted in a letter that "foul-mouthed and gap-toothed old
dog", Emerson; he cruelly parodied Lytton and Browning;
and his Shakespearian criticism was the signal for a war with
Furnivall of the New Shakespeare Society which was to
continue for many years.

True to the enthusiasms of the past, he had once more
begun to devote himself to the study of the early English
dramatists which in boyhood and adolescence had captured
his admiration. "I am now," he wrote to Gosse in January
1875, "at work on my long-designed essay or study on the
metrical progress or development of Shakespeare as traceable
by ear and *not* by finger, and the general changes of tone
and stages of mind expressed or involved in this change or
progress of style. I need hardly say that I begin with a
massacre of the pedants worthy of celebration in an Icelandic
saga—'a murder grim and great'. I leave 'the finger-
counters and finger-casters' without a finger to count on or
an (ass's) ear to wag." The publication of some instalments
of this work in *The Fortnightly Review* for May 1875 and
January 1876, instalments which controverted the official
views of the New Shakespeare Society which Furnivall had
recently founded, began a ridiculous guerrilla warfare which,
in 1880, upon the publication in volume form of *A Study of
Shakespeare*, flared into a pitched battle. Furnivall behaved
with astonishing imbecility, referring to Swinburne's "shallow
ignorance and infinite self-conceit" and to his ear as "a

poetaster's, hairy, thick and dull". He wrote libellous postcards to Swinburne's friends and excommunicated from his society several important mutineers — including the Duke of Devonshire—with a printed "I am glad to be rid of you". He referred to Swinburne himself as "Pigsbrook". Swinburne, on the other hand, expended much ingenuity in infuriating his opponent. He composed "flagellant notes"; he retorted to "Pigsbrook" with "Brothelsdyke"; and henceforth always described his manuscript paper as "Furnivallscap". The pedants, indeed, had surprisingly refused to submit to massacre.

Nevertheless, during these years he was slowly collecting the poems that were to be published as *Poems and Ballads: Second Series*, in 1878. Many of the poems had been written before 1872, such as *Ave Atque Vale*, the circumstances of whose composition have already been described, and which was by far the most distinguished poem in the book, ranking, as it does, amongst Swinburne's masterpieces. Many more were translations, essays in literary technique or necrological poems. Biographically, interest is centred in some half-dozen lyrics composed during the period. These, mostly written in lucid intervals in the country, where from time to time long stays were made necessary by the state of his health or the condition of his finances, are informed with a new, an unimpassioned, an almost quietist emotion. Many critics, emerging shocked and battered from the tumultuous flood of the earlier poems, have been tempted, reassured by the safe poetic harbours of nostalgia and melancholy, to discover in these exquisite lyrics the perfection of Swinburne's mature genius. There is, indeed, a certain tremulous sorrow, a wistfulness of retrospection, a calm, an almost lethargic, regret evident in their elaborate cadences.

> *I hid my heart in a nest of roses,*
> *Out of the sun's way, hidden apart;*
> *In a softer bed than the soft white snow's is,*
> *Under the roses I hid my heart.*

And it is not only in *The Ballad of Dreamland* that there is side by side with the melancholy an undercurrent of longing

—for rest was it, for safety? The note is struck again in
*Sestina*:

> *I saw my soul at rest upon a day*
> *As a bird sleeping in the nest of night.* . . .

Indeed, it is not straining interpretation unduly to see in
these poems a reflection of the physical conditions in which
they must have been composed. His health was rapidly
deteriorating; he suffered the heart-searchings of remorse;
he feared the future. And from that fear sprang the ache
of nostalgia for the vibrant past. In *A Vision of Spring in
Winter* he pleaded for its recapture:

> *The morning song beneath the stars that fled*
> *With twilight through the moonless mountain air,*
> *While youth with burning lips and wreathless hair*
> *Sang toward the sun that was to crown his head,*
> *Rising; the hopes that triumphed and fell dead,*
> *The sweet swift eyes and songs of hours that were;*
> *These may'st thou not give back for ever; these,*
> *As at the sea's heart all her wrecks lie waste,*
> *Lie deeper than the sea;*
> *But flowers thou may'st, and winds, and hours of ease,*
> *And all its April to the world thou may'st*
> *Give back, and half my April back to me.*

But the climax of retrospection in these poems is attained
in *On the Cliffs*, which was published in *Songs of the Springtides* in 1880. The poem itself was written at Holmwood
in the summer of 1879. The house was about to be sold;
Swinburne was about to enter The Pines—to use a verb
associated with institutions. It marks the end of a period.
Listening to a nightingale, the poet bares his soul with
a new certainty, a new subtlety of analysis. The poem
is marked by a fluidity of rhythm, a laxity of metre, which
is to be met with practically nowhere else in his work. In it
are recapitulated the vain regrets for a life spent without
the comfort of mutual love. He is resigned to being a
"barren stock"—a phrase which appears several times in
the letters of this period:

*Thee only of all; yet can no memory say*
*How many a night and day*
*My heart has been as thy heart, and my life*
*As thy life is, a sleepless hidden thing,*
*Full of the thirst and hunger of winter and spring,*
*That seeks its food not in such love or strife*
*As fill men's hearts with passionate hours and rest.*
*From no loved lips and on no loving breast*
*Have I sought ever for such gifts as bring*
*Comfort, to stay the secret soul with sleep.*
*The joys, the loves, the labours,· whence men reap*
*Rathe fruit of hopes and fears,*
*I have made not mine; the best of all my days*
*Have been as those fair fruitless summer strays,*
*Those water-waifs that but the sea-wind steers,*
*Flakes of glad foam or flowers on footless ways*
*That take the wind in season and the sun,*
*And when the wind wills is their season done.*

It is interesting to compare *On the Cliffs* with *Thalassius*, composed the following year from the safe anchorage of Putney. Avowedly autobiographical, conceived some time before but its execution postponed, there is, nevertheless, an absence now of any wistfulness. Sure harboured, the uncertainties of life's passage now resolved, there is a tendency to treat the self-revelation dramatically. In contrast to *On the Cliffs* it is possible to detect a certain coarsening of perception, a failing of sensitivity. It is tempting to see an infiltration, an advance guard of Watts-Dunton's massive influence already at work. The poet meets "the great god Love":

*And seeing him lovely and like a little child*
*That well nigh wept for wonder that it smiled*
*And was so feeble and fearful, with soft speech*
*The youth bespake him softly; but there fell*
*From the sweet lips no sweet word audible*
*That ear or thought might reach:*
*No sound to make the dim cold silence glad,*
*No breath to thaw the hard harsh air with heat;*
*Only the saddest smile of all things sweet,*
*Only the sweetest smile of all things sad.*

*And so they went together one green way*
*Till April dying made free the world for May;*
*And on his guide suddenly Love's face turned,*
*And in his blind eyes burned*
*Hard light and heat of laughter; and like flame*
*That opens in a mountain's ravening mouth*
*To blear and sear the sunlight from the south,*
*His mute mouth opened, and his first word came:*
*"Knowest thou me now by name?"*
*And all his stature waxed immeasurable,*
*As of one shadowing heaven and lightening hell;*
*And statelier stood he than a tower that stands*
*And darkens with its darkness far-off sands*
*Whereon the sky leans red;*
*And with a voice that stilled the winds he said:*
*"I am he that was thy lord before thy birth,*
*I am he that is thy lord till thou turn earth:*
*I make the night more dark, and all the morrow*
*Dark as the night whose darkness was my breath:*
*O fool, my name is sorrow;*
*Thou fool, my name is death."*

The plaintive note discernible in the lyrics of this period echoes not only a conscious regret at declining inspiration—a decline of which he must at moments have been well aware—but a melancholy dissatisfaction with his way of life. Gradually during these years his existence, which he had never been altogether competent to conduct, became increasingly unmanageable. Little by little he came subconsciously to long for some change in its rhythm, some haven, perhaps, from which the sharp angularities might be viewed objectively as once he had looked upon stormy seas from the windows of East Dene. As already with failing inspiration he had capitulated in his art, so now with failing health he was to capitulate in his life. Submission was to become the dominant trait in his character. But it was a long process —a process, indeed, which might never have come to fruition but for a number of fortuitous circumstances and, above all, the patient, tactful, almost feline resilience and perseverance of Watts-Dunton.

Walter Theodore Watts (the Dunton was not added till 1896) was some five years Swinburne's senior, having been

born in 1832. The son of a country solicitor of St. Ives,
Watts studied the law in order to carry on his father's business.
But the respect of a local community was not enough.
Behind that placid, slightly pompous exterior was a streak
of romanticism, a certain mystical delight in the mysterious. The Gothic novel proved more sympathetic than
conveyancing, and Scott than mortgages. *Lavengro* was
overwhelming. A new ambition dawned. Was it, could it
be possible that he, Watts, might become acquainted with
its author? Who knew to what castles in Spain such a
friendship might not lead? With assiduous tenacity he
pursued his first literary capture. Hunted down on Wimbledon Common, Borrow was brought to bay in the surf at
Whitby. What transpired between the country solicitor
and the cantankerous literary celebrity? "My life," Watts
recorded, "has always been singularly exposed to beautiful
influences." Borrow's we may suppose to have been the
first. Others followed: Ruskin and the romantic charms
of Pre-Raphaelite art. His ambitions soared. Visits to
London imperilled his business, but he was not to be deterred.
At last the glad day dawned. Dr. Gordon Hake, a mutual
friend, introduced him to Rossetti.

It was a happy moment for both of them. Rossetti's
affairs were in that state of chaos that generally followed
upon entrusting such matters to Howell. Watts placed his
legal knowledge, his integrity, and his business capacity at
the artist's disposal. And then there was the matter of a
cheque for £50 that had been forged in Rossetti's name—
"a most vexatious discovery". Rossetti did not wish to
prosecute as he had "reason to fear that the forger is a
member of a family known to me from childhood". Watts
helped to settle the matter. "I hardly know," wrote
Rossetti, "how to thank Mr. Watts enough for the extremely
kind trouble he has taken in that unpleasant bank business."
The only thanks Watts required was to be admitted as a
friend into Rossetti's circle. In this he succeeded. They
could not do without him.

With this rosy future in view—a future which held all
the prospects of continuous contact with artistic celebrity—
Watts threw up the business in St. Ives and settled in

London. That same year, 1872, he met Swinburne, probably at the house of Madox Brown. *Atalanta* and *Poems and Ballads* had impressed him; so had their notoriety. Here, unquestionably, was genius. Watts pressed the acquaintanceship. But Swinburne was not much given to casual acquaintanceships; besides, what could he have in common with this earnest, provincial, middle-class solicitor? There was a tragic moment when to Watts "the door of hope seemed closed". Nevertheless, he persevered. Events favoured him. Swinburne was still in difficulties with Hotten. The publication of *Songs before Sunrise* by Ellis had led to no final settlement. Hotten maintained that, though he had waived his rights to that particular volume, he was still entitled to *Bothwell* and various other works. To whom could Swinburne turn for help? Watts, obviously, was the answer. By the end of 1872 they were in regular correspondence.

Indeed, during these years Swinburne was much in need of a friend. As already indicated, many of his old intimacies had by now cooled. Rossetti, already far gone in his addiction to chloral, resented some criticism which Swinburne had innocently made of his work. "To this day," wrote Swinburne, "I am utterly ignorant and unable to conjecture why, after the last parting in the early summer of 1872, he should have chosen suddenly to regard me as a stranger." And soon his friendships with Howell and Lord Houghton were to show the same tendency. The former, indeed, was to end with Howell's "habitually amusing mixed companies of total strangers by obscene false anecdotes about my private eccentricities of indecent indulgence in real or imaginary *lupanaria*." But "thank something," Swinburne wrote in January 1877, "there are spirits of another sort— and I have met with my share of them as well as of Houghtons and Rossettis (D.G.)". Amongst these "spirits of another sort", which included such old friends as Nichol, W. M. Rossetti, Knight, Madox Brown and, more recently, Edmund Gosse, possibly the most important influence during these years was that of Jowett, whose rather startled reactions to the intractable undergraduate had gradually grown into affection for the poet. Constantly inviting

Swinburne to stay with him at Pitlochry, West Malvern, in Cornwall, or at Oxford, Jowett endeavoured to counteract the ill effects of London by exposing the poet to the influences of respectable society.

For indeed, as Lady Jane had realized, it was impossible to keep Swinburne permanently away from London. After the breakdown of 1871, due to the Admiral's insistence, he had no longer had rooms there but, nevertheless, by March 1872 he was again engaging furnished rooms at 12 North Crescent, and after a visit to Scotland with Jowett in July and August, where he was encouraged to swim in the burns, to the great benefit of his health, he was renting in September new lodgings at 3 Great James Street. This was to be his last independent address.

Moving house, he found, as always, an intolerable strain. The practicalities of ordinary life were almost beyond his powers to sustain. They could drive him to the verge of frenzy. Besides, he had a very nice sense of property. His visitors would be led from piece to piece of his furniture and expected to express admiration. The pictures of Mazzini and Orsini, preserved from Oxford days, were necessary to his existence. From time to time he would give little skips in the air in order to impress a fleeting kiss upon their glass. How could he ensure that they would not be damaged in the transit from lodging to lodging? And might not the serpentine candlesticks go astray? These were very perturbing considerations. And then there was the odious and unfortunate Mrs. Thompson, a former landlady. "I . . . wholly repudiate and flatly deny the existence of any claim on her part, especially when backed up by two deliberate and impudent lies. . . ." But what had she done with the movable filter and the Turkey carpet? And where, moreover, was the latchkey?

There was, too, a carpenter's bill that remained unpaid. It was one of many. For some years Swinburne had been living beyond his income. This was certainly well under £400. His allowance was "just £200 a year" and he could not "count on making as much annually" by his writings. Pursued by bills he retired to Holmwood. Prolonged stays in the country became financially necessary. As Lafourcade has pointed out, lack of money probably saved his life. In November 1872 he was writing to Morley: "I am at present in a fair way to be pressed to death by unpaid bills." And in December to George Powell: "I must look to pounds just now as I am pressed by duns and am still worth £200 less than nothing." He dared not go to London and one may suspect that the Admiral was not particularly eager to mitigate an insolvency that had so desirable a result. Nevertheless, his father paid some of the more pressing bills though "to return to town, I must have *some* money at my bankers to go on with . . . I shall have none in the ordinary way till Midsummer". Instead, he went to Oxford, where Jowett introduced him to the Bishop.

The gratification this meeting caused him—symptomatic, perhaps, of a new-found desire for the respectability which he may now have felt was slipping from him—was offset by a disturbing conversation with Walter Pater. Its subject was the unfortunate behaviour of Simeon Solomon. The painter had graduated from the companionship of Swinburne to the more enduring, if less highly charged, aestheticism of Pater, Oscar Browning, Symonds, and the undergraduate Oscar Wilde. There had been rumours and scandal. He was now to suffer a term of imprisonment. He was, so it appears, both a pervert and a flagellant. Nothing shows the change that was taking place in Swinburne during these years more clearly than his reaction to the news. Swinburne, who ten years before had composed the *Hermaphroditus*, who had noted in 1871 with evident approval that Solomon's painting showed "the latent relations of pain and pleasure, the subtle conspiracies of good with evil, of attraction and abhorrence", who had been the recipient of Solomon's account of a famous case of 1870, the Queen *versus* Boulton and others, in which Solomon described "Lais"—or was it "Antinous"?—as "remarkable—he is not quite beautiful but supremely pretty . . .", Swinburne, who had been Solomon's intimate friend and perfectly aware of his aberrations, now wrote to George Powell: "I saw and spoke with a great friend of poor Simeon, Pater of Brasenose. . . . I suppose there is no doubt the poor unhappy little fellow has really been out of his mind and *done* things amenable to

law such as done by a sane man would make it impossible
for anyone to keep up his acquaintance and not be cut by
the rest of the world as an accomplice?" Concern for his
reputation was growing upon him. The pressure of Victorian
morality was cumulative in its effect. By 1879 he was
writing of Solomon as "a thing unmentionable alike by men
and women, as equally abhorrent to either—nay, to the
very beasts—raising money by the sale of my letters to him
in past years, which must doubtless contain much foolish
burlesque and now regrettable nonsense never meant for any
stranger's eye who would not understand the mere childish-
ness of the silly chaff indulged in long ago". And in 1905,
when Solomon died of chronic alcoholism in St. Giles'
workhouse having, as an obituary notice expressed it,
"stepped back into the riotous pages of Petronius", did it
occur to Swinburne as he sipped his daily glass of beer in
the placid ambience of The Pines that he was perhaps not
altogether blameless for the tragic life which had now drawn
to so pitiful a close?

Undoubtedly Jowett's influence was in part responsible
for this growing concern with reputation and respectability.
The Master of Balliol did all he could to wean Swinburne
from Pater and such other influences as he considered subversive, frequently at Oxford tracking him down and leading
him back to Balliol with all the authority of, in Gosse's
words, "an indignant nurse". He endeavoured, too, to
attach the poet to him by the bonds of mutual interests.
Swinburne was persuaded to help Jowett, much to the surprise of some other of the poet's friends, in the compilation
of the *School and Children's Bible*; he was encouraged to
revise the Master's version of the *Symposium*—an honour,
indeed, and which led to such vivacious, almost impertinent
criticisms as: "Another howler, Master!" to which Jowett
would reply with a benign and tactful: "Thank you,
Algernon, thank you!" And upon the other side, Swinburne
is recorded as flinging himself upon the floor at Jowett's
feet and saying: "Master, I feel I have never thanked you
enough for cutting *four thousand* lines out of Bothwell!"

After spending July 1873 at Grantown, with Jowett, he
was in London in August and again in October. But again

his health gave way and he was compelled "to leave town suddenly and everything in my rooms at sixes and sevens". He returned but comparatively rarely to Great James Street during the next three years. His life was made up of visits to Jowett and long months at Holmwood. Outwardly there is but little to record. In June 1874 he met, while on a short visit to London, John Trelawny. The visit might well have proved disastrous. Trelawny had been instrumental in placing Swinburne's name on the Byron Memorial Committee without his consent. Byron at this time was, in the somewhat curious ebb and flow of his reputation with Swinburne, at the lowest ebb. Trelawny called to apologize. Evidently old age had not impaired his ability to charm genius. "The piratical old hero calls me the last of the poets," Swinburne wrote. Besides, was he not "a magnificent old Viking to look at"? Flattery and old age proved an irresistible combination: the nerve of hero-worship quivered. Trelawny became "the one Englishman living I was really ambitious to know". And in 1880 that "very famous veteran of the sea" received, not inaptly, the dedication of *Songs of the Springtides.*

The summer and autumn months of 1874 were spent with some other members of his family at Niton in the Isle oi Wight, where lived his uncle, Sir Henry Gordon. He was making a study of Chapman, an author for whom Swinburne retained always an enduring enthusiasm. Here, too, outswimming his strength as he had so often done in the past, he was very nearly drowned, being hardly able to regain the shore, "and even", as he wrote to Morley, "had I been drowned, as I reflected on regaining land in rather a spent condition, could not have enjoyed the diversion of reading the notices of my death in the papers, which is an unreasonable dispensation of Providence". After a stay in London, Christmas, the season of "Galilean orgies", was spent at Holmwood.

After a visit to Jowett at West Malvern in January 1875 he came to London in February to celebrate at "a pleasant private party . . . with the same libations, both the two great men [Lamb and Landor] who loved and admired each other in life, and whose memories might fitly and gracefully be mingled after death in our affectionate recollection". The "pleasant private party", due possibly to Swinburne's insistence on organizing it without assistance, failed, according to Gosse's description, to attain any very high level of conviviality, while the bill proved unexpectedly large in the eyes of indigent men of letters. Swinburne, indeed, was probably the least able to afford it since, though his finances had been to some extent restored by the Admiral, it was only with the grestest difficulty that he was able to remain in London for a period as long as, on this occasion, three months. Nevertheless, he probably minded it less than the others, having no sense of money as he himself very well understood. "Of my own or my friends' finances," he once wrote to Gosse, "I never professed to be a judge (God—or something better—help my friends if I did!)."

After a short stay at Oxford, he was back in Holmwood by the middle of June, where his stay was happily prolonged by "a badly sprained foot" which kept him in bed for some days as he wrote on 4th July: "I sprained it trying to climb and jump from a garden fence . . . and the consequence has been worse than twenty swishings." In August he wrote to Gosse wishing him, upon his marriage, "all the joy and good fortune . . . without admixture of envy of that particular form of happiness which I am never now likely to share. I suppose it must be the best thing that can befall a man, to win and keep the woman that he loves while yet young; at any rate I can congratulate my friend on his good hap, without any too jealous afterthought of the reverse experience which left my own young manhood 'a barren stock'—if I may cite that phrase without seeming to liken myself to a male Queen Elizabeth".

August was spent with Jowett at West Malvern. Here, amidst mutual raptures at Captain Webb's unprecedented feat of swimming the Channel, *Erechtheus* was begun. Having made certain of its classical correctitude, Swinburne left Jowett and went to Southwold to join Watts. By now, 1875, Watts had become not only the indispensable man of business but a close friend as well. By imperceptible stages the transformation had taken place over the previous three years. Constant tact and limitless perseverance had been necessary.

The difficulties in acting as intermediary between Swinburne
and Hotten, two tiresome and temperamental principals,
would have reduced a lesser man to despair. But had Watts
not sworn that Swinburne should enjoy the financial fruits
of genius? Ellis, who had agreed to become Swinburne's
publisher, offered to buy Hotten's stock. Watts set about
trying to extract a financial statement from Hotten and come
to an amicable arrangement. But *Songs before Sunrise* sold
so slowly that Ellis backed out and refused to buy the stock.
What was to be done? Watts found another publisher,
named King. But still no financial statement could be got
from Hotten. Watts was contemplating legal action against
Hotten. King was still anxious to consider the matter. But
Swinburne discovered that King had published the *Collected
Works* of Robert Buchanan. His "surprise and disgust"
was poured out upon the head of Watts. That head was
bowed but with supreme tact he replied: "I admire your
indomitable pluck . . . I understand your feeling." King
was dropped and Watts approached Chapman & Hall.
"You will get," Watts wrote, "the cash you want. But
don't show you need it. Mr. Chapman is not likely to take
a mean advantage (he is a gentleman). But it is wonderful
how practical gentlemen are in business matters. . . .
Imperceptibly to himself, Mr. Chapman would be more
anxious to deal liberally with you if he thought we didn't
care a damn whether he dealt with us or not. He himself
has lost a card or two, by exhibiting his own anxiety to treat.
As a man, I like him the more, but as a trader, I respect him
the less." Indeed, Chapman & Hall offered very liberal
terms, proposed to bring out a cheap edition of Swinburne's
works, and had a specimen page printed and submitted to
him. To Swinburne it seemed that his "insecurity and
ill-luck in all business matters" had now come to an end.

Hotten, however, resolutely refused to part with
Swinburne's works, for which he claimed he had an "oral
contract". The fact that another publisher was prepared
to take them over tended to enhance their value in his eyes.
He was prepared to litigate. Nor, curiously, did Watts
receive quite the support he expected from Swinburne
himself. The "oral contract" was denied, but hardly with

the expected force. Watts was, no doubt, somewhat disconcerted; but did he suspect the reason? Swinburne attempted to keep it from him: "But of course," he wrote to Howell, "you would say nothing to anyone, least of all men to Watts." Indeed, Swinburne found himself in something of a delicate position. He had supplied Hotten with "a list drawn up in my hand of scenes in school which he was to get sketched for me on approval by a draughtsman of his acquaintance . . . in which list I had explained the posture and actions of 'swishing'". He now feared that, if forced to litigate, Hotten would take his revenge by publishing these descriptions in some "History of Flagellation" or "Romance of the Rod". No wonder that Watts found that "This business is most harassing".

In the meantime Chapman had heard that Hotten had a stock of five thousand unsold volumes. The prospect of taking these over was rather more than he had bargained for. There was, however, the possibility of Hotten becoming bankrupt and Chapman suggested that Watts should wait a few weeks before proceeding further. In the end the whole business settled itself with the sudden death of Hotten from "a surfeit of pork chops"—which Swinburne considered refuted Burton's theory of cannibalism—in June 1873. His successor, Andrew Chatto, a man of unblemished character, became, upon Watts' advice, Swinburne's publisher and the Chapman scheme was dropped.

Besides these infinitely complicated negotiations with publishers, Watts frequently acted as literary agent for Swinburne in the day-to-day selling of articles and poems to various editors of reviews. He was able to extract more money from them than Swinburne could do on his own. For this, considering the state of his finances, Swinburne was infinitely grateful. Within a year Watts was accepted as a friend. In March 1873 Swinburne was already writing "we might begin mutually to drop the Mr. in writing as friends". It was typical of the tact and diplomacy of Watts that he should have allowed the suggestion to emanate from Swinburne. And, indeed, Swinburne was beginning to feel that in his precarious and unsatisfactory existence there was one friend at least upon whom he could count. But even then Watts had to be careful in spreading the net; a little too much insistence, a word of gratuitous or unacceptable admonition, and the startled quarry retired once more into his private thickets. "I am astonished at your suggestion," Swinburne wrote on one such occasion, "the points on which I am undecided are those only on which I asked your advice in my last letter." Watts humbly hastened to apologize.

By 1875, as we have seen, the friendship had ripened to a point of intimacy where they could holiday together. Watts, too, had moved into lodgings in Great James Street and had improved his literary standing by becoming a leading critic upon the staff of *The Athenaeum*. This last event increased his usefulness to Swinburne. "I took the poem to MacColl," he wrote in January 1876, "who has accepted it for £20 for the *Athenaeum*. I am to meet him in town about the other poems you left with me, one of which I shall offer him. . . . Do not, pray, forget that I am to have the manuscript of *Erechtheus*. Where is it? The manuscript, too, of the present poems I understand you have promised me — *n'est-ce pas?*" And in 1877 Swinburne's letters were filled with references to Watts' opinions: "As my friend Watts knows . . ." and ". . . Watts also was most strongly of the same mind". While Watts himself in the same year was the recipient of a letter which apostrophized him as "last in date among my closest friends but certainly not least in my love and trust and gratitude". Watts had joined those "spirits of another sort". And if Watts' life was exposed to a beautiful influence, it was becoming increasingly clear that Swinburne's was exposed to a practical one. Nevertheless, those influences were by no means yet secure. *A Year's Letters*—in spite of "my friend Watts' horror at the inconceivable idea of my so 'debasing myself'"—was published anonymously in *The Tatler*; while *Lesbia Brandon*, again in the face of opposition and though incomplete, was sent to the printers. And this lack of domination in Swinburne's literary activities was matched by Watts' lack of control over his life. Like Mazzini before him, Watts realized that the whole of this carefully cultivated friendship might well be jeopardized by any premature attempt at interference. The moment for that was not yet come.

In spite of Watts' efforts, however, there was still fortunately insufficient money to permit Swinburne to live continuously in London. Thus, practically the whole of 1876 was spent at Holmwood. He would have liked to work in the British Museum but the doors were closed to him by the authorities, in spite of appeals to Gosse and Watts to approach them on his behalf. "I cannot," he wrote, "expose myself to be addressed like a schoolboy suspected of pilfering or convicted of carelessness." In May he went with Nichol on a holiday to the Channel Islands. Hugo, unfortunately, was not in Guernsey but the islands, so he wrote to Mallarmé, charmed him, and from Sark he drew the inspiration for the *Garden of Cymodoce*. In June he was back at Holmwood and, in the middle of the month, on a visit to London, received a subpoena to appear in the Buchanan-Taylor case. In October he wrote to Gosse that he had been ill for some time—"I don't know whether you heard from any quarter of my being accidentally poisoned some months since by the perfume of Indian lilies in a close bedroom—which sounds romantic, but was horrible in experience, and I have not yet wholly recovered the results, or regained my strength."

It seemed, indeed, in the early months of 1877 as if Swinburne might settle permanently at Holmwood—from the point of view of his family and friends a most desirable prospect. In January he was writing quite happily: "I am not likely to be in town for months and have not been since the middle of September." But in March an unexpected event changed everything: his father died, and was buried at Bonchurch. By his will Swinburne was left £5000 and, upon the death of Lady Jane, the ultimate possession of his books and manuscripts valued at a further £2000. After the funeral he returned to Holmwood but was shortly planning in his new independence to go to London. Another reason for this early determination to depart may well have been his resentment, in spite of the fact that in dispassionate moments he was well aware of his own business incapacity, at his younger brother, Edward, being appointed an executor under the will instead of himself. Early in June he was back in Great James Street.

There now followed two years of increasing physical

prostration. Increasingly, too, he cut himself off from his friends. At Great James Street he lived in a large sitting-room and bedroom. His breakfast was served to him in his rooms, but for his other meals he had to go out, and might have been seen with punctual regularity, oblivious of the traffic, crossing Holborn on his way to the London Restaurant by Chancery Lane. Sometimes, but seldom, Gosse records, he or Watts were invited to dine with the poet. Casual acquaintances he never made. Bouts of drinking increased in their severity and there was no Admiral now to come rushing up to London and carry him away when he had made himself ill and was too weak to resist any more. Already in September 1877 he was writing to Karl Blind that he could "hardly hold his pen". In October he wrote to Howell that he had been "prostrate for weeks". Was it at this time that the strange encounter took place with George Moore recorded in the letter published in an appendix to Gosse's *Algernon Charles Swinburne*? "I opened a door," wrote Moore, "and found myself in a large room in which there was no furniture except a truckle bed. Outside the sheets lay a naked man, a strange, impish little body it was, and about the head, too large for the body, was a great growth of red hair. The fright that this naked man caused me is as vivid in me to-day as if it had only occurred yesterday, possibly more vivid. . . . I had no idea what Swinburne's appearance was like, but there was no doubt in my mind that the naked man was Swinburne. How I knew it to be Swinburne I cannot tell. I felt that there could be nobody but Swinburne who could look like that, and he looked to me like a dreadful caricature of myself. . . . It seemed to me that at the end of a ball, coming downstairs at four o'clock in the morning, I had often looked like the man on the bed, and the idea of sitting next to that naked man, so very like myself, and explaining to him that I had come from William Michael Rossetti frightened me nearly out of my wits. I just managed to babble out, 'Does Mr. Jones live here?' The red head shook on a long thin neck like a tulip, and I heard, 'Will you ask downstairs?' I fled and jumped into a hansom."

Indeed, he would lie prostrate on his bed for weeks, and

in the winter of 1877–1878 it appears that he fell into prolonged fits of physical and mental torpor. Appalling disorder prevailed in his rooms: letters and manuscripts were lost: business communications remained unanswered. In January he wrote to P. H. Hayne: "After an intermittent illness of some months' duration, I find on turning over a fearful mass of unsorted papers, proofs, correspondence, etc., etc., a note from you dated as far back as October 12th. . . . During my illness . . . my books, papers and parcels have got into such confusion that for two days I thought I had lost the most important manuscript I have. . . . That has turned up—but many other things are missing. Among these I fear must be the biographies you mention of Edgar Poe. . . . Generally I am as yet, being still somewhat of an invalid, quite unable to say what has or has not come to hand here during the last few months."

In February, by an effort of will, he mustered sufficient strength to visit Nichol in Glasgow. He was the professor's guest at 14 Montgomerie Crescent, Kelvinside. Here he read some of John Davidson's unpublished poems, received him with solemnity and, remembering perhaps his own youthful interview with the august Rogers, placed his hand upon Davidson's head while addressing him as "Poet". He was to be seen, too, so Alexander Hedderwick told Gosse, "marching about the Quadrangle" of the University "very fashionably dressed, in a loose-fitting long Melton coat of dark blue, and the neatest of little shoes, his top hat balanced on his great mop of hair." And there were other diversions: he was shown some "erotic correspondence and Priapic poetry of Burns which are simply sublime. Oh! how frail are *our* attempts on the Chastity of the Muses to that 'large utterance of the early Gods'". Amid these excitements he prepared his forthcoming volume of the second series of *Poems and Ballads*.

By the end of the month he was back in London and in March his health broke down again. On 11th April he wrote: "I am hardly yet recovering from a very tedious and painful attack of sickness . . . which resulted in depriving me for weeks of all natural sleep and appetite—nay, well-nigh of all power to swallow or digest anything. . . .

I literally *can* write no more this morning." And on 27th
May, though he was playing with the idea of accepting
Hugo's invitation to represent English Poetry at the
Centenary Commemoration of the death of Voltaire, it was
clear that he was too ill to go. "I have been," he wrote,
"a bed-ridden invalid for many days—this being the first
I have crawled out into the open air—but I think this
summons would raise me like a second Lazarus from the
very grave. If it be physically possible, I will go." But the
months crept unhappily on with Swinburne in the grip of
"his fearful propensity". In July Lady Jane received an
alarming letter from Lord Houghton. But in the same
month he was fleetingly well enough to pay Jowett a visit.
In August, however, his friends again became alarmed. He
refused to see them, to leave London or, even, to answer
their letters. "I feel great anxiety about the Bard," wrote
Powell. "I have had no answer to several cards and gifts.
Has the old tempter seized him? What is the matter?"
In November Lady Jane was writing in distress to Watts.
Could Swinburne be "induced . . . to do something that
might do him permanent good"? Should she come to
London and fetch him? It was of no avail. For months,
in increasing exhaustion, he lay in his rooms, tended only
by the devoted Mrs. MacGill.

And what, one may well ask, was Watts doing all this
time? It is clear that he was able to watch developments
from closer at hand than anyone else. He lived in the same
street; he managed the poet's affairs; he was in correspondence with Lady Jane. Why did he wait to act till
June 1879? He knew that Lady Jane would be only too
grateful to be relieved of an appalling anxiety. But Watts
was cautious and wise. To assume what had once been the
Admiral's prerogative a moment too soon might, he suspected,
be met with resistance and resentment. Who can say he was
not right? And when the moment came, and from Great
James Street he removed a dying Swinburne, utterly prostrate,
who had taken no food for days, the poet was no longer
capable of objection. And when Watts did act, he acted
with great promptitude. Taking Swinburne to his sister's
house at Putney, Ivy Lodge, he at once informed Lady Jane.

She replied on 10th June: "I am so glad Algernon is out of town. Bring him on Thursday. Tell me what I had best do about his treatment." The Press reported that he was "at death's door", but only a month later, with his marvellous powers of recuperation, he was writing to Lord Houghton: "My mother has just shown me your note to her enquiring after my health; so I add a line of acknowledgement to her reply. I *was* very unwell for weeks together before I left London, and a good deal reduced in strength by prolonged insomnia and consequent loss of appetite and exhaustion; but a day or two at a friend's house near Putney Heath, with plenty of walking exercise thereon and thereabouts, sufficed to set me up—higher I may say than I had been for many months. Thence I came down here to see the last of this place [Holmwood], which we leave for good in October." He was working at *Tristram*, *Mary Stuart* and his *Study of Shakespeare*.

But what, Lady Jane may well have asked—though it was the last time she was ever to need to do so—was to be done with Algernon? Holmwood was on the point of being sold. Obviously he could never be allowed to live in London by himself again. Where could he go? Watts supplied the answer. He had decided to annex permanently and for himself the "beautiful influence". A *régime* would be established, the distressing traits eliminated from the poet's character and he, Watts, would attain to that once seemingly impossible ambition: he would live in the closest communion with genius, indeed he would be its confidant, its guardian. But how was genius to be persuaded? Fortunately the poet was again in financial difficulties, and now the Admiral's library was to be sold. Lady Jane was prepared to let him have at once half the eventual sum that was to be his due. And this £1000 was conditional on "his giving up his lodgings in London" to live with Watts. "This," she said, "is absolutely necessary." Swinburne had no alternative. In the meantime Watts had rented No. 2, The Pines, Putney Hill. The poet became quite reconciled to the idea and remarked that the view was "really very nice". Society had claimed a rebel. And this happy and desirable event had, ironically, been due to alcoholic poisoning.

# CHAPTER IX

## (1879–1909)

BEHIND the prim suburban façade of No. 2, The Pines, life was from the first calm, regular and orderly. But it was Watts' life; it was the life of a retired provincial solicitor with literary interests; it was a life in which routine became hallowed and incident was rigorously excluded. The sharp pangs of rebellion and revolt, the disorders of excess, the eccentricities of genius were deftly suppressed. With what determined tact, with what soft yet unremitting persuasion Watts laboured to tame his captive poet, to reform his genius to the accepted moral standards of the Victorian middle class! And with what extraordinary success his labours were crowned! At last Swinburne had been persuaded to "do something that might do him permanent good." The practical circumstances which had brought this about are clear. For the moment there was no alternative. But how was the permanency achieved? How was it that Swinburne accepted this dominion for thirty years?

One year during which he did not leave The Pines was sufficient to restore him to health. Watts instituted a precise regularity into the day's programme. By a process of suggestion, infinitely subtle, he proceeded to cut off alcohol by slow and steady degrees. Brandy was disposed of; they drank port—the true poet's drink. But should not Swinburne drink the wines of his beloved France? Claret was substituted. But what, after all, could be a more romantic beverage than "Shakespeare's brown October, our own glorious and incomparable British beer"? Bottled ale, and in small quantities, became the poet's most violent dissipation. In October 1880, when Lady Jane visited The Pines, she was astonished at the change. "I am so glad," she wrote to Watts, "to have seen my son well and happy. . . . What a contrast to former days!" In one thing, however, she was to be disappointed. "The return to the religious faith of

187

his youth," she wrote, "I feel is so much more hopeful when that fatal tendency from which he has suffered so much is got the better of." Even Watts was never quite able to effect this.

But this one year of convalescence achieved, his health perfectly restored, what persuaded Swinburne to continue subject to this jealous guardianship? For a jealous guardianship, arrogant and self-assertive under the tact, the wariness, the delicacy of its application, it was. "From this moment . . .," Watts boasted, "Swinburne's connection with Bohemian London ceased entirely." And behind the solicitude for Swinburne's health, for his reputation, for his finances, for his manuscripts, there was a proprietary air which was determined to create a Swinburne according to the Wattsian mode. Hence he was jealous of Swinburne's past—a past that must be eliminated, denied, repudiated, so that the genius of Swinburne might become a projection of Watts. And this, in effect, it very nearly did. For, indeed, once installed, there was never any question of Swinburne's leaving The Pines. If any clear picture of his extraordinary character should have by chance emerged from the preceding pages, it will have been seen that imperceptibly, from the period of Mazzini's domination—not to give too precise a date to it—the emphasis was shifting from the sadistic in his character to the masochistic, from rebellion to submission. These two compensating traits had always been there, had, indeed, been the basis of his temperament, the motive forces in his life to a degree exaggerated beyond the normal. The controversial discords, related in the last chapter, were but the final—and superficial—manifestations of revolt. And now, with the sharp lessons of self - induced ill - health, mortgaged dignity and failing genius he had no longer the strength of will to assert his right to an independent but unmanageable existence. His temperament found its solace in a subjection which, if less impassioned, less ecstatic than his relations with Mazzini, was fuller, deeper, wider, which included not only his mind and his art, but every detail of his life, his eating, his drinking, his exercise and his rest, even the visitors he might receive. And Watts did something else too, he restored his faith in his genius.

What, one is tempted to ask, was there about Watts that
enabled him to exercise this curious domination? Could
anyone else have achieved precisely this? For all that has
been written about him, all that is recorded of him both by
enemies and admirers, Watts remains an essentially elusive
character. Can the two following quotations, written from
very different points of view, be made to throw any light on
the problem? Mrs. Watts-Dunton—a young lady to whom
Watts was married in 1905 at the age of seventy-three—wrote
in description of the poet's attitude to her husband: "The
almost adoring expression which came into Swinburne's eyes
when he looked at Walter made me realize how deeply and
gratefully conscious he was of the incalculable blessing the
*magnetic* presence of his friend had been to him all the happy
years he had spent under his roof." While Gosse, in a letter
to T. J. Wise dated 29th May 1921, wrote less amicably
(Gosse always felt that Watts had ruined the most fascinating
friendship of his life): "What you say about the hold Watts-
Dunton had on him is very true. It was a sort of rattlesnake
fascination, which left the victim as helpless as a rabbit.
Lord Redesdale, who had a remarkable experience of Watts-
Dunton's business ways, always held that he exercised over
nervous persons a directly *magnetic* influence." It will be observed that the word *magnetic* appears in both accounts. But
how does a "magnetic presence" or "a magnetic influence"
square with Sir Max Beerbohm's "dear little old man",
with the "something gnome-like", with the "chubbiness",
and the "eternally crumpled frock-coat", or with A. C.
Benson's vision of a "clotted" moustache? No, the adoring
wife and the antagonistic acquaintance have fallen into the
same error for opposite reasons. Watts' "magnetism"
—whatever exactly that may mean—can be dismissed.
There was a will of iron concealed behind a façade of
exquisite tact, illimitable consideration. And if from time
to time Watts thwarted an ambition, or forbade a pleasure,
the pang of disappointment suffered by the poet but bound
him the closer to its author. "I must say," so Swinburne
expressed his feelings, "I do feel the want of a God (of faith
and friendship) to whom I might offer sacrifice of thanks-
giving for the gift of such a good friend as I have in you."

Having captured his genius, the "old horror of Putney",
as Gosse called him, set about directing his activities into
proper channels. Watts was determined that Swinburne
should become not only a success financially and socially—
that is by standards of middle-class propriety—but also, one
cannot help but feel, in a manner that would be worthy of
Watts himself. The more immediate results were necessarily
visible in Swinburne's social life. There were, of course,
good reasons for not permitting the poet to go about London
as before. And this, indeed, Swinburne realized very well
himself. "In the atmosphere of London," he wrote, "I
can never expect more than a fortnight, at best, of my usual
health and strength." While already he "never was fresher
or stronger or happier at twenty than now and for many
weeks back". But this embargo was imposed, too, upon
visits of any duration to friends outside London. His
presence at the celebration of the Eton ninth jubilee, which
has already been referred to, was forbidden. Watts had,
naturally, not been invited. Were the old "scholastic
associations" really likely to cause irreparable backsliding
in a single night? Or was it that Watts, being excluded, was
jealous? Except for one visit to Jowett, in August 1883,
only Lady Jane was permitted to entertain the poet un-
accompanied by Watts. And this she regularly did, until
her death, in the various houses she inhabited after the sale
of Holmwood, and thus Swinburne stayed for considerable
periods at Bradford-on-Avon, Cheltenham, Aston, Chestal
and Solihull.

Accompanied by Watts, however, excursions to the sea
were not in these early years forbidden. In 1882 they went
to Guernsey and Sark, which Swinburne was delighted to
show to his companion. Hugo, as usual, was not there. It
was the accustomed disappointment. Would he never meet
the third of the three great men—Landor, Mazzini, Hugo
—whom he had spent his life in hero-worshipping? And
then, on his return to London in October, he received a
summons to attend the fiftieth anniversary of the first
performance of *Le Roi s'Amuse*. Watts had but little
admiration for Hugo; he raised objections. But even he
could not deter Swinburne from doing homage to this

particular god. There was only one alternative: Watts must go too, in spite of his toothache. On 20th November they were in Paris.

Was the meeting the anti-climax that has been asserted? There have been stories that would tend to make it appear so: the Master, now eighty years old, responding to Swinburne's flow of adulation with "Mais qu'est-ce qu'il me raconte là? Qu'est-ce qu'il me raconte?" and his displeasure at Swinburne's enthusiastic breaking of the glass out of which he had drunk the Master's health. Indeed, there is absent from Swinburne's letters the frenzied worship that followed his meetings with Landor and Mazzini. But he was older now, and perhaps no longer capable of such exalted emotions. His regard for Hugo never wavered, as is shown in his passionate grief at Hugo's death three years later. In fact the meeting seems to have gone off very well, though the hereditary deafness from which he was now suffering detracted something from his pleasure. Hugo said on receiving him: "Je suis heureux de vous serrer la main comme à mon fils." Swinburne dined with him and, "after dinner, he drank my health with a little speech, of which— tho' I sat just opposite him—my accursed deafness prevented my hearing a single word. This, however, was the only drawback—tho' certainly a considerable one—to my pleasure". Two days later, at the Théâtre Français, Swinburne and Watts attended the performance of Le Roi s'Amuse. Between the third and fourth acts Swinburne was invited into Hugo's box. The Master asked him, "Etes-vous content?" and Swinburne, though unable to hear a word of the performance, said he was indeed content. This seems to have been the extent of their relations. Literary Paris was en fête and Hugo the centre of the celebrations. Nevertheless there were compensations. "During the past few days," wrote a journalist, "he [Swinburne] has been the lion of some exotic blue-stocking salons, and the journalist poets, like Catulle Mendès, have written wonderful articles on his 'strange silhouette', his 'measureless brow', his 'pale lips' and 'the striking mobility of the features of the bizarre artist'." Could recognition of fame go further? Then there was Tola Dorian, "the translatress of some of my verses into

French—a Russian princess by birth [Princess Mestchersky] and—*need* I add—a nihilist by creed and practice". And when the nihilist princess proved also to be extremely rich and the possessor not only of "a most lovely little daughter" —his passion for babies was already in the ascendant—but of "a magnificent stud . . . Russian and Arabian horses", well might he exclaim: "Fair owner: spirit, fire, grace!" At her house, too, he had the pleasure of meeting "a very noble and amiable old man"—Leconte de Lisle. Altogether, they proved to be "five of the most memorable days of my life".

They were, too, to be the last spent beyond the shores of England. Watts disliked foreign travel. Soon Swinburne was agreeing with him that nothing could beat the English coast. Year after year Watts led his charge to the sea like a horse to the water—to Sidestrand, to Eastbourne, to Lancing-on-Sea. The poet was permitted to swim under Watts' anxious eye and, since even holidays should be turned to account, he was encouraged to write descriptive verses. This was "Mr Swinburne's later development as a nature lover and poet of the sea"—a development which, unfortunately, was totally alien to his genius. But, indeed, Watts seems to have cared but little for the aesthetic merits of his captive's work. Propriety was the touchstone by which they were judged. Could not Algernon see the danger of ill-advised words, the mire into which lack of proper principles so inevitably led? Those appalling letters, for instance, which kept cropping up on the deaths of their recipients like a recurring nightmare—how much better if they had never been written! Indeed, what might not the consequences to Algernon have been had Walter not been there to manage the delicate negotiations for him? For after Rossetti's death, in 1886, Fanny Schott became possessed of a correspondence which had at all costs to be bought back from her; and after Howell's, a still more compromising packet fell into the hands of a publisher called George Redway, and it required the exercise of all Watts' business acumen to exchange it for the copyright of *A Word for the Navy*. Besides, look at the results of publishing *Poems and Ballads*! Could not Algernon realize how unnecessary and impolitic

SWINBURNE AND WATTS-DUNTON AT THE PINES

it was to flout the public's sense of decency? And Swinburne
was now predisposed to listen to this constantly reiterated
theme. At length he began to think that possibly some of
his early poems had indeed been composed in error. Ought
he perhaps to suppress them? But then would this not
merely direct fresh interest towards them? Watts agreed
that it might. But were there not other mistakes in the past
which could be more conveniently set right? *Whitmania*
(1887) disposed of one "unhealthy" admiration (Watts
"hated him most heartily") and *Mr. Whistler's Lecture on
Art* (1888) of another. Concerning the latter Watts admitted
that he had "persuaded Swinburne to write the really
brilliant article" which, as Gosse notes, is a typical
example of Swinburne's later and depressing prose style.
It was published in *The Fortnightly Review* and was an
onslaught on Art for Art's sake and, indeed, the whole
of Whistler's aesthetic theory which he himself had once
so devoutly shared. Whistler replied in *The World*: "Have
I shot down the singer in the far off when I thought
him safe at my side?" And no doubt Watts was gratified
to read the decisive sentence: "I have lost a *confrère* and
gained an acquaintance, one Algernon Charles Swinburne,
outsider, Putney." The breach, after thirty years of friendship, was thus made complete and Watts felt that another
pre-redemption influence had been satisfactorily disposed
of. Baudelaire, too, was ultimately to be denied. In 1901,
writing to William Sharp concerning the Tauchnitz volume
Sharp had edited of *Selections* from his poems, Swinburne
would "have preferred on all accounts that *In the Bay* had
filled the place you have allotted to *Ave Atque Vale*, a poem
to which you are altogether too kind in my opinion, as
others have been before you. I never had really much
in common with Baudelaire. . . ." Was there no cock
to crow? But by then he was no longer capable of
judging his own works save through the eyes of Watts.
*Erechtheus* would, he thought, "have been a better and
a fairer example of the author's works" for inclusion
than—*Atalanta*!
During these last years his industry was prodigious.
After 1880 some twenty-four volumes were published during

his lifetime and a further five posthumously, while from
T. J. Wise's vast collection of manuscripts, now in the
British Museum, something approaching one hundred were
edited and privately printed.   There were, too, between 1882
and 1909, two hundred and twenty-three contributions
to reviews, magazines and newspapers.   Watts approved.
Indeed, what could be more satisfactory?   Swinburne was
happy and busy, while the financial results, under his own
able management, were really quite gratifying.   But into
this vast overwhelming flood it is neither possible, nor
desirable, to do more than dip.   The mere contemplation
of its bulk induces a certain lassitude, while its perusal
culminates in an extraordinary tedium.   Nor are the reasons
for this far to seek.   His technique was at least as good as it
had ever been, the astonishing music of which he was capable
still poured out in endless, insistent metrical stresses.   But
now there was no longer any essential experience to com-
municate.   As verse is piled upon verse, stanza upon stanza,
with an incredible virtuosity of rhyme, alliteration and
assonance, it becomes increasingly clear that there is no
outline to the flood of his distressing fluency.   Words,
phrases, stanzas have no meaning beyond their musical
sound: nothing is conveyed.   It is as if we were
contemplating the exquisite convolutions of a carved
marble chimney-piece — the same indeed that we gazed
upon with so much admiration in former years—but now
it has lost all meaning: the hearth is empty, the fire has
gone out.

And Watts was always at hand with advice and encouragement.   "For the last thirty years," wrote Watts in 1910,
"his thoughts had been mainly absorbed in two subjects.
The first of these was the study and contemplation of nature
in various localities.   The second . . . was childhood."
And if the contemplation of nature led to an unbridled and
meaningless fluency, the presence in the household of Watts'
nephew, Bertie Mason—of whom Swinburne was already
writing in 1884: "When my forthcoming volume [*A Midsummer Holiday and Other Poems*] is out, I shall have
published fifty poems on a single child"—led to a no less
distressing bathos:

*A baby shines as bright*
*If winter or if May be*
*On eyes that keep in sight*
        *A baby.*

*Though dark the skies or grey be,*
*It fills our eyes with light*
*If midnight or midday be.*

*Love hails it, day and night,*
*The sweetest thing that may be,*
*Yet cannot praise aright*
        *A baby.*

And as each mechanical composition was struck off by the
machine Watts was on hand to assure the author that it was
"*the* best poem I ever wrote". Indeed, from the moment
Swinburne went to live at The Pines there seems never to
have been a doubt in his mind as to the quality of his productions. Watts at least gave him the happiness, whatever
he may have come to think about some of his early work, of
complete certainty in his present genius. Nevertheless, even
this last period produced, if no great poetry, at least work
of merit. Outstanding in the interminable procession of
his compositions is *Tristram of Lyonesse*. This work, which
had been lingering in his mind since 1858, he intended to be
his masterpiece. In 1871 he wrote the sonorous invocation
to Love which forms the Prelude, but the forced labour of
*Bothwell* and other avocations interfered with the poem's
immediate completion. It lay on his hands too long and
when, after "parcels of Tristram" had been composed at
intervals, he set himself in the summer of 1881 to complete
it, the inspiration had faded. As always the narrative or
epic form eluded him and he was brought to realize that in
fact it had become "a succession of dramatic scenes and
pictures with descriptive settings of backgrounds". In its
totality it cannot be considered an unqualified success. It
is likely, too, that Watts was instrumental in toning down
some of the more frankly amorous passages, while he insisted
upon its being published in the same volume together with a
number of morally unimpeachable verses which Swinburne
designated "Songs of Innocence" and which were not

calculated to enhance the major poem's effectiveness. *The Tale of Balen*, published in 1896, is also not without merit. His imagination played about the vivid freedoms of Northumberland which once he had known, and "a sun more blithe, a merrier breeze" stirred and illumined the drab hangings of the Putney villa. Perhaps for a moment he was really able to persuade himself that he lived "close to the edge of a noble down". And in two of the closing stanzas, with the dying Balen, he recaptured, with a wistful, insistent nostalgia, the surge and lifting of a boy's heart.

> *And there low lying, as hour on hour*
> *Fled, all his life in all its flower*
> *Came back as in a sunlit shower*
> *Of dreams, when sweet-souled sleep has power*
> *On life less sweet and glad to be.*
> *He drank the draught of life's first wine*
> *Again: he saw the moorland shine,*
> *The rioting rapids of the Tyne,*
> *The woods, the cliffs, the sea.*
>
> *The joy that lives at heart and home,*
> *The joy to rest, the joy to roam,*
> *The joy of crags and scaurs he clomb,*
> *The rapture of the encountering foam*
> *Embraced and breasted of the boy,*
> *The first good steed his knees bestrode,*
> *The first wild sound of songs that flowed*
> *Through ears that thrilled and heart that glowed,*
> *Fulfilled his death with joy.*

The same note of wistfulness is to be found in *To a Seamew* which appeared in *Poems and Ballads: Third Series*, published in 1889.

> *When I had wings, my brother,*
> *Such wings were mine as thine:*
> *Such life my heart remembers*
> *In all as wild Septembers*
> *As this when life seems other,*
> *Though sweet, than once was mine;*
> *When I had wings, my brother,*
> *Such wings were mine as thine.*

*       *       *       *

*We are fallen, even we, whose passion*
  *On earth is nearest thine;*
*Who sing, and cease from flying;*
*Who live, and dream of dying:*
*Grey time, in time's grey fashion,*
  *Bids wingless creatures pine:*
*We are fallen, even we, whose passion*
  *On earth is nearest thine.*

Otherwise the volume, except for a number of Border ballads composed a quarter of a century earlier, and some dignified necrological poems, which were naturally tending to become increasingly frequent, was undistinguished.

In politics, too, Watts was gradually able to exercise an ameliorating influence. Were visions of the Laureateship for his charge already hovering in that far-seeing brain? The difficulty was that Swinburne had taken up a very definite attitude towards Russia. The Czar, the "waxing" evil, had become fixed in Swinburne's mind as the prototype of all tyrants, had indeed taken the place in his troubled political mythology that Napoleon III had once occupied. And this was a sentiment that Watts had not the time to eradicate before irreparable harm had been done. The Laureateship passed Putney by on the official grounds of insult offered to a foreign crowned head. The question remains: had that offer been extended, would Swinburne have accepted it, or would he have refused it as he did Curzon's offer, some years later, of an honorary Oxford degree? It is probable that Watts set but little store by the latter honour, but the Laureateship would have been a very different matter. And who, indeed, by 1892, as we shall see, was better fitted than Algernon to celebrate in dignified and faultless stanzas such public events as were deserving of immortal commemoration? It was unfortunately true that his favourite exclamation of emphatic denial was: "May I die a Poet Laureate!" But this was a relic of pre-redemption days, and even if the sentiment behind it was still strong, could not Watts have influenced it as he had influenced so much else? This, we shall never know, since, after much delay, Alfred Austin proved to be the superbly inept official choice.

In fact, Swinburne's political views on foreign affairs

were, from Watts' point of view, completely out of hand.    It
is probable that Watts had no very clear views on this
subject himself and, therefore, was the less able to influence
Swinburne's. He was forced to content himself with
endeavouring to suppress the more violent outbursts and
even in this was not always successful.    The most notable
development during these years was a gradually increasing
Francophobia.    He had, it is true, never altogether recovered
from his disappointment at the Conservative tendencies of
the Third Republic.    But his "inherited loyalty" to France
had remained reasonably secure during Hugo's lifetime.
But now, with the Master's death, he no longer felt under
any obligation to make undue allowances:

> Quenched is the light that lit thee; dead the lord
> Whose lyre outsang the storm, outshone the sword.

And it was becoming quite clear to him that France was
behaving in an exceedingly objectionable manner.    In the
first place the comments in the Parisian Press on the subject
of Stead's famous articles in the *Pall Mall Gazette* in July
1885—of which the paragraphs that dealt with sadism ("Why
the cries of the victims are not heard" and "Strapping girls
down")made a particular impression in France—did not hesitate to link Swinburne's name with the practices described.
This was bad enough, and called forth from Swinburne the
*Rondeaux Parisiens*, which, however, were so violently
vituperative that no journal would print them; but when
in 1886 it became clear that France had allied herself with
that despicable despot Alexander III in a Franco-Russian
*entente* he was impelled to write three sonnets, *The Russ
and the Frenchman*, which were followed in the next year,
1887, by *Russo Gallia*. Watts was able to withhold these
effusions from publication; but in them Swinburne had
established his new attitude to the land from which, so he
had once imagined, he had derived "particles of my blood".
Nor was this attitude in any way ameliorated by the criticism
of England that became common in the French Press, some
years later, at the period of the Boer War.

*Falsehood, thy name is France!*

The rise of German militarism and her apparently increasing autocracy did not pass unnoticed at The Pines. The Kaiser gradually became in Swinburne's view a counterpart of the Czar, and his indignation reached its culmination when those two monarchs met with mutual grandiloquence in 1905. And so it began to seem to him that England, though by no means perfect, was surrounded by nations whose governments were infinitely less democratic than, and possibly even dangerous to, the Empire which, much to Watts' satisfaction, was gradually taking the place in his mind of that now discarded "universal republic" as the bright hope for the proper governance of the world.

However disastrous Swinburne's attacks on foreign crowned heads may ultimately have proved to have been, the gradual formation of this attitude in foreign politics was of considerable assistance to Watts in the proper ordering of the poet's views in the realm of home affairs. As he did not fail to point out: if the tolerant spirit with which the British Empire was governed was the hope of the world, calumny from outside must not be reinforced by criticism from within. But there were formidable difficulties to be overcome. In the first place Swinburne in his Mazzinian distrust of all monarchies and perhaps from some romantic hereditary feeling for the Stuarts—a not uncommon paradox —had no love for the Hanoverians. The Queen had, fortunately not publicly, been consistently treated with scant respect. This Watts considered must be changed. While in the second place, as has been recorded in the previous chapter, Swinburne was in the difficulty of disliking Mr. Gladstone, who led the party he was popularly supposed, owing to his volume of 1871, to support. This was a dilemma Watts set himself ardently to resolve.

As regards the Queen, Watts' diplomacy had some prospect of success. Had not Swinburne already replied, with what appeared to be a hopeful spontaneity, to "some insolent lines addressed by a Russian poet to the Empress of India" by composing *The White Czar* in 1877? Watts took every opportunity of bringing to Swinburne's notice the attacks which appeared in the foreign Press upon the Queen who was, after all, the representative of the country. He pointed out

that the office she held was in direct succession to Elizabeth
and Cromwell, rulers whom Swinburne permitted himself
to admire.   And then, on 2nd March 1882, there occurred an
event which stimulated all Swinburne's chivalrous instincts.
A lunatic, Roderick MacLean, fired a pistol at the Queen as
she was driving in Windsor and was promptly arrested with
the assistance of Eton boys.   The combination of the Queen's
calm courage, his nostalgia for Eton, and the romantic
youth of her defenders, was overwhelming.   He marked his
change of attitude with a sonnet:

> No braver soul drew bright and queenly breath
> Since England wept upon Elizabeth.

And five years later Watts prevailed upon him to write a
song for the Jubilee, though "Watts wished me to say, and
thinks I should have said, more about the Queen than the
little word I did say".   However, Watts was able to feel
satisfaction at the progress made.

The reorientation of Swinburne's views in politics was
not of course a process that could be immediately achieved.
The growing dislike of Mr. Gladstone was, however,
enhanced by two quite separate events.   The first was his
alleged callousness in leaving General Gordon to his fate in
a besieged Khartoum.   Gordon had been elevated by the
Press into exactly the kind of romantic hero that Swinburne
most admired.   Steadfast, chivalrous and betrayed, he had,
in Swinburne's opinion, been "nailed up and spat on like the
head of Christ", owing to the treachery of Mr. Gladstone
and his government, who were "Irresolute, instable as water
—Yea and false as water":

> Forsaken, silent, Gordon dies and gives
> Example: loud and shameless Gladstone lives,
> No faction unembraced or unbetrayed,
> No chance unwelcomed and no vote unweighed. . . .

These explosive satires Watts was able to suppress.   But
there was another and more purely political event which
aroused Swinburne's anger: Mr. Gladstone announced his
policy of Home Rule.   To this policy Swinburne was
violently opposed.   Without doubt the basic reason for his

opposition was, though in his public statements he condemned the methods of the Fenians, his feeling that the English race had a "mission" and that its strength would be impaired by any disunity in the United Kingdom. He was thus thankfully able to give his support to Chamberlain's new Unionist party in the election of 1886 and published *The Commonweal, A Song for Unionists*, in which he attacked Mr. Gladstone and Parnell. And in *The Jubilee*, published in 1887, he makes the idea of a "mission" quite clear. How could it be otherwise when in England, the "Crowning nation", "The watchword Freedom fails not . . ."? It followed from this, of course, that smaller nations must be liberated by being brought within the Empire—by force if necessary. From this point Swinburne's political utterances were perfectly logical. They culminated in his poems on the Boer War, where he gave encouragement:

> *To scourge these dogs, agape with jaws afoam,*
> *Down out of life. Strike, England, and strike home.*

The Mazzinian revolutionary had, Watts might congratulate himself, become the Jingo imperialist.

After 1890 the monastic retirement of The Pines became more complete. The visits to the seaside, except for one ultimate expedition to Cromer in 1904, ceased. The visits from friends which up till this time had, though heavily invigilated by Watts, still been reasonably frequent, now came to an end. Indeed, there were no longer many old friends to come: death had accounted for Rossetti and Powell in 1882, for Lord Houghton in 1885, for Philip Marston in 1887, for Inchbold in 1888, for Burton in 1890, and in the next eight years Jowett, Madox Brown, Nichol, Morris and Burne-Jones were all to pass away. And where death had been unsuccessful Watts had triumphed. The occasional readings of his own works, which had till now been permitted, Watts decided were too exciting. Private reading from Dickens was substituted, and Watts submitted with a sigh of mingled boredom and relief to listening during these last years to the thrice-repeated Complete Novels. The ordered life of The Pines, too, took on a new, a more exacting symmetry. Every hour of the day was properly employed, suitably organized. It was the only anodyne to what must otherwise have become an excruciating boredom. "Nothing," wrote Gosse, "could be more motionless than the existence of 'the little old genius, and his little old acolyte, in their dull little villa'." Their life was "spent almost as if within a Leyden jar". Mrs. Watts-Dunton has recorded the poet's daily time-table, which became set in an unvarying routine, a sort of elaborate, royal etiquette, as if the sovereign *ennui* of Versailles had come to rest, shorn of its grandeur, in a melancholy suburb. The poet, never an early riser, would breakfast alone in his library on the first floor at ten o'clock, enjoying *The Daily Telegraph*. At eleven he would go across Putney and Wimbledon Common on a walk which lasted two hours, winter and summer, rain or fine, "pelting along all the time as hard as I can go", whenever he was not peering sentimentally into perambulators or, as he preferred to call them, "pushwainlings". On the way home, un-varyingly, he would stop at the "Rose and Crown", where a glass of beer would be ready for him. Luncheon followed, and at two-thirty he retired to rest until four. From four till six he would work in his library and then came the readings from Dickens till dinner at eight. After dinner he again worked in his library till bedtime.

The death of his mother in 1896 cloistered him still further. Even the change of scene his visits to her had afforded him was now cut off. The days passed in indis-tinguishable procession. "I am beginning," he wrote in 1904 to W. M. Rossetti (who survived him by ten years), "to lose count of time," and then added pathetically: "They have got me a really beautiful type for the forthcoming edition of my poems in six volumes: of course it will be sent to you—but not to anyone else—or hardly. Who is there to send them to, for that matter?" Indeed, there was no one; and so he sat up in his room, remote from the world of men, indulging in a limited literary correspondence, unable to believe that it was not the common practice to read at least one Elizabethan or Jacobean drama every day—a relaxation which he varied with the vicarious excitements of novels from the lending library—living, indeed, in an intellectual vacuum which insulated him from the achievements of the new generation of writers. He disliked Stevenson, harshly criticized Yeats, never mentioned Kipling, and wrote to Hardy, who had sent him *The Dynasts*: "I trust you do not mean to give over your great work in creative romance even for the field of epic or historic drama."

Indeed, his intellectual pleasures, his enthusiasms, remained constant, formed ultimately, as it were, part of the etiquette of The Pines. To the few carefully selected visitors— handpicked by Watts for their talents or their enthusiasms, such as Sir Max Beerbohm, William Rothenstein and T. J. Wise (Swinburne's future bibliographer)—he was shown off by that devoted and possessive presence as if he had been some rare and delicate *bibelot*. His mind lingered in the literary past; he lived in the history of his art. Feuds a century old were more real to him than the events of last week. A reckless guest would be reproved by Watts: "We don't mention Hazlitt's name here." Had he not attacked Coleridge? And upstairs in the library the fortunate visitor would be shown the collection of quarto plays and given an enthusiastic discourse on their respective beauties or, perhaps, fired by a chance word, there would be a flow of panegyric, a spate of eulogy, on Shelley, Landor, or Victor Hugo, till Watts anxiously hurried the visitor out. Excitement was another stimulant that must be rationed.

In November 1903 Swinburne caught a chill while walking in the rain which developed into pneumonia. Had the mothering presence of Watts failed to notice the dampness of the poet's clothes, or had the poet in one of his childish fits of disobedience neglected to change them? Sir Thomas Barlow was called in and saved his life. His lungs remained delicate but he had still six years to live; placid years in which he continued to compose verses, as he admitted, "to escape from boredom". But at Easter in 1909 an epidemic of influenza attacked the household of The Pines. Watts was confined to his room. Swinburne, with no one to watch over him, again contracted a chill to which he paid no attention. Watts did not even realize he was ill till one morning he failed to get up and refused food. His lungs were almost immediately affected. Very quietly he lay in his bed without, so it seemed, any desire to recover. Indeed, there was no longer anything to live for; the links which bound him to the world had been severed one by one; calmly he awaited the resolution of the mystery. Nothing could reconcile him to God, but was there a life after death? "I do now," he had written in 1882, "on the whole, strongly incline to believe in the survival of life—individual and conscious life—after the dissolution of the body." And now he would find out, for by 1st April he was dying. Sir Douglas Powell was called in consultation, but without avail. On 10th April at 10 A.M., in his seventy-third year, Swinburne died.

> Death, if thou wilt, fain would I plead with thee;
> Canst thou not spare, of all our hopes have built,
> One shelter where our spirits fain would be,
>    Death, if thou wilt?

And perhaps, at the last, "the trumpets", unmuted by Watts-Dunton, "sounded for him upon the other side".

The only survivor of his immediate family was his youngest sister, Isabel. Her religion was narrow and fierce. She immediately entered into correspondence with Watts concerning the funeral rites. But Watts, who was still confined to his bed—and was, indeed, unable to attend the funeral —was adamant. "Up to his last moment," he wrote, "he cherished the deepest animosity against the creed which he felt had severed him from his most beloved ties. Up to now I have kept from you this bitter fact, but now I recall a promise I made to him that the burial service *should never be read over his grave.* . . . If he had made a slight matter of his antagonism against Christianity as so many freethinkers do it would have been different, but with him it increased with his years and at the last (if I must say what I am sorry to say) it was bitterer than ever. Cannot those broad-minded clergymen friends of yours do something to relieve the matter?" They could indeed. A compromise was reached. Instead of over the grave the lines of the Burial Service were read as the coffin left the hearse. Of his family only Sir John Swinburne (whom he had heartily disliked) and Mrs Disney Leith, were present in Bonchurch churchyard.

A further cause of tension between Watts and Swinburne's family was the poet's will. Everything was left to Watts; no relatives were even mentioned by name; and this they regarded as a public slight. The pictures, works of art, and most of the books remained at The Pines till Watts' death in 1914. The manuscripts were sold from time to time to various collectors. T. J. Wise ultimately secured nearly every document or manuscript of importance. And these, upon his death, passed with the Ashley Library to the British Museum.

# BIBLIOGRAPHY

(To give more than a list of useful authorities would be supererogatory. It is to be noted that there are still unpublished Swinburne letters in private hands to which access has so far been denied. There is no reason to suppose them to be of particular significance. In addition to the main biographical, bibliographical and critical works dealing specifically with Swinburne, an arbitrary selection has been made of those which seemed particularly relevant from the numerous biographies and memoirs making incidental mention of the poet, as well as of one or two more general works elaborating the literary and aesthetic background to the period.)

ADAMS, Henry: *The Education of Henry Adams.* 1919.

BEERBOHM, Sir Max: *And Even Now:* [*No. 2 The Pines*]. 1922.

BROWNING, O.: *Memories of Sixty Years.* 1910.

BURNE-JONES, Lady: *Memorials of E. Burne-Jones.* 1904.

BURTON, Jean: *Sir Richard Burton's Wife.* 1942.

CHEW, S. C.: *Swinburne.* 1929.

DRINKWATER, John: *Swinburne: an Estimate.* 1913.

GAUNT, William: *The Pre-Raphaelite Tragedy.* 1942.

—— *The Aesthetic Adventure.* 1945.

GOSSE, Sir Edmund: *Portraits and Sketches.* 1913.

—— *The Life of Algernon Charles Swinburne.* 1917.

—— *Swinburne: an Essay.* 1925.

GOSSE, Sir Edmund, and WISE, Thomas J.: *The Letters of Algernon Charles Swinburne.* 2 vols. 1918.

HAKE, Thomas, and RICKETT, A. Compton: *The Life of Watts-Dunton.* 1916.

—— *The Letters of A. C. Swinburne: with some Personal Recollections.* 1918.

HARDMAN, Sir William: *A Mid-Victorian Pepys: Letters and Memoirs.* Ed. S. M. Ellis. 1923.

KERNAHAN, Coulson: *Swinburne as I Knew Him.* 1919.

LAFOURCADE, Georges: *La Jeunesse de Swinburne.* 2 vols. 1928.

—— *Swinburne: a Literary Biography.* 1932.

LEITH, Mrs. Disney: *The Boyhood of A. C. Swinburne.* 1916.

LUCAS, E. V.: *At "The Pines": a Visit to A. C. Swinburne.* 1916.

MACKAIL, J.W.: *Swinburne: a Lecture.* 1909.

NICOLSON, Harold: *Swinburne.* 1926.

PENNELL, E. R. and J.: *The Life of James McNeill Whistler.* 2 vols. 1908.

—— *The Whistler Journal.* 1921.

PRAZ, Mario: *The Romantic Agony.* 1933.

REUL, Paul de: *L'Oeuvre de Swinburne.* 1922.

ROSSETTI, W. M.: *Dante Gabriel Rossetti—His Family Letters with a Memoir.* 2 vols. 1895.

RUTLAND, W. R.: *Swinburne: a Nineteenth-Century Hellene.* 1931.

SCOTT, William Bell: *Autobiographical Notes.* 2 vols. 1892.

THOMAS, Edward: *Algernon Charles Swinburne: a Critical Study.* 1912.

WATTS-DUNTON, Clara: *The Home Life of Swinburne.* 1922.

WAUGH, Evelyn: *Rossetti.* 1928.

WELBY, T. Earle: *A Study of Swinburne.* 1926.

WISE, Thomas J.: *A Bibliography of the Writings in Prose and Verse of A. C. Swinburne.* 2 vols. 1919.

—— *A Swinburne Library.* 1925.

—— *Catalogue of the Ashley Library.* 11 vols. 1922–31.

WRATISLAW, Theodore: *A. C. Swinburne: a Study.* 1900.

# INDEX